An American Critic in Canada

An American Critic in Canada

The Literary Memoirs of Morton L. Ross

NeWest Press
Edmonton

© Copyright 1999 the Estate of Morton L. Ross
© Copyright 1999 William Bartley—Foreword
© Copyright 1999 Robert Kroetsch—Eulogy
First Edition
All rights reserved. The use of any part of this publication reproduced, transmitted in any form or by any means, electronic, mechanical, recording or otherwise, or stored in a retrieval system, without the prior consent of the publisher is an infringement of the copyright law. In the case of photocopying or other reprographic copying of the material, a licence must be obtained from the Canadian Reprography Collective before proceeding.

Canadian Cataloguing in Publication Data

Ross, Morton.
   An American critic in Canada

ISBN 1-896300-44-8

1. Ross, Morton. 2. Critics—Canada—Biography. 3. College teachers—Canada—Biography. 4. Canadian literature—History and criticism. 5. American literature—History and criticism. I. Title.
PN75.R67A3 1999   810.9   C99-910241-9

 Canadian Patrimoine
Heritage canadien Canada

Editors for the Press: Diane Bessai and Christopher Drummond
Cover and book design: John Luckhurst / GDL
Front and back cover photographs: Courtesy the Estate of Morton L. Ross

NeWest Press acknowledges the support of the Canada Council for the Arts for our publishing program. We also acknowledge the financial support of the Government of Canada through the Book Publishing Industry Development Program (BPIDP) for our publishing activities.

Special thanks to: Janis Watkin, Michael Ross, Donald Kerr, and Valerie Green.

Every effort has been made to obtain permission for quoted material.
If there is an omission or error the publisher would be grateful to be so informed.

Printed and bound in Canada

NeWest Publishers Limited
Suite 201, 8540-109 Street
Edmonton, Alberta T6G 1E6

Table of Contents

Editors' Preface – *1*
Foreword: Morton Ross As an Education – *2*

Critical Preliminaries
    The Common Pursuit of True Judgment (1973) – *8*

The Edmund Kemper Broadus Lectures:
American Public Styles: Community and the Private Heart (1982)
    The American Puritans: Piercing the Private Heart – *20*
    Benjamin Franklin: Masks for Meeting Community – *33*
    Ralph Waldo Emerson: Unsettling Community – *47*
    Nathaniel Hawthorne: Restoring Community – *59*

American Essays: Pedagogy, Provocation, and Preaching
    Poor Richard and *Playboy*: Brothers under the Flesh (1967) – *74*
    Thoreau and Mailer: The Mission of the Rooster (1971) – *80*
    Moby-Dick As an Education (1974) – *89*
    Walt Whitman and the Limits of Embarrassment (1968) – *102*
    Bill Gorton, the Preacher in *The Sun Also Rises* (1972) – *113*
    A Memorial Note for Ralph Ellison (1994) – *122*

Western Canadian Literature
    What Do You Know about Canadian Literature?
        Shame On You! (1979) – *126*
    The Canonization of *As For Me and My House*:
        A Case Study (1978) – *135*
    Robert Kroetsch's Early Novels (1973) – *150*

Some Personal Essays, Mainly Western and Canadian
    Praise to the Albany (1975) – *164*
    For John Quentin Cook, Historian (1968) – *171*
    Toward the Margin: Notes in Passing (1991) – *172*
    Introduction to a Memoir (1992) – *182*
    A Passion of Poets (1993) – *187*
    Where I Was Coming From (1994) – *198*
    A Memorial Note for Marian Engel (1985) – *206*

Eulogy for Mort Ross (1995) – *207*

Writings of Morton L. Ross – *211*

Acknowledgements – *216*

Editors' Preface

The writings of Morton Ross derive from his teaching in America and Canada. First he taught American literature to Americans, then in 1968 (in the thirty-sixth year of his life) American literature to Canadians; then Canadian literature to Americans; and finally, Canadian literature to Canadians. This progress is only slightly obscured in the order of the writings that follow. We begin with a paper that lays out Mort's classroom procedures and defends his pedagogical purposes. There follow the four Broadus Lectures (a series delivered annually in the English Department of the University of Alberta) that sum up for a Canadian audience Mort's insights into American literature in its first three centuries. Then we print some of Mort's many papers on American literature, written for both American and Canadian audiences, on the whole course of American literature into the twentieth century, containing some unique insights into its continuity and interrelationships—Franklin and Hefner, Thoreau and Mailer, Ecclesiastes and Hemingway. The three themes that occupied Mort throughout his scholarly life are treated here under the topics of pedagogy, provocation, and preaching, matters that also appear in the Broadus Lectures. There follow three papers that testify to Mort's developing interest, after his immigration, in Canadian literature, especially Western Canadian literature. This section begins with his chastisement of Americans for knowing almost nothing about what he, after 1968, discovered to be the thriving literature of Canada, and concludes with two essays on Western Canadian novelists. The fifth section contains more personal essays about his friends and experiences, including three parts of a Memoir that most regrettably Mort did not live to complete, but whose parts should excite interest in both his American and Canadian experiences. We conclude with Robert Kroetsch's moving funeral eulogy for his friend Mort, which complements William Bartley's equally moving account of the impact Morton Ross had on his students, especially on his Canadian students. Robert Kroetsch was Mort's old Alberta friend from their graduate student days in Iowa City, and William Bartley was Mort's younger Alberta student from his teaching days in Edmonton. The tie in Mort's life between America and Canada was of long duration.

One last piece of evidence that testifies to Mort's devotion to Western Canada was the assiduous work he performed for the NeWest Press in his capacity as fiction editor. Many writers acknowledge the graceful help he gave them.

Finally, we gratefully acknowledge the intrepid help that Mort's friend James Marino gave us in preparing for publication one of Mort's last efforts, the essay entitled "Toward the Margin: Notes in Passing."

Foreword: Morton Ross As an Education

The most important advice Morton Ross gave me while I was writing my Ph.D. dissertation under him came in the form of an exhortation: "Have the courage to be arbitrary." There is a surprising echo here of Ralph Waldo Emerson's "Self-Reliance," surprising since Mort was skeptical of the optimism behind Emerson's famous exhortations to "Trust thyself," and to write "on the lintels of the door post, *Whim*." But in keeping with that skepticism, even as he echoes Emerson, Mort's appeal for self-reliance is a counter to Emerson's facile program of human perfection in which trusting oneself is the initial move. As I understood it, having the courage to be arbitrary requires one to acknowledge imperfection—without being at ease with it—as an inescapable condition of the risky business of choosing and judging. This means mustering the nerve to trust how much one knows but also to acknowledge that one knows very little. I learned that one usually doesn't do justice to an object of inquiry, but it *can't* be done without this surrender to the inevitable surplus of what one doesn't know.

My chief fear in writing about Mort is that I won't do him justice, but I will gladly trust the value of how much indeed I do know about him, and how much I can say about why the generations of undergraduate and graduate students who met him during his twenty-six years in Canada (and, before that, his years in Wyoming, Illinois, and Iowa) were so very lucky. I was far from knowing why, when in 1978, I took Mort's class in nineteenth-century American fiction. Initially, I didn't like this man very much. Mort did not flatter his students. He had no wish to please or ingratiate, a disposition not easy to square with his distantly gentle, avuncular manner, not condescending but not inviting, in short, a quality of self-possession that proved very confusing if not threatening to young students. He rarely told jokes, and if he did they were too witty and adult. The gap could not be closed by discipleship, because his almost ritualistic formality simply forbade even that degree of contact. Not until I was thirty-three years old did he ask me to stop calling him Professor Ross and, at the same time, for the first time ever, he addressed me by my first name. This breakthrough came at the conclusion of my dissertation defence when he emerged from the examination room to tell me that I had passed. Its status as a ritual was confirmed by the fact that we rehearsed it beforehand. "If you pass," he said, "this is what I will say and this is how you will respond." All of this seems rather quaint, but this gracious if studied courtliness has its point. It embodied as it protected a candour and generosity which implied, among other things, a profound rejection of the manners of the academic world, with its professionalized rituals of affability and nastiness, so inimical to speaking truly and fearlessly. It is a world too in which Mort's genuine affability and warm courtesy could be misunderstood, and would prove—and this I find astounding—an occasion to underestimate his noble and acute intelligence. Apart from the company of his very closest friends, Mort exercised that intelligence in the formal theatricality of classroom teaching, where its intact and unalloyed display mattered most of all, and where perhaps Mort was most perfectly himself.

The closest one could get to him was by speaking in class, but the first time I did (we were doing *The Scarlet Letter*) I said something youthfully fatuous, to which he replied: "Have we read the same novel, Mr. Bartley?" Such dismissals, firm, but patient, eventually persuaded us that he cared for us (I wasn't the only one he dismissed) but without sacrificing his care for the complexities of the texts he gave us to read and of the subject at hand. The equipoise between the two cares he maintained never interfered with doing justice—were in fact constitutive of it—and we got what we deserved, the full measure really of the care he felt for us. This sense of justice motivates the single compliment he gave me: after I had finished sitting my comprehensive examinations, I believed I had done well, but submitted without much resistance to Mort's adjustment: "Competent, not brilliant."

To the more resistant student, Mort could indeed be rough, but he was just, and so always with the right touch of care. A case in point—a graduate student in my department, Jason Mighton, who was among the last group of students Mort would teach before he retired (and whose father was also Mort's student) tells a story that can stand for all the other stories we could tell about him. A young woman in the class loudly dismissed Mort's wonderful insight (offered to support a point about a novel) that one can change one's mind about a person unpredictably and suddenly—how a well-timed joke, a turn of phrase, a shift in tone, a gesture, a quick unspoken exchange with the eyes, can, for reasons that arrive only after the fact, damage or launch a friendship, could even deprive one of an enemy. His response (immediately, without his breaking stride) to her rudeness was to tell a story (of which he had at that moment been reminded) of meeting a young woman whom he uncharitably thought wouldn't amount to much because she seemed to have an ugly spirit, until one day he saw her smile unguardedly, and the loveliness of that smile changed his mind unalterably. Was this a free offer of unmerited grace?

Without protest, the young student took the point, as Mort, in this gesture of habitual probity, refused to evade a "teaching moment," as they say now in faculties of Education.

As that young student may have learned, Mort demonstrated his care for us and for the text simultaneously by showing us how to read. How exciting that was—as we learned how to move back and forth through the layers and textures of a text, to trace patterns and structures, to develop an eye for the choice passage, to think heuristically. He taught us, that is, to see how great novels "educe the wonderful from the sensuously palpable" to borrow from his praise of Melville (in his essay, arguably his best, "*Moby-Dick* As an Education"). But he himself was an elegant practitioner of the art of eduction, the art, that is, of drawing out, of bringing into view. All of this was a preparation for something more important—to move from how novels worked (and how they can fail to work) to why we need to honour the novel as *thought*, to see that novels could be true, and that novelists could be wise, to consider that our deepest and richest moral insights are most subtly discovered in the processes of the literary imagination—notions that were as exciting and professionally retrograde then as they are now.

That excitement would shield us from the dictates of academic professionalism which would require students, as those of us who pressed on to graduate school would discover, to choose between the frigid polarities of what Gary Saul Morson distinguishes as "semiotic totalitarianism" (the dogmatic certainty of Marx, Freud, structuralism, Northrop Frye, Foucault, Althusser) and "village relativism" (the dogmatic skepticism of Derrida, de Man, Stanley Fish). But recognizing the novel as an instrument of knowledge, inasmuch as a novel is a hypothetical exploration of a human problem, led us to rest anxiously content with the only sort of insight available—the *probable* insight, educed from the complex, scarcely tractable mess of contingency, lodged somewhere between certainty and skepticism, which provides the basis for our choices, profound or quotidian. That unstable middle ground had its own courageous defenders: twenty years ago, with the help of Mort and his friend and brilliant colleague C. Q. Drummond, we read F. R. Leavis, Yvor Winters, and George Whalley. We wanted to learn how to live in that middle ground, and this meant of course that, whatever our success, we could never become, as Primo Levi puts it, "beadle-technicians" of Theory.

A related and no less valuable emphasis. Mort also helped us understand that there was more at stake in studying American literature than recognizing it as a great national literature. As he made clear, it was especially urgent for *Canadians* to study American literature, a perspective quickened by the fact that Mort was an American expatriate, and who, now a Landed Immigrant, brought his Americanness to bear on the problem of capturing a workable sense of the Canadian identity. How could Canadians fail to see the adaptability to Canadian experience of Henry James's famous remark about the problematic relationship between America and Europe? "It's a complex fate," says James, "being an American, and one of the responsibilities it entails is fighting against a superstitious valuation of Europe." As America is to Europe, so Canada is to America, not to mention Europe. It would take an expatriate's initiative to get us to think about our superstitious valuations of America—whether they yielded a shrill contrariness or slavish imitation. It would take an expatriate's initiative to direct our attention to two of our own most intelligent explorers of the Canadian identity—George Grant and W. L. Morton. Grant reminds us that Canadians are "still enfolded with the Americans in the deep sharing of having crossed the ocean and conquered new land." Mort would argue that the American experience, beginning with that of the Puritans of Massachusetts Bay, was a "particularly audacious effort at such conquest," especially as it became the prototype, as Morton said, of America as a messianic nation that knows no natural limits. Canadians need to understand this if "we are to strengthen our commitment to avoid being enfolded in the audacity if not the effort." The weight of this argument is still considerable, especially since Canada, as wasn't quite apparent in 1978, has ceased to value its English-Anglican and French-Catholic antecedents as a counterweight and as a necessary point of departure towards a middle ground between America and Europe—the fragile promise of the more complex fate of being a Canadian. How fragile that promise is now, for as Mark Steyn, a Canadian expatriate, has put it, "with its history obliterated, its symbols trivialized, and its government mythmaking descending deeper into banality," Canada, at least as an idea having any intellectual strength and vitality, may indeed be a lost cause. We were warned.

But the larger point that emerges here points to what I think is the essence of Mort's legacy. He led us forcefully, in his formal and passionate generosity, to the view that our fates are complex, ranging as we do, if we choose to be free and responsible men and women, in the middle ground—in that risky territory of probable insight and provisional judgement, educing (again that word) truth from circumstance, and testing truth against circumstance. The consolation I take now in this awareness (which scarcely makes my fate less complex) is as great as the pain of growing into it. Only with that awareness are we enlivened to the possibilities of being arbitrary in the special sense that I believe Mort, in a typical gesture of beautiful economy, meant it. And just as Mort made the case to the young people of Alberta—he knew he had no more important a task—so will I—perhaps with the double care I learned from him, if not his acuity—to the young people of Saskatchewan.

William Bartley
University of Saskatchewan

Critical Preliminaries

The Common Pursuit of True Judgment

I have borrowed my title from T. S. Eliot's essay called "The Function of Criticism," which first appeared in 1923. In this I follow F. R. Leavis, who used the first three words of the phrase in 1953 as the title for a collection of essays in which he attempts to demonstrate that the common pursuit of true judgment is the central and proper business of the literary critic. I wish to extend Leavis's point, as he himself has done in other works, in order to insist that the common pursuit of true judgment is the central and proper business of any classroom now devoted to the serious study of literature. Indeed such pursuit is the *only* legitimate function of those who propose or profess to teach literature.

Let me, then, suggest the terms of the argument by some necessarily brief attention to the components of Eliot's phrase. Let's start with the very thorny notion of true judgment. And here I will proceed by way of case history, although, admittedly, one that is a bit shaped and tailored.

It has been my habit to introduce freshman literature courses by asking students to compare their differing judgments about Henry James's character, Daisy Miller. Frequently the comparison condenses into an issue, the two sides of which are roughly that 1) Daisy Miller is an irresponsible flirt and therefore to be condemned, and that 2) Daisy Miller is a courageous opponent of snobbishness and therefore to be celebrated. But, having created the issue, the students now seem reluctant, even unwilling to resolve it, even under pressure of my cries of outraged logic—"But she *can't*, for pity sakes, be *both*! Come now," I continue, "You all seem interested in her; why can't we work to decide which of these two opposing judgments may be the true one, or whether both are inadequate as true judgments." But they remain stubborn. The timid ones, believing apparently that my Ph.D. gives me access to that secret file at English Central where all the solutions are kept, wait for me to resolve the issue they have helped to create. The more energetic, believing either that there is no disputing about taste or that everything is relative, insist that such an issue can't be resolved. And all of them believe, with a fine democratic righteousness, that they have their own opinion already and, by the Bill of Rights and be damned, they are entitled to it.

At this juncture I endure an annual temptation to play the philosopher. After all, the student's fears and objections about moving from his personal opinion to a collaborative quest for true judgment are genuine and far-reaching in implication. They can't be dismissed. They can't be ignored. The epistemological and ontological problems they raise are at least as old as Western civilization, receiving one of their classic formulations in Plato's dialogue "Meno." There the key questions are put like this: "You say you're in quest of a true judgment. If you don't already know what is true, how are you going to recognize the truth when and if you find it? If you already know what true is, why are you looking?" Socrates then struggles to answer and the answers have been increasing in desperate sophistication ever since. Yet it is tempting to join in this philosophical effort, if only to get the students to examine their first, and often hasty opinions. If I could only find the arguments that will convince them that true judgment exists and can be arrived at by something akin to Socratic dialogue, then things will go swimmingly. I confess I have occasionally given way to this temptation. The results were that the students, Henry James, Daisy Miller, and I all foundered, as the text and the actual making of judgments about it were gradually submerged in exclusively metaphysical speculations about whether or not we are ever capable of arriving at true judgments.

But, on the other hand, if I successfully resist this temptation, the class has reached what I consider to be a perilous impasse. If, for our various reasons, we refuse to open the relatively simple question of how we can know which of two opposing judgments has the greater claim to being true, we have in effect denied that there is any standard by means of which we can discriminate among all the possible responses to James's story, deciding which is adequate or inadequate, better or worse, true or false. We have conceded in effect that the proper response to literature consists in what Eliot has called "listening to our inner voice," and that, finally, "we can not only like whatever we like to like, but we can like it for any reason we choose." Such a concession makes me unhappy for a number of reasons, but, self-restrained from too many philosophical arguments, I now move to another tactic—a low and cunning appeal to my students' self-interest, an appeal which goes like this: "We must submit our personal, initial judgments to some standard by which we may discriminate among them, and we *must* do this in order to avoid a painful alternative, that is, the prospect of incredible boredom. If we are to be reduced and confined to a simple exchange of our personal opinions—to a succession of statements about how Daisy makes each of us feel, or what she makes each of us think, then we have sentenced ourselves to a series of Wednesday night prayer meetings in which we each in turn testify as our inner voice directs us: "I feel Daisy Miller is good—Amen, brother." "I'm sure she is misguided—Amen, sister." "I think she is just dumb—and again, Amen." In recent years, I've updated the prayer meeting metaphor by reference to an experience I had in 1968 when I encountered a far-out student just back from a giant zap-in in Golden Gate Park. On one of the few occasions we spoke at any length, he was moved to tell me of a great underground classic he had discovered—James Fenimore Cooper's novel, *The Prairie*. When I asked him why he was so high on it, he replied that it was outa sight, and, when pressed further, would sometimes go as high as three successive outa sights. I was delighted with his enthusiasm and we resonated for a time with the happy vibrations of a shared interest, but the vibrations weren't very helpful in satisfying my curiosity about exactly what *The Prairie* is or what it is good for—questions which had persisted since my first brush with that very odd novel. While I don't underestimate the value of good vibrations—or of prayer meetings, for that matter—neither does much to advance the understanding of a novel, the experience of which we had had in common. By confining himself to personal testimony, my far-out friend has presented me with only an interesting fact about himself. It was a *fact*: he liked Cooper's novel. And I accepted it as fact because it was indisputable. One would be a fool to argue that he really *didn't* like the novel; only he could know for sure whether or not he was reporting his reaction correctly. Quick to generalize from this experience, I now assure my students that if we are content to conduct our meetings as round-robin reports of individual reactions, we will be left in the end with just such a collection of indisputable facts—which will hold as long as nobody changes his mind, and which will be about as useful and interesting to us as the latest Gallup Poll. If we retain any interest in the text, we can use these facts only to calibrate Daisy's popularity among us, but we might as well confess that our interest has shifted from the text to ourselves, and recognize that we have become a genteel version of a Sensitivity Training Group. And here, my students challenge me once again by eagerly embracing the notion of constituting ourselves as an encounter group—a notion that I had half-intended as a put-down.

At this juncture I endure an annual temptation to play the encounter group leader. One of the legacies of the sixties to the seventies has been the enormous proliferation of techniques for raising the level and capacities of human consciousness. These range from drugs, through the various Oriental disciplines of meditation, to the group techniques developed by the human potential movement. These last depend largely on the interaction of a small, self-conscious group to generate intense experience. The hope is that such activity, however painful, boring, or joyous, will ultimately refine the perceptive capacities so that one's experience in future may be heightened and enriched. And there is nothing wrong, after all, in conducting classes in a manner which promotes the skills of perception.

Both Eliot and Leavis make the assumption that one of the major results of the common pursuit of true judgment is just such an improvement in the reader's capacity for sensitive and intelligent response. The reason, then, for resisting the Sensitivity Group temptation is not this emphasis on the subjective aspect of human experience; the trouble comes, rather, with the corresponding deemphasis of the objective source of experience, that is, stimuli from outside the individual consciousness. And the specific trouble is that too many practitioners of raised consciousness are singularly undiscriminating about the objects that fall into the way of their perception. I have seen devotees, their sensibilities honed and sandpapered by abrasive encounters, in rapt contemplation of everything from the back of their own eyelids to a freshly picked radish. In the face of such apparent ecstasy, it is folly to argue that the stories of Henry James might offer a more rewarding experience. The response is too often a smile of serene indifference. In truth, this new hedonism seems dedicated to being thrilled by virtually anything, the more trivial and nondescript the better; thus the ability to get kicks from a radish becomes a positive virtue, and Henry James is valued, if at all, only insofar as he provides a jolt of comparable voltage.

This state of affairs has several unfortunate consequences, only one of which I will touch on. It is illustrated by the kind of curricular tinkering that often accompanies the new hedonism when it is transported into the classroom. The argument runs that if our primary responsibility is to reach and improve the subjective sensibilities of our students, then it follows that we must offer them exercise in responding to works which are both familiar and easily accessible to them—that are, in effect, presold. Edward M. White, the editor of Norton's *The Pop Culture Tradition*, mounts a respectable version of this argument in his introduction:

> ... popular art is unusually appropriate material for the study of analysis—in some ways even more appropriate than the 'fine' arts. Popular art is generally accessible—is everywhere about us—and familiar; it is interesting for what it is and for what it unconsciously reveals about the culture it expresses. In a sense, to examine our popular art is to examine the forces that have helped make us what we are.

Under the protection of such argument, one sees the lyrics of Bob Dylan and Leonard Cohen replacing those of John Donne and Ben Jonson as objects of study. Please let there be no mistake here. I am not objecting to those who would argue that the poetry of Bob Dylan is superior to the poetry of John Donne. I have heard such an argument and while I found it, finally, unconvincing, I had great respect for the proponent who made and defended his judgment in a serious and responsible manner. I have considerably less respect for those who make this replacement on grounds of accessibility and familiarity, even while privately conceding that Donne is a far better poet than Dylan. This seems at best, a condescending treatment of students, at worst, a fraudulent one, for it confesses that the inferior work, simply because it is somehow more accessible and more familiar, is to take the attention withdrawn from the superior. To return, then, to my case study, I try to resist the temptation to play encounter group leader. While I remain concerned to help my students improve their capacities for perception, I can't shake my conviction that Donne is better than Dylan and that Henry James is superior to the best radish in California. My responsibility is, then, as much to the superior qualities of Donne and James as it is to my students. But if we have now moved from our original impasse at all, it is only because the students, stung by my slighting references to pop heroes, now challenge me to defend such exclusive attention to the more traditional classics of English literature.

And at this juncture I endure an annual temptation to play the literary scholar. It is, after all, a role for which I was trained, by the most uncompromising set of literary historians you'd ever want to meet. And it would reestablish my shaken confidence within the most traditional claim our profession has to be called a discipline. But more importantly, it would get me off the horns of those dilemmas about true judgment which I have been rehearsing, for scholarship provides a manageable number of facts which come as close as any to being indisputable, and, unlike the reports of our personal preferences, they have, haven't they, the virtue of being objective. Supplied by painstaking research, supported by the weight and rules of evidence, and sustained by the authority of eminent scholars who are forever checking on one another, such facts can at least illuminate obscure places in the text even if they aren't much good for correcting errors in taste. So persuasive are the arguments for acting the literary scholar in the classroom that one wonders why we ever worried about conflicts in judgment in the first place. Here, for example, is Northrop Frye, in an essay called "On Value-Judgements" which appeared in 1968:

> One cannot pursue [the study of literature] with the object of arriving at value-judgements, because the only possible goal of study is knowledge. The sense of value is an individual, unpredictable, variable, incommunicable, indemonstrable, and mainly intuitive reaction to knowledge.

Thus assured that the judgment of value is so capricious, one can safely confine oneself to dealing out knowledge, and, if there remains any lingering worry that differences in judgments about a work's value may yet be important enough to try to resolve, Frye continues to be reassuring: "When two value judgements conflict, nothing can resolve the conflict except greater knowledge." May we not, then, be content with what can be known with certainty and communicated with security?

There is, however, a serious danger here, and one that Frye himself illustrates. Anyone familiar with his magisterial and panoptic system of generic categories, first developed in *The Anatomy of Criticism*, will know that Professor Frye is a scholar of formidable learning and even more formidable authority. It takes close reading and the penetration of a judicious critic like John Fraser to see that Frye's majestic offering is really a very elaborate apologia for a most conventional academic taste. Behind his scorn for evaluative critics and his effort to give literary study the stability of a science, Professor Frye is actually defending a canon of great writers whose greatness is alleged to need no defence, being, as it were, self-evident. The test case is Milton. Professor Frye is on record as simply dismissing those who have dared to argue that Milton's poetry is disfigured by very grave flaws: "Ezra Pound, T. S. Eliot, Middleton Murry, F. R. Leavis, are only a few of the eminent critics who have abused Milton. Milton's greatness as a poet is unaffected by this: as far as the central fact of his importance in literature is concerned, these eminent critics might as well have said nothing at all." By confining his rebuttal to an insistence on Milton's widely acknowledged position within the developing history of English poetry, Frye has simply missed the point. None of these critics deny the established facts which demonstrate that Milton had an enormous influence on his successors; what they do assert is that Milton's poems have serious defects which compromise their value for a reader, and the compelling question thus raised is whether these assertions are right or wrong. John Fraser provides a paradigm which neatly captures the way in which Frye evades this question: "The garbage stinks." "Nonsense! That garbage can was made by my great-grandfather." Frye's procedures are unfortunately typical of what happens when one yields too easily to the temptations of scholarship. Especially in an age of publish or perish, the industry needed to recover even more arcane facts about an author is too often justified by unquestioning faith in his worth. One can't really excuse a search for Milton's lost laundry tickets, unless one can be secure from serious doubts about his greatness. Furthermore, once recovered, those laundry tickets add their weight to the already impressive brick-work of facts about Milton, a structure which, by its very solidity, begins to function as a fortress for defending him against those who would raise rebellious doubts. At this extreme, then, the possibility of argument in the classroom gives way to the authoritative delivery of fact. One can't really object to such delivery because it is authoritative, for the essence of scholarly facts is that they are publicly verifiable and thus have all the earmarks of being objectively true. But one can object to such delivery because of what it does to the study of literature in the classroom, for, in practice, it removes both the literary work and the student from active participation in the process. Scholarly fact is most relevant to what is called the background or context of a work. For those who agree with Frye that judgments about a work's value are individual, capricious, and incommunicable, the effort to supply background by the facts of biography, literary history, and the history of ideas commands first place. At another remove, such facts are justified by talk about methods of approach to a literary work, routes by which a reader may sneak up on it. What happens of course is that preoccupation with background too often allows the foreground to slip away and concentration on methods of approach often obscures a direct sight of that which we are alleged to be approaching. Exhibit A of these tendencies for me will always be one of my graduate school friends. Obsessed with his suspicion that there were hidden allegories in Henry James's novels, he took a year off to study computer techniques which might help him to establish a full context of allegorical possibilities. He is now of course an editor of that journal called *Computer Studies in the Humanities*; he speaks Fortran, lectures for IBM at fat honoraria, and hasn't read Henry James in fifteen years.

But if the primary work recedes before this devotion to scholarly method or fact, so does the student. The verbal offering of the scholar's information in the classroom, traditionally in the form of a lecture, is quite obviously inefficient. Since the invention of the paperback and of the photocopier, conveying necessary information to students is as inexpensive as it is convenient. It would be insulting to remind you of this truism if it weren't also true that new techniques are often used to perpetuate the old methods. Witness the now proverbial case of the professor who taped his lectures for delivery at seminar meetings scheduled during his absence from campus. Returning unexpectedly, he arrived at a meeting to discover only a room full of tape machines, his own sending away, and his students' machines all wired to receive. This electronic miracle, from which all active mind has been removed, is the most modern fulfillment of Eliot's earlier worry that, if misapplied, scholarship will supply opinion to the passive instead of educating active taste, or, as Leavis puts it, will "abet the reader's desire to arrive without ever having travelled." One should, then, resist the temptation to play the scholar in the classroom. Again, let there be no mistake. The discipline of scholarship is important, even basic to literary study, but we must keep it in its place, as only ancillary to the proper work of the classroom.

And what, finally, is that work. The functions of the philosopher, the encounter group leader, and the scholar are first suspect either because they direct attention away from the text itself, or because they fail to engage the student fully, or both. But finally they must be resisted because these failings impede the demanding but necessary work of making accurate decisions about the literary object—the work of arriving at a true judgment of the object's value. I have touched on some of the theoretical problems which make true judgment so difficult to come by in actual practice. In the face of these problems, the case for persisting in such practice ultimately rests on three hard facts, facts which to my mind make the common pursuit of true judgment absolutely necessary. And the first of these is the unlovely but undeniable fact that we all must die. I had a professor once who could scare the bejammers out of me; fixing me with his eye, he would say: "Mr. Ross, you are exactly thirty-seven minutes closer to death than you were when you entered this classroom." Theatrical, I admit, but of course he was right, and his point was preliminary to a serious argument about choice. If one didn't have to die, there would be no necessity to discriminate among the rush of objects and experiences vying for our attention. One could relish the radish and dig Dylan for as long as they fascinated, and still have all the time needed to become inward with the reaches of Henry James.

But of course we don't have the time for everything, and this leads directly to the second hard fact. Given our human inability to experience everything from the worst to the best, it is our basic propensity to want only the best and to make only those choices which will ensure that we get it. Indeed some moral philosophers defend the absolute proposition that, when presented with alternatives for choice, the human being will always choose what at that moment seems best to him. The kicker here is, of course, the word "seems," and this leads me to the third hard fact: that is, we are all fallible—too often frustrated in our desire for the best by our apparently endless capacity to be wrong about what the best really is.

If we now consider these interlinked facts as they necessarily govern our response to literature, we can see, I think, that together they compel the enterprise of the evaluative or judicious critic. And the best definition of the critic defined by those adjectives is obtained simply enough by pointing to that relatively small handful of critics whose evaluative accomplishments have merited the term. Within the history of English literature, these include Dr. Johnson, Coleridge, Matthew Arnold, and T. S. Eliot. In contemporary letters, the two preeminent examples are Yvor Winters of Stanford University and F. R Leavis, long associated with Cambridge University. To cite the work of Winters and Leavis as outstanding examples of the evaluative enterprise is also to expose its still controversial nature, for they are easily the most vilified of modern critics. The charges against them range from academic bad manners, through arrogant elitism and dogmatism, to arbitrary impressionism, although it is also fair to say that their methods and positions inspire a blind and cultish loyalty as often as they do outrage and indignation. This is not the place either to defend them or to assess the particulars of their work. For my present purpose, they are useful in illustrating the attitudes and procedures I am recommending for use in our classrooms.

First of all, Leavis and Winters have shown themselves to be extraordinarily dedicated readers, passionately devoted to the conviction that the possibilities of human experience are most available to us as they are revealed, shaped, and explored in the language of great literature. If you think about this for a moment, you will see that it is a conviction not now widely shared, even in this profession. But for Leavis and Winters, it means that the accurate judgment of literary works has a direct and determining effect both on the quality of life and of civilization. Without pausing to debate these assertions, let me say that I find the degree of serious commitment revealed by them salutary both for myself and for my students. Too often students come to a course in literature hoping for casual, but high-toned diversion, looking upon their reading as what Leavis has called "an elegantly virtuous dissipation." And too often I ease into professionalism, that pose of aloof dispassion which makes an equally elegant virtue of what is really indifference. It is useful, then, to be shaken up—to be provoked by men for whom poems, plays, and novels are important enough to demand that full justice be done to them, and who therefore undertake the strenuous task of valuing each work exactly as it deserves.

And this unremitting attention to the work itself is the second attitude Leavis and Winters so effectively illustrate. And here, they need to be distinguished first from the New Critics among whom they have occasionally been lumped, and thereby from the familiar charges against the New Criticism of a too exclusive and insular attention to the individual poem or novel. Both men seek to place the individual work with respect to comparable productions within literary history, but, unlike the traditional literary historians preoccupied with the train of sources and influences, they focus attention so that works are tested and measured against one another with the hope, finally, of establishing a clear and defensible hierarchy of valued objects. This is not simply a process of sorting books into fixed pigeon holes of good and bad, best and worst. For both men, propositions that assert that something is good or bad are only summary, short-hand, and often naïve forms for the more complex process of deciding exactly what that something is and exactly what that something does.

It is this process that Leavis and Winters have practiced with forthright and unswerving deliberation. In so doing, they have been called presumptuous, for they presume to guide our reading by printing their decisions and discriminations. In an age of democratic self-reliance, such presumption is doubly glaring. In fact the age has created a paradox in which we teach and guide others so that they may resist the guidance of others—and we may have succeeded too well. But to test the alleged presumption of these critics is really simple enough; read some things they recommend and see if they are right—and if they are, you have already begun to assemble reasons for trusting them further. Winters, for example, has made himself notorious for recommending as excellent some poems by very obscure poets like Jones Very and Adelaide Crapsey, and I used to snigger about this with my colleagues until I took the trouble to read these poems myself.

I was chastened to discover that Winters was right about them, but even when I believe he is wrong, as he has been on other occasions, I have sharpened my own ability to make and defend judgments by abrasion against the clarity of his. Thus Winters performed an even more important service for me, for my encounters with his judgments, however grating at first, gradually helped convince me that the study of literature is most rewarding when it is conducted as a collaborative enterprise. And this leads me, finally, to that other component of Eliot's phrase, the common pursuit.

We would all concede, I think, that the most important things that happen in the study of literature happen privately, at the moment the reader experiences and reacts to the text before him. The process of evaluative criticism begins quite simply with the articulation of one's honest reaction to the text. Since, under pressure of time, we desire the good, we need to inspect our reaction so as not to be self-deceived. This careful inspection is what I think is meant by responsible judgment, that is, active thought motivated by an urgency to fully understand and adequately appreciate what has happened to us, what the stimulus of the text has done to us. It is not easy, but I think no one will deny it is absorbing, and it leads invariably to that moment when we are satisfied that we comprehend the text and our reaction to it. It is, however, too easy to mistake this satisfying moment for the end of literary study. Rightly seen, it is just here that the proper work of the classroom begins.

The hardest of my three elementary facts to make inward is the fact that we are fallible, but once we muster the humility to retain it, it follows that we need not only to form and examine our judgments privately, we need also to test them against the judgments of others. Leavis has formulated this procedure as an exchange in which the first speaker says: "This is so, is it not?" prompting the second speaker to reply: "Yes, but...." What saves such exchange from being simply exercise in debate, or in polemics, or in the rhetoric of persuasion is that it *be* governed by my admitting that I may be wrong and you may be right, and by an effort, we may get nearer the truth. If we do nothing more than promote this attitude in our classrooms, we will have performed a valuable service. But what makes the common pursuit of true judgment, as it is conceived by Leavis and others, most exciting is the possibility that the quest for truth may have been traditionally misconceived. It may *not* be those fixed and absolute Platonic forms of truth, always glimmering ahead and always eluding us, for which we are looking. We may instead be actually creating meaningful and useful truths in the very act of pursuing them in common. This is the possibility, at least, that Leavis holds out when he defines the creative process of criticism as "that interplay of personal judgments in which values are established and a world created that is neither public in a sense congenial to science, or merely private"—but a fully human world in which experience is not objectified, quantified, or averaged, but assessed, savoured, and understood as it can be shared. Leavis goes on to say that it is this common pursuit, this "collaborative-creative process," which sustains the existence of literature in English, "a living whole that can have its life only in the living present, in the creative response of individuals, who collaboratively renew and perpetuate what they participate in—a cultural community or consciousness." This is, then, the proper work of our classrooms. This is so, is it not?

The Edmund Kemper Broadus Lectures

American Public Styles: Community and the Private Heart

The American Puritans: Piercing the Private Heart

Every year the English Department invites the community to gather for some public discourse in honour of Edmund Kemper Broadus, the first professor of English at the University of Alberta. It is a pleasant custom, and I'm honoured to be this year's speaker, but the occasion should also remind us that the community we now take for granted had once to be created, and that it was created in part by a special kind of public discourse. In an essay called "Small Beginnings," Professor Broadus recalled the task facing Henry Marshall Tory and his four-man faculty just seventy-five years ago in 1908, the task of "getting into touch with these scattered three hundred thousand [citizens] and persuading them that there really was a university in their province." The principal means of accomplishing this task was "the extension lecture," which took them, as Professor Broadus put it, "to every little rabbit-path of a settlement in the province," once for him to a southern town on a Saturday night where he competed with a dance at the Oddfellows' Hall and the weekly moving-picture show. His audience consisted of three grim ladies who lacked dancing partners and four "wriggling little boys" who lacked a dime for the movies. But despite these difficulties, Professor Tory also believed that an unbroken tradition of British and European respect for learning helped them in establishing the new community. Perhaps because the history of the United States is a history of broken traditions, what may have been difficult in Alberta has been even more difficult below the border. Certainly that history is less one of community than of challenges to community.

A catalogue of Americans speaking for and against community would illustrate both the variety and the vitality of American styles of public discourse. Its point would be to underscore the frequency and persistence with which American men and women have tried to create community by the sheer force of public language, and it could read like this: stump speeches, filibusters, whistle-stops, Congressional boilerplate, and Fourth of July, spread-eagle operations; toastmasters, moderators, interlocutors, valedictorians; spellbinders, high-binders, steamrollers, and stemwinders; the pitch, malarky, the spiel, hogwash, whitewash, buncombe, and bushwah; the soapbox, the rostrum, the crackerbarrel, the caucus; fancy cussing, and tall tales, fireside chats and testimonials, the Chautauqua tent, the union hall, circuit riders, and camp meetings; obsequies, lyceums, open forums, and town meetings; commencement addresses, booster luncheons, and prayer meetings; Bible-thumpers, pulpit-pounders, Gypsy

Smith, Billy Sunday, Billy Graham, Billy Joe Haggis, and William Jennings Bryan, the Silver-Tongued Orator of the Platte, who aroused the entire west with a single phrase: "You shall not crucify mankind on a cross of gold." In the face of such riches, I can tell only part of the story; I will consider four American public styles as they worked to create—or to destroy—community. These are the preaching of seventeenth-century American Puritans; the eighteenth-century journalism of Benjamin Franklin; the lyceum lecturing of Ralph Waldo Emerson, and the storytelling of Nathaniel Hawthorne. I begin with the Puritans.

The most famous early expression of a hope for genuine community in the American new world is a lay sermon by John Winthrop, governor of the Massachusetts Bay Company. He delivered it in 1630 to those on board the *Arbella*, the flagship of the fleet carrying the first great Puritan migration to the Bay colony. Under the title "A Model of Christian Charity," Winthrop followed one standard form of the Puritan sermon by beginning with a statement of the doctrine to be expounded or "opened":

> God Almighty, in his most holy and wise providence, hath so disposed of the condition of mankind, as in all times some must be rich, some poor, some high and eminent in power and dignity; others mean and in subjection.

To a modern ear, especially the one tuned by Marx, this sounds like the condition for endless class warfare rather than community, but Winthrop, in giving the reasons for this wise Providence, argues that God creates such inequality so "that every man might have need of other, and from hence they might be all knit more nearly together in the bond of brotherly affection." Winthrop is traditional in his view of society; here the individual is defined and valued, not as or for himself, but for his worth and function as an interacting member of a corporate body. Winthrop thus frames his imperatives for communal effort:

> We must be knit together in this work as one man, we must entertain each other in brotherly affection, we must be willing to abridge our selves of our superfluities, for the supply of others' necessities; we must uphold a familiar commerce together in all meekness, gentleness, patience, and liberality; we must delight in each other, make others' conditions our own; we must rejoice together, mourn together, labor and suffer together, always having before our eyes our Commission and Community in the work, our community as members of the same body.

The reward for such concerted effort, Winthrop ends by promising, is that the God of Israel "shall make us a praise and a glory, that men shall say of succeeding plantations: the Lord make it like that of New England: for we must consider that we shall be as a City upon a Hill, the eyes of all people are upon us."

The eyes of conventional historians, on the one hand, have generally seen the history of the Bay colony as the frustration of Winthrop's plans for a model community. They have measured the first twenty years of the town's life against the governor's sermon, and have found a tragedy in which Winthrop's ideals are brought low, chiefly by the gathering forces of individualism. Historians of ideas, on the other hand, have been fascinated by the intricacy of the Puritans' visionary city upon a hill. They have tended to treat the inevitable discrepancy between Puritan ideals and New England actuality as irrelevant; the most extreme case is Sacvan Bercovitch's claim in *The American Jeremiah* (1978) that the Puritan vision "survived through a mode of ambiguity that denied the contradiction between history and rhetoric." Bercovitch is the most prominent successor to Perry Miller who, in his pioneering and still authoritative study of the seventeenth century *The New England Mind* (1939), first celebrated the Puritan enterprise in America as a remarkable intellectual synthesis—a synthesis which was itself evidence of the existence of genuine community. So frequent are Miller's assertions of successful synthesis that his expositions of Puritan thought begin to sound a bit like a pitchman's spiel for a highwire act. For instance, Miller judges the American Puritan theories of salvation in these words: "One of the most amazing achievements of the Puritan mind, a unification of inherited science and intense piety, containing at one and the same time all the advantages of order and all the charms of caprice, all the security of an assured income and all the fascinations of a gamble." Miller's successors in the field have adopted and broadened his images of balance precariously achieved, so much so that Bercovitch virtually exhausts the vocabulary of synthesis. In his book, *The Puritan Origins of the American Self* (1975), Bercovitch displays the coherence of what he calls the American Puritan Vision by repeatedly asserting that its elements are integrated, converging, transmuted, converted, subsumed, interacting, blended, blurred, merged, transformed, conjoined, conflated, fused, or collapsed into one another, most often with the implication that because disparate elements are so met, they are necessarily well met. Such language seems useful in rescuing the wit and ingenuity of Puritan thinkers from ninteenth-century historians—historians like Charles Francis Adams, who dismissed Puritan writing as "a literature of forgotten theology and unreadable homilies," of "utter intellectual aridity." But the language of synthesis can be misleading as well; it occasionally smudges together elements that remained unreconciled in the Puritan experience, or at least in such dangerous tension as to subvert their enterprise. One such pair of opposing elements, in fact, shaped the Puritan public style in America.

The American Puritan preachers evolved a public style that served incompatible and finally irreconcilable ends. To put it as simply as possible, insofar as their public style was bent to instruction, it assumed and fostered a sense of community; insofar as it relied on provocation, it worked to separate and isolate the individual from community. One way to focus this problem is to point out contradictory judgments that grew out of Miller's study of the New England mind. Miller notes at one point that "the figure of the pious and trembling individual closeted alone with his Bible, of the solitary walker with God, is often taken to be the true symbol of the Puritan spirit," and he concedes that after the collapse in England of the Puritan political program, this was indeed the case. Puritanism now focused on the inward spiritual quest of the individual sinner, as Bunyan's *Grace Abounding* attests. In seventeenth-century New England, however, as Miller points out, Puritan theory was public and social rather than private and individualistic, an amalgam of the civil and the ecclesiastical, stressing public discourse in the form of scriptural explication to the covenanted church. As Miller says, congregations heard the word of God ". . . not as it is written in revelation, but as it was expounded by the ministry, refashioned into doctrines, reasons, and uses." But Miller's view of a puritan community united by public discourse remains suspended over his recognition that one thrust of that discourse was to isolate the individual from community. Miller argues that the doctrine of regeneration, for example, made the Puritans "experts in psychological dissection and connoisseurs of moods before it made them moralists," forcing them into "solitude and meditation" by the need to cast up their moral accounts. To support his claim Miller quotes the American puritan Thomas Hooker: ". . . but in a solitary Desert place, he will allure us, and draw us into the wilderness, from the company of men, when he will speak to our heart." Miller's considerable achievement has been to establish the ingenuity of the Puritan thinkers' efforts to bridge this space between the communal city on the hill and the solitary desert place, but that achievement hasn't dimmed the recognition among scholars that Puritan public discourse did as much to create that space as to bridge it.

The best illustration in New England of the incompatible aims of the Puritan public style is found in the work and career of John Cotton, the first man appointed to the post of teacher for the original congregation gathered at Boston. Already a preacher of great repute when he migrated to new Boston in 1633 at age forty-nine, Cotton was arguably the most learned among the first generation of Massachusetts leaders. He was one of only two New England divines who held the degree of Bachelor of Divinity, his from Emmanuel College, Cambridge, which then required seven years of study beyond the B.A. His grandson, Cotton Mather, called him "a most universal scholar, and a living system of the liberal arts, and a walking library." Although he was famous for spending twelve hours a day alone in his study, he did much to determine the shape of community in the new colony. He was among the first overseers of Harvard College, founded in 1636 to insure a continuing supply of learned clergy. He was author of a large part of the colony's legal code, and of the most popular New England catechism, titled *Milk for Babes, Drawn Out of the Breasts of Both Testaments*. He became the colony's ablest defender when its unique system of Congregational church government came under attack from English Presbyterians on the right and from separatists like Roger Williams on the sectarian left. Moses Coit Tyler, the most prominent ninteenth-century historian of American literature, recognized Cotton's civic authority in New England by calling him "the unmitred pope of a pope-hating commonwealth."

But from 1612, the year in which Cotton left Cambridge University to become vicar of St. Botolph's Church in old Boston, Lincolnshire, he had devoted most of his public energies to preaching. In that year he apparently made a deliberate decision to shape his public style to the needs of a wider audience. His contemporary, Thomas Allen, later explained that Cotton "had a great conflict in himself about the composing of his sermons, viz., whether after the plain and profitable way, by raising of doctrines, with propounding the reasons and uses of the same, or after the mode of the University at that time, which was to stuff and fill their sermons with as much quotation and citing of authors as might possibly be." Cotton's choice was to follow the plain and profitable way as it had been set out most notably in William Perkins' manual called "The Art of Prophecying." There Perkins had distilled what he termed "The Order and Summe of the sacred and only method of preaching" under four headings, all of them designed for instruction:

> 1. To read the text distinctly out of the Canonical Scriptures. 2. To give the sense and understanding of it being read, by the Scripture itself. 3. To collect a few and profitable points of doctrine out of the natural sense. 4. To apply (if he have the gift) the doctrine rightly collected, to the life and manners of men in a simple and plaine speech."

Perkins' methods were the practical implementation of Puritan intentions to replace the traditional sacraments and ceremonies of the church with the authority of the word alone as the bond of community; the minister's principal task would thus become public explication, the opening and exposition of central texts for common understanding and use. In the new world, during nineteen years of Sunday sermons and weekday lectures, John Cotton exercised these methods in explicating, by the reckoning of his grandson, Cotton Mather, "the Old Testament once, and a second time as far as the thirtieth chapter of Isaiah; the whole New Testament once and a second time as far as the eleventh chapter of Hebrews," with, adds Mather, "innumerable other scriptures on incidental occasions."

One piece of evidence that Cotton was effective in this instruction is that most of the fourteen volumes of his sermons that survive in print do so as reconstructions from careful notes taken by those who heard them. This may also account for Moses Coit Tyler's judgment of Cotton's writings as devoid of any interest except the pedagogical:

> These are indeed clear and cogent in reasoning: . . . but that is all. . . . One wanders through these vast tracts and jungles of Puritanic discourse—exposition, exhortation, logic-chopping, theological hair-splitting—and is unrewarded by a single passage of eminent force or beauty, uncheered even by the felicity of a new epithet in the objurgation of sinners, or a new tint in the landscape-painting of hell.

Tyler's tastes are clearly romantic, but by preferring sublime evocations—as in novel tints for the landscapes of hell—he undervalues the preachers' concern to strengthen the powers of the believer's understanding. Some later Puritan thinkers, using faculty psychology, had argued that unregenerate men inherited a form of insanity from Adam who, at the moment of the fall, had suffered a massive derangement in the proper ordering of his faculties. By his act of disobedience, Adam's reason had toppled from its position of command and control, thus enslaving his will to complete direction from his basest emotions; this genetic defect marks all of Adam's descendants. But God will save his elect and He does so through a curative process of regeneration. God's free gift of unmerited grace is the agency of this regeneration, the means of restoring mental and spiritual health. Its first task is to reinvigorate the understanding so that it may regain control over the emotions and the will. Because the Puritans regarded the sermon as the principal means by which God conveys saving grace to unregenerate men, its first appeal is to the understanding.

Here, for example, is Michael Wigglesworth's formulation: the proper rhetoric will, says Wigglesworth, "secretly convey life into the hearer's understanding, rousing it out of its former slumber, quickening it beyond its natural vigor, elevating it above its ordinary conceptions." It is this effort to revive the understanding that dictates the shape of John Cotton's sermons, what some have called an obsessive style. This is in essence Coit Tyler's description, updated and flattened out by modern psychoanalytic talk, but no less dismissive. But for all their complaints about obsessive rationality in the recorded sermons, both Tyler and recent commentators recognize that such judgments simply do not square with the reports of those who actually heard them. The testimony of Cotton's associate and occasional rival at First Church, Boston, the pastor John Wilson, is typical: "Mr. Cotton preaches with such authority, demonstration, and life that, methinks, when he preaches out of any prophet or apostle, I hear not him; I hear that very prophet or apostle. Yea, I hear the Lord Jesus Christ speaking in my heart." What Tyler found was the carefully preserved record of Cotton's public instruction; what Wilson and others report is the living force of Cotton's provocation—a process Cotton often referred to as the piercing of the private heart.

For Cotton, as for most Puritan ministers, instruction in the meaning of God's word was essential for the creation, guidance, and preservation of the holy commonwealth, but insufficient for the complete regeneration of his hearers unless accompanied by the work of the holy spirit. Cotton expounded the point at great length, especially in six sermons preached on Acts 2:37. Cotton concentrated on the first part of this text which reads: "Now when they heard this, they were pricked in their hearts. . . ." Cotton first explains the most important reason for "hearing the word": "It has pleased the Lord much to delight in this ordinance, and to make it a principal sovereign means for the piercing of the hearts of his people." As Cotton carefully explains, the target here is not the understanding, but the human will itself: "By the heart you must not understand the fleshy part of the body. . . . It means the will of a man, which lies in the heart." In the process of explaining why the depraved will must be subject to such violent assault, Cotton defines the limits of rational instruction: "Men may change our minds, by giving us better reasons for things than we discerned before, and may alter our judgments and opinions by strength of reason, but no man is able to change the heart but only God." Here then is the limit of the minister's learning; he may and he must instruct the understanding, but he can only pray that God will use his words, inspirit them, for the more violent attack necessary in piercing the sin-hardened heart. Cotton takes assurance from Scripture that this is exactly God's intention: "By ordaining the breath of the word to be the breath of the spirit; whenever his word is dispensed he will accompany it with the breath of his own spirit, which sets an edge upon it, so as they shall sink deeply; it is the spirit of God that gives it a point." Cotton then continues to draw out the figure of piercing, reminding his audience of the Scriptural evidence that the word is sharper than a two-edged sword, that it is compared to goads and nails, to sharp and keen arrows. Students of Cotton's style have found him more restrained than other New England ministers in brandishing the rhetorical sword, but even his gentler modes suggest that Cotton discovered more than one way to provoke and pierce the heart. One of his favorite texts for sermons was The Song of Solomon, and he manipulated its erotic imagery, always explaining as he did so, in order to woo, soften, and otherwise seduce the stony heart. William Hubbard, writing in 1680, very aptly recognized that Cotton's intent to penetrate the heart was the same in both his militant and his erotic modes: "Mr. Cotton had such an insinuating and melting way in his preaching that he would usually carry his very adversary captive after the triumphant chariot of his rhetoric."

Whatever the method of provocation, its success was signaled when the listener felt the full trauma of the experience: Cotton concludes one of his sermons on Acts 2:37 by asserting: "Had saving grace seized upon thy will, thy heart would have been pierced and broken." This was only one expression of Cotton's conviction, evident especially during the American years, that the only true signs of election or salvation were matters of intense, often painful private feeling. With most Puritans, Cotton held that because the covenant of works had been broken by Adam's fall, unregenerate man could do nothing to insure his own salvation. The gracious gift of saving faith to God's foreordained elect is extended not because the individual merits it, but because God has freely and mercifully chosen to give it. It follows that the performance of good works can not earn salvation. And it is just here that the Puritans encountered one set of their celebrated dilemmas. Psychologically, although the believer might accept the doctrine that he could never be absolutely sure of his election, he needed hopeful signs lest he fall into despair or moral fatalism. Publicly, the problem was even more acute; in New England the migrating Puritans had undertaken to establish a holy commonwealth based on a gathering of the elect into the visible church. Church membership, the right to vote and hold office, were all determined by the community's ability to discern and separate the elect from the unregenerate, however provisionally, a separation that required reliable and public tests.

One solution to these problems was to reintroduce the performance of good works, now not as the means of earning grace, but rather as one visible sign that enabling grace had already been received. Puritan thinkers, studying case histories of the saintly, had evolved elaborate morphologies of conversion as guidelines by which the individual believer might chart his spiritual status; one version summarized the process of regeneration as marked by three stages: 1) justification, in which the believer experienced a relieving sense that his sins had been forgiven, 2) vocation, by which he felt a new sense of calling in both his secular and spiritual occupations, and 3) sanctification, virtually a life-long stage in which the justified believer accumulated evidence that he was growing in sanctity, in the ability and the desire to perform good works. This last stage came to be accepted by most New England leaders as a continuing and public evidence of election, available for inspection by anyone in the community.

John Cotton is notable for his rejection of this view; he argued that the community's reliance on sanctification was doctrinally unsound because it revived the broken covenant of works. He further argued that it was psychologically and morally dangerous because it encouraged self-righteousness and hypocrisy. For Cotton, the true and only test of election was an active faith, the presence of the holy spirit felt working within the believer's heart; any consequent gifts, like a renewed ability to behave well, were to be praised, but since good behavior was within the capacity of unregenerate men as well, it was beside the point as a test of election. "It is the desire of my heart by the grace of Christ," Cotton wrote, "to provoke Christians (in this country of universal profession) not to rest in any changes of graces, duties, or ordinances." He goes on: "I would not wish Christians to build the signs of their Adoption by Christ upon any Sanctification but such as floweth from faith in Christ Jesus; for all other—righteousness may be mortal seed." Other Puritan leaders in New England had rather automatically assumed that morality argued piety, that public propriety was a visible index of saving grace, and that continuing good citizenship was practical evidence of election. Thus Cotton, by insisting that genuine election could only be felt intensely and subjectively as a private experience, still faced the problem of public tests, a problem that had been solved to others' satisfaction. Cotton's solution was to become the principal architect of an innovative practice in the churches of New England, the requirement that applicants for church membership make, in addition to the standard confession of faith, a public declaration of their subjective experiences with the saving work of grace.

Edmund Morgan has traced the history of this practice in his book *Visible Saints* (1963), where he describes its procedures, and offers evidence which suggests the difficulty of determining whether or not such a narration was genuine. He reports how some of these accounts that have been preserved strongly indicate that the narrators were familiar with the forms of conversion. So strict were these forms one might even call them stereotypes. Some elders apparently found this stereotyped testimony reassuring because it helped avoid the excesses of enthusiasm, something universally warned against in the seventeenth century and defined by Henry More "as nothing else but a misconceit of being *inspired*." Others deplored the stereotypic repetitions as smacking of the rote formulas of confession associated with detested Catholic practice, but even they must have been a bit startled by the confident testimony of one Captain John Underhill, who asserted that saving grace had come to him while he was enjoying a pipe of the good creature tobacco. It was not unusual for congregations to reject such testimony. There was one occasion when the leaders rejected a petition for a new church in Dorchester because of a whole range of unsatisfactory expressions of the work of grace from the would-be founders. John Winthrop explained in his Journal: "The reason was for that most of them had builded their comfort of salvation upon unsound grounds, *viz.*, some upon dreams and ravishes of spirit by fits, . . . others upon duties and performances." Winthrop's objections here illustrate the two extremes—excessive enthusiasm and excessive reliance on good works—between which the American Puritans were trying to walk a middle way. As Cotton himself put it: "Zeal must be according to knowledge, knowledge is no knowledge without zeal, and zeal is but a wild-fire without knowledge." Cotton's problem was that while shared knowledge was the only secure basis for community, zeal remained a property of the private heart.

But if the community laboured with the problem of distinguishing the elect from the unregenerate, Cotton himself had ample evidence that his efforts to provoke his parishioners as well as to instruct them had been inspired with the capacity to convey the experience of saving grace. His considerable harvest of souls had begun rather impressively back in his university days when his preaching had converted John Preston, a promising student at Cambridge who later became master of Emmanuel, a favorite of James I, and one of the most sought-after preachers in England. In 1633, the year of Cotton's arrival in new Boston, John Winthrop reported in his Journal that because of Cotton's preaching "more were converted and added to that church than to all the other churches in the Bay. . . . Divers profane and notorious evil persons came and confessed their sins, and were comfortably received into the bosom of the church." But the full effect on the community of Cotton's provocation is best illustrated by his most famous convert, Mistress Anne Hutchinson.

Mrs. Hutchinson had been Cotton's parishioner in old Boston and had become so dependent upon his preaching that she followed him to New England. There she had formed the habit of gathering people in her home to study Cotton's sermons, a practice not uncommon in Boston. Her twice-weekly meetings became popular and soon the group was not only studying, but criticizing the sermons of other ministers, particularly those who put public sanctification before Cotton's own emphasis on saving faith as a private experience. Soon the group was charging that only Mr. Cotton preached the true covenant of grace while all others in the Bay were preaching a covenant of works. They were especially critical of Cotton's colleague at First Church, the pastor John Wilson, and soon the growing dissension in the congregation spread to other churches. As was to be expected in the holy commonwealth, the issue very soon became political as well. The controversy raged for some two years and finally reached a climax when Mrs. Hutchinson was brought to trial before the General Court in November of 1637. Governor Winthrop had taken note of Mrs. Hutchinson in his Journal a year before and had been brisk about her errors: "One Mrs. Hutchinson, a member of the church of Boston, a woman of ready wit and bold spirit, brought over with her two dangerous errors: 1. That the person of the Holy Ghost dwells in a justified person, 2. That no sanctification can help to evidence to us our justification."

In the intervening year the issues had become so tangled that Winthrop opened her trial with only the most general of charges: "you are called here as one of those that have troubled the peace of the commonwealth and the churches here." During the first day, Mrs. Hutchinson confounded her examiners by demanding more specific charges and stricter rules for the admission of hearsay evidence. Furthermore, she claimed that her views were simply those of her teacher, Mr. Cotton. But on the second day, under the badgering of the assembled magistrates and ministers, she gave them what they were looking for. The record reads as follows:

> Mrs. Hutchinson: If you please to give me leave, I shall give you the ground of what I know to be true.... I bless the Lord, he hath let me see which was the clear ministry and which the wrong.... Now if you do condemn me for speaking what in my conscience I know to be truth I must commit myself unto the Lord. Mr. Nowell: How do you know that that was the spirit? Mrs. Hutchinson: How did Abraham know that it was God that bid him offer his son, being a breach of the sixth commandment? Deputy Governor: By an

immediate voice. Mrs. Hutchinson: So to me by an immediate revelation. Deputy Governor [and here the text uses an exclamation mark]: How! an immediate revelation. Mrs. Hutchinson: By the voice of his own spirit to my soul.

And with this her fate was sealed. After asserting that she was guilty of "the most desperate enthusiasm in the world," Governor Winthrop pronounced the verdict:

> Mrs. Hutchinson, the sentence of the court you hear is that you are banished from out of our jurisdiction as being a woman not fit for our society, and are to be imprisoned till the court shall send you away. Mrs. Hutchinson: I desire to know wherefore I am banished? Governor: Say no more, the court knows wherefore and is satisfied.

And indeed Governor Winthrop, the author of "A Model of Christian Charity," did know wherefore. In a later account he makes the reason for her banishment very clear:

> For here she hath manifested that her opinions and practice have been the cause of all our disturbances, and that she walked by such a rule as cannot stand with the peace of any state; for such bottomless revelations, as either came without any word, or without the sense of the word (which was framed to humane capacity) if they be allowed in one thing, must be admitted a rule in all things; for they being above reason and Scripture, they are not subject to control.

Although John Cotton tried to soften the judgments against Mrs. Hutchinson, he finally repudiated her and joined those who added censure and excommunication from her church to her banishment from the colony. Commentators have differed in their judgments of Cotton's role in the controversy. Perry Miller sees his action as a cowardly compromise to save his standing in the community. Perhaps, however, we should judge Cotton not so much a coward as a naïve scholar. Whatever the proper judgment, it seems clear that in the case of Mrs. Hutchinson and her followers, who persistently claimed Cotton as their teacher, it was his provocation rather than his careful instruction that had most moved them. By claiming direct revelation from the Holy Spirit implanted within them, they had separated the piercing spirit from the guiding authority of the word; they had thus abandoned and subverted the communal force of Cotton's patient instruction in reason and the Scripture. The result, as Cotton's own epigram had foreseen, was a zealous wildfire that almost consumed the infant commonwealth.

Thus the Puritan public style opened a breach between communal knowledge and private insight that can be traced in American life since the seventeenth century. In the second lecture, we will consider a curious expression of this breach in the *Autobiography* of Benjamin Franklin.

Benjamin Franklin: Masks for Meeting Community

Benjamin Franklin was born in Boston in 1706 and, as he reports in his *Autobiography*, "my parents had early given me religious impressions, and brought me through my childhood piously in the dissenting way," that is, in the New England Puritan way. That way was still sustained and directed by public preaching, and Franklin confesses that the habit of attending sermons stayed with him, however reluctantly and sporadically, throughout a long life. But in its reports of preachers and sermon-going, the *Autobiography* also records profound changes in that American public style. Franklin tells of one Philadelphia preacher who

> used to visit me sometimes as a friend, and admonish me to attend his administrations. . . . Had he been, in my opinion, a good preacher perhaps I might have continued. . . . But his discourses were chiefly either polemic arguments, or explications of the peculiar doctrines of our sect, and were all to me very dry, uninteresting, and unedifying, since not a single moral principle was inculcated or enforced, their aim seeming to be rather to make us Presbyterians than good citizens.

Franklin then offers as an example a sermon preached on a text from Philippians:

> . . . I imagined, in a sermon on such a text, we could not miss of having some morality: But he confined himself to five points only. . . . 1. Keeping holy the Sabbath day. 2. Being diligent in reading the holy Scriptures. 3. Attending duly the publick worship. 4. Partaking of the Sacrament. 5. Paying a due respect to God's ministers. These might be all good things, but, as they were not the kind of good things that I expected from that text, I despaired of ever meeting with them from any other, was disgusted, and attended his preaching no more.

Franklin imposes standards here which respect only one of John Cotton's homiletic aims, public instruction, the inculcation and enforcement of moral principles by which good citizens are made. The preacher's talk of the means of piety, of the agencies by which the private heart might be pierced or provoked, may be talk about good things, but dwelling on them disgusts Franklin and he simply quits listening.

Although Franklin's father had originally intended him for "the service of the Church," the pressure of events made him a printer instead of a preacher, and in that occupation he acquired and came to represent in America a public style that was to rival and finally to supplant preaching as the dominant public medium of the American eighteenth century. In the process, John Cotton's pious intention to pierce and provoke gave way to its opposite in Franklin's deliberate effort to avoid provocation. In order to do this, Franklin carefully trained himself in all the techniques of public ingratiation, and the resulting style is best described as obliging, civil, engaging, urbane, easy, affable, familiar, and agreeable. But let Franklin himself explain: ". . . as prose writing has been of great use to me in the course of my life, and was a principal means of my advancement, I shall tell you how, in such a situation, I acquired what little ability I have in that way." He begins this account by recording his conviction that the discourse of preachers offered bad models for imitation. He speaks of his early fondness for argument, and then says:

> Which disputatious turn . . . is apt to become a very bad habit, making people often extremely disagreeable in company, by the contradiction that is necessary to bring it into practice, and thence, besides souring and spoiling the conversation, is productive of disgusts and perhaps enmities where you may have occasion for friendship. I had caught it by reading my father's books of dispute about religion. Persons of good sense, I have since observed, seldom fall into it, except lawyers, university men, and men of all sorts that have been bred at Edinborough.

If Franklin knew what to avoid, he was guided by what he seems to have recognized immediately as a proper model for style: "About this time I met with an odd volume of the *Spectator*. It was the third. I had never before seen any of them. I bought it, read it over and over, and was much delighted with it. I thought the writing excellent, and wished, if possible, to imitate it." Franklin wrote this account in 1771, anticipating in print by ten years the advice given by Dr. Johnson in *The Life of Addison*: "Whoever wishes to attain an English style, familiar but not coarse, and elegant but not ostentatious, must give his days and nights to the volumes of Addison." And Johnson's carefully balanced judgments of Addison's prose as "the model of the middle style" seem generally apt for Franklin's as well: "On grave subjects not formal, on light occasions not groveling; always equable and always easy, without glowing words or pointed sentences." With certain allowances made for its homespun, provincial context, there is little doubt that at its best Franklin's public style deserves these judgments, and that he earned them through the assiduous labor which Johnson recommends. Franklin tells us that he worked at improving his writing at night, before and after work, and especially on Sundays, "evading as much as I could the common attendance on public worship, which my father used to exact of me when I was under his care. . . ."

Franklin's preference for schooling from the *Spectator* rather than the preachers, and his choice of the vocation of printer-publisher-man of letters, signals the increasing authority, especially among the aspiring, of journalism in the eighteenth century. It was within this republic of letters, not within a theocracy, that Franklin both made his own fortune and became an influential public voice with the marked success of his several journalistic ventures, most notably *Poor Richard's Almanack*. He considered the *Almanack* to be "a proper vehicle for conveying instruction among the common people, who bought scarcely any other books." "I considered my newspaper, also, as another means of communicating instruction, and reprinted in it extracts from the *Spectator*, and other moral writers; and sometimes published little pieces of my own. . . ." Thus Franklin became the principal American representative of the *Spectator*'s effort *not* to implant grace in the believer, but to reform his manners; not to provoke piety, but to promote civility.

Dr. Johnson explained it well: "Before the *Tatler* and *Spectator*, . . . England had no masters of common life. . . . We had many books to teach us our more important duties, and to settle opinions in philosophy and politicks; but an *Arbiter Elegantiarum*, a judge of propriety, was yet wanting, who should survey the track of daily conversation, and free it from thorns and prickles, which tease the passer, though they do not wound him." Johnson then sets out the tasks for such an arbiter: "To teach the minuter decencies and inferior duties, to regulate the practice of daily conversation, to correct those depravities which are rather ridiculous than criminal, and remove those grievances which, if they produce no lasting calamities, impress hourly vexation." Johnson concludes: "The *Tatler* and *Spectator* adjusted . . . the unsettled practice of daily intercourse by propriety and politeness."

The virtues Johnson touches on here were collectively manifested in an agreed convention in the eighteenth century, the acceptance by all classes of the conversation of gentlemen as the best model for discourse, written and spoken. Franklin aspired to and achieved those virtues by force of imitation, but in the major record of that achievement, the

Autobiography, there is a tension between two sets of those virtues that raises serious questions about his public style.

The art of the eighteenth-century gentleman was to speak his mind clearly and exactly without raising his voice or otherwise giving offence. On the one hand the demand was for candour, an open and straightforward frankness of expression; on the other were the demands of courtesy, the need to secure and maintain the respect and cooperation of other parties to the conversation. These two demands on the gentleman's style are not necessarily incompatible, but the *Autobiography* offers strong evidence that Franklin avoided the strain of meeting them both by simply sacrificing candour to ingratiation. This seems especially true in his accounts of his self-education in the proper style. Having prudently given up his disputatious turn because it was "productive of disgusts and perhaps enmities where you may have occasion for friendship," Franklin goes on to detail his imitation of another famous model.

> While I was intent on improving my language, I met with an English grammar ... at the end of which were two little sketches of the arts of rhetoric and logic, the latter finishing with a specimen of a dispute in the Socratic method; ... I was charmed with it, adopted it, dropt my abrupt contradiction and positive argumentation, and put on the humble inquirer and doubter.
> I continued this method some few years, but gradually left it, retaining only the habit of expressing my self in terms of modest diffidence; never using, when I advance anything that may possibly be disputed, the words, *certainly, undoubtedly*, or any others that give the air of positiveness to an opinion. ... This habit, I believe, has been of great advantage to me when I have had occasion to inculcate my opinions, and persuade men into measures that I have been from time to time engaged in promoting.

Franklin is quite candid here, but candid about a public mask deliberately put on from motives we have to call calculating rather than courteous. Franklin's shrewdness in contriving various favourable and ingratiating public masks for himself is in fact so often the subject of the *Autobiography* that it raises the question of whether Franklin's public style is properly ingenuous, a word which for Dr. Johnson and the eighteenth century was synonymous with openness and candour, or whether that public style was finally and deeply disingenuous.

This question is especially pointed in trying to understand the first segment of the memoirs, written in 1771 when Franklin was sixty-five years old. Franklin intended this part only for the audience of his immediate family; he addressed it directly to his eldest son, William, then the royal governor of New Jersey. Franklin explains that

> having emerged from the poverty and obscurity in which I was born and bred, to a state of affluence and some degree of reputation in the world, . . . the conducing means I made use of, which, with the blessing of God so well succeeded, my posterity may like to know, as they may find some of them suitable to their own situations, and therefore fit to be imitated.

This part of the *Autobiography* is by far the liveliest and most interesting, largely because the reader is treated with the apparently guileless intimacy appropriate to family reminiscence. The narrative is organized to display the means of his success as a model fit to be imitated. Ostensibly the principal means thus recommended are the practice of industry and frugality, the prudential or squirrel virtues that Franklin never tired of inculcating in the public mind through the pages of his *Almanack*. Yet it also becomes clear that Franklin takes most delight in selecting details which illustrate his shrewd manipulation of his ranking within the eighteenth-century lottery of patronage. There is little reason to doubt Franklin's personal industry and frugality, but there is every evidence to suggest that they might have been insufficient for his business success without the considerable aid of his self-advertisement—his careful management of public opinion in securing for himself a favourable reputation. What sustained his business was not the capital produced by his hard work and frugal ways, but the public confidence, private loans, generous patronage, and increasing custom produced by his public image. "In order to secure my credit and character as a tradesman, I took care not only to be in *reality* industrious and frugal, but to avoid all *appearances* of the contrary." It is this latter principle which acts to select a surprisingly large number of the details by which Franklin charts the oscillations of his early career. Franklin's famous account of his poor-boy entry into Philadelphia is the most vivid dramatic image in the book, but this one is only a shade less so: "to show that I was not above my business, I sometimes brought home the paper I purchased at the stores through the streets on a wheelbarrow. Thus being esteemed an industrious, thriving young man, . . . I went on swimmingly." Even Franklin's lapses are reported with an eye to public response: "I drest plainly; I was seen at no places of idle diversion; I never went out a-fishing or shooting; a book, indeed, sometimes debauched me from my work, but that was seldom, snug, and gave no scandal." This is mild debauchery, to be sure, but the emphasis is on "snug" rather than "seldom" as Poor Richard once put it: "Men take more pains to mask than mend." Franklin is equally candid in recording occasions when public opinion resisted his efforts to control it. He explains his competition with the old Philadelphia printer, Andrew Bradford, in these terms:

> ... as he kept the Post Office, it was imagined he had better opportunities of obtaining news, his paper was thought a better distributer of advertisements than mine, and therefore had many more, which was a profitable thing to him and a disadvantage to me. For tho' I did indeed receive and send papers by post, yet the public opinion was otherwise; for what I did send was by bribing the riders who took them privately....

Franklin may be implying here that had his private act of bribery been better known, it might have corrected public opinion to his advantage.

Franklin's concern for public image in this first section of the *Autobiography* generates additional models for his readers by operating as a prime criterion for judging the behaviour of his friends and competitors alike. His partnership with young Hugh Meredith discouraged two patrons who were willing to advance needed capital because Meredith "was often seen drunk in the streets, and playing at low games in alehouses, much to our discredit." Franklin is apprehensive about another of his rivals, David Harry, not because of Harry's skills as a printer, but because "his friends were very able, and had a good deal of interest," but Harry scandalously abused his public image: "He was very proud, dressed like a Gentleman, lived expensively, took much diversion and pleasure abroad, ran in debt, and neglected his business, upon which all business left him." The accumulation of such details seems meant to suggest the precarious nature of young Franklin's enterprise; the image he contrived to project seems fragile enough, at least in his mature memory, to have required constant vigilance.

It would be wrong, I think, to see Franklin's public masks as false faces. They seem crafted more to call public attention to his genuine virtues than to disguise his occasional lapses from them. For the most part, he simply avoided appearances contrary to the desired ones. But it also seems true that Franklin's candour in exposing the mild stratagems of his practice upon the good faith of public opinion is less the result of a manly and straightforward frankness than it is an old man's relish for his youthful cleverness, a relish now indulged within the private, snug, and no-scandal confines of a family communication.

In any case, this judgment may be easily tested against the second and more famous segment of the *Autobiography* in which the same issues are raised under much more public circumstances. The pressure of events forced Franklin to abandon his memoirs at the point of recounting his first entry into civic affairs. When he resumed writing them thirteen years later, in 1784, he did so at the urging of two friends whose letters have been made part of the *Autobiography*. They assured Franklin that "all that has happened to you is also connected with the detail of the manners and situation of a rising people," and they reminded him of "the chance which your life will give for the forming of future great men." They were of course accurately prophetic on both counts. "What follows," Franklin writes, "was written ... in compliance with the advice contained in these letters, and accordingly intended for the public."

The most famous feature of this second segment of the *Autobiography* is the account of what Franklin calls his "bold and arduous project of arriving at moral perfection." The account in the memoir of his plan for perfecting himself sets out what is less an art than a technology of virtue, a system of moral bookkeeping to ensure the proper conduct of the endeavour. The plan includes the famous list of the thirteen virtues to be cultivated, his timetable for concentrating on one virtue at a time, his division of the year into quarters for a complete rotation of the virtues, his debit and credit columns for toting up his progress, his daily schedule systematically allotting his activities, even his concern to save paper by using the ivory leaves of a memorandum book in which he could rub out the calculations when he was finished with them.

The question that plagues thoughtful readers of this account is how Franklin means us to take all this. Is it simply the calculating business ethic of a small tradesman naïve to the point of crassness, or is it another of Franklin's masking put-ons? That it might be the latter is suggested by his cheerful confession that he achieved only partial success in arriving at moral perfection,

> for something that pretended to be reason, was every now and then suggesting to me that such extreme nicety as I exacted of myself might be a kind of foppery in morals, which, if it were known, would make me ridiculous; that a perfect character might be attended with the inconvenience of being envied and hated; and that a benevolent man should allow a few faults in himself, to keep his friends in countenance.

This is preparing a face to meet the faces that you meet by adding some warts to it, and this has to be irony, doesn't it? Certainly Franklin's reasoning here is consistent with what A. O. Lovejoy (1948) defines as one way in which the eighteenth century used the word "pride": "'Pride,' then, in an especially important sense, meant a sort of moral overstrain, the attempt to be unnaturally good and immoderately virtuous, to live by reason alone." And this of course is Franklin's point, but notice that the corrective for such pride offered here is not candour about one's limitations, but the need to pander to the limitations of others in order to keep them in countenance.

Critics of Franklin have become fascinated with his skillful eighteenth-century habits of manipulating literary personae to achieve various ironies. But the effect, however skillfully achieved, is still disturbing. If the initial plan for moral perfection is offered in tones of ironic naïveté, that innocence is now exposed by another voice, but it is the voice of a worldlywise cynic who seems equally repellent. The reader may be reassured, however, about Franklin's own stance in all this by the passage that follows this one: "But on the whole, tho' I never arrived at the perfection I had been so ambitious of obtaining, but fell far short of it, yet I was, by the endeavor, a better and happier man than I otherwise should have been if I had not attempted it. . . ." He adds, "It may be well my posterity should be informed that to this little artifice, with the blessing of God, their ancestor owed the constant felicity of his life, down to his seventy-ninth year, in which this is written." If Franklin is only offering "this little artifice" as a model for conducting campaigns of self-improvement rather than recommending the impossible goal of moral perfection, it is pretty harmless, and we can rest easier. And the reader might have rested here had not Franklin further complicated matters by returning to a point he had already detailed thirteen years before in the first section of the memoirs:

> My list of virtues contained at first but twelve; but a Quaker friend having kindly informed me that I was generally thought proud; that my pride showed itself frequently in conversation; that I was not content with being in the right when discussing any point, but was overbearing, and rather insolent, of which he convinced me by mentioning several instances; I determined endeavoring to cure myself, if I could, of this vice or folly among the rest, and I added Humility to my list, giving an extensive meaning to the word.
>
> I cannot boast of much success in acquiring the *reality* of virtue, but I had a good deal with regard to the *appearance* of it.

As in his earlier use of this formula, Franklin pointedly emphasizes the discrepancy by underscoring the key words. He then repeats the steps by which he cultivated the stylistic appearance of humility:

> I made it a rule to forbear all direct contradiction to the sentiments of others, and all positive assertion of my own. I even forbid myself . . . the use of every word or expression in the language that imported a fixed opinion, such as *certainly, undoubtedly,* etc., and I adopted, instead of them, *I conceive, I apprehend,* or *I imagine* a thing to be so or so; or it so appeared to me at present. When another asserted something that I thought in error, I denied myself the pleasure of contradicting him abruptly, and of showing immediately some absurdity in his proposition; and in answering I began by observing that in certain cases or circumstances his opinion would be right, but in the present case there *appeared* or *seemed* to me some difference, etc. I soon found the advantage of this change in my manners. The conversation I engaged in went on more pleasantly. The modest way in which I proposed my opinions procured them a readier reception and less contradiction.

Franklin then goes on to make even more extravagant claims for his adoption of the mask of humility, and here, I think, we have to imagine a massive wink from the speaker:

> And this mode, which I at first put on with some violence to natural inclination, became at length so easy, and so habitual to me, that perhaps for these fifty years past no one has ever heard a dogmatical expression escape me. And it is to this habit (after my character of integrity) I think it principally owing that I had early so much weight with my fellow-citizens when I proposed new institutions, or alterations in the old, and had so much influence in public councils when I became a member.

This second segment of the memoir concludes with what was, by the time it was written, another eighteenth-century commonplace about human pride:

> In reality, there is, perhaps, no one of our natural passions so hard to subdue as pride. Disguise it, struggle with it, beat it down, stifle it, mortify it as much as one pleases, it is still alive, and will every now and then peep out and show itself; you will see it, perhaps,

often in this history; for, even if I could conceive that I had completely overcome it, I should probably be proud of my humility.

And what have we here? Is the speaker now taking off the mask of humility by revealing a humble awareness of his pride? Or is this another theatrical gesture of unmasking, producing an even more clever appearance of humility?

This is the place to return to the questions I raised earlier—the questions of whether Franklin's public style may be said to maintain the correct eighteenth-century balance between candour and courtesy, or whether the *Autobiography* exposes the creation of a public style by the deliberate sacrifice of frankness to ingratiation. These questions have puzzled critics, but some of them, curiously enough, have found a measure of agreement which allows them to answer "yes" to both questions. That measure is in the phrase "disarming candour" used as a judgment of Franklin's procedures in the memoirs—a phrase used in turn by many critics. What they all mean to point to is the fact that although Franklin's public style, as its creation is revealed in the *Autobiography*, is a conscious, deliberate, and life-long imposture, its exposure as such is so good-natured, open, and candid that our natural suspicions in the face of social fraud are quieted and disarmed. I doubt, however, that eighteenth century readers would have been so easily disarmed. The pervasive eighteenth- century conviction was that public imposture is a particularly serious threat to the good order and coherence of society. At the beginning of the century, Archbishop Tillotson had defined "sincerity" in this way: ". . . it signifies a simplicity of mind and manners in our conversation, and carriage towards another; singleness of heart, discovering itself in a constant plainness and honest openness of behavior, free from all insidious devices, and little tricks and fetches of craft and cunning; from all false appearances and deceitful disguises of ourselves in word or action." Later Dr. Johnson castigated the "perpetual disguise of real character by fictitious appearances" as one of the stratagems of pride and one that merited universal contempt. He regarded it as a species of fraud: "Whoever commits fraud is guilty not only of the particular injury to him whom he deceives, but of the diminution of that confidence which constitutes not only the ease but the existence of a society." Although some today may be disarmed by Franklin's candour in exposing his social masks, we can't really avoid the distrust—that diminution of confidence warned of by Dr. Johnson. We may wonder what the man who appears humble hopes to gain by his appearance. Indeed, if the appearances are false, we may never discover from all the masks whether there is anything behind them.

Finally, it must be said, if we abandon the kind of moral concerns expressed in the eighteenth century, we do so by celebrating Franklin's aesthetic skills as a creator of ironically interlinked personae. In the process, the moral relationship between personae and character, the question of where the real Franklin is to be located among his play with social masks, becomes irrelevant. Those who submerge the author in his impersonations are the vanguard of the deconstructionists who may soon descend on Franklin's writing in force. But to be fair, let it be said that the historians may have got there first. Carl Becker, writing the entry by Franklin for the *Dictionary of American Biography* in 1930, makes Franklin into something of a master gamester, expressing his own uneasiness about the elusive Franklin by stationing him somewhere above his own life and work:

> In all of Franklin's dealings with men and affairs, genuine, sincere, loyal as he surely was, one feels that he is nevertheless not wholly committed; some thought remains uncommunicated; some penetrating observation held in reserve. . . . He manages somehow to remain aloof, a spectator still, with amiable curiosity watching himself functioning effectively in the world. After all, men were but children needing to be cajoled; affairs a game not to be played without finesse."

Other historians have treated Franklin's impersonations as striking manifestations of ideological pressures. Max Weber, in his well-known treatment of the Protestant ethic (1930), speaks of "the really unusual candidness of Franklin's autobiography" in order to defend him against the charge that "this striking case" confirms "the impression of many Germans that the virtues professed by Americans are pure hypocrisy," but Weber also explains that, for Franklin, ". . . the surrogate of mere appearance is always sufficient when it accomplishes the end in view. It is a conclusion which is inevitable with strict utilitarianism."

John William Ward, also a historian, seems even more chilling when he writes in *Red, White, and Blue: Men, Books, and Ideas in American Culture* (1969): "Yet it is this . . . very difficulty of deciding whether we admire Franklin or suspect him, that makes his character an archetype of our national experience." Ward sees Franklin's life-story as "a witness to the uncertainties about social status that have characterized our society, a society caught up in the constant process of change." Ward's numbing conclusion is this: "The question, 'Who was Benjamin Franklin?' is a critical question to ask of Franklin because it is the question to which

Franklin himself is constantly seeking an answer." Ward has completely defeated the hope of Franklin's friend Benjamin Vaughan, whose letter of appeal moved Franklin to make his memoir public. Vaughan had written: "Considering your great age, the caution of your character, and your peculiar style of thinking, it is not likely that any one besides yourself can be sufficiently master of the facts of your life, or the intentions of your mind." If Ward is right, even this source of those facts and those intentions is compromised. It is, I think, not surprising that these various modern commentators have found so many ways to lose Franklin among his public styles and masks. Because his *Autobiography* is the archetypal story of a self-made man making himself, a confusion between the self that is made and the self doing the making may be inevitable. But the *Autobiography* also offers a final clue which may allow us to characterize Franklin's public style not as a confusion among selves, but as an almost total collapse of the private self into the public style.

In the last two parts of the *Autobiography*, Franklin turns his attention to accounts of his civic projects, his practice of public benevolence. Whereas the story of early business success in the first two sections emphasized the crafts of public ingratiation and self-promotion, such details are abandoned in the last two parts because, by this stage in his career, the desirable public image achieved had accomplished its purpose, helping to secure for him substantial wealth and leisure. It is to his credit that he continues the memoir, now in 1788 when he was eighty-two years old, and now offering his career as a model for the responsible use of the rewards which the self-serving virtues had brought him. What is most interesting about these final sections is that Franklin's public enterprises are now conducted largely by the means of deliberate and systematic self-effacement, the adoption of stratagems designed to conceal rather than to publicize or to ingratiate. Here, for example, he reports the method used in raising funds for a library:

> The objections and reluctances I met with in soliciting the subscriptions, made me soon feel the impropriety of presenting one's self as the proposer of any useful project that might be supposed to raise one's reputation in the smallest degree above that of one's neighbors when one has need of their assistance to accomplish that project. I therefore put my self as much as I could out of sight. ... In this way my affair went on more smoothly, and I ever practised it on such occasions; and from my frequent successes, can heartily recommend it.

In one sense, this is simply another social mask—the appearance of humility has reached a limit in the deliberate appearance of anonymity—but these attempts at self-effacement are also reflected by a change in the texture of the narrative. Franklin still delights in reporting his manipulation of public opinion, but now these displays are restrained by an often weary sense of obligation very unlike the zesty records of self-promotion and ingratiation in the first two parts. If the early parts of the *Autobiography* show Franklin as manipulator, successfully imposing his impersonations on the public, the last two parts reverse this pattern, for they show him as manipulated, often playing reluctantly the roles imposed upon him by the public: "When I disengaged myself ... from private business, I flattered myself that by the sufficient tho' moderate fortune I had acquired, I had secured leisure during the rest of my life for philosophical studies and amusements; ... but the public now considering me as a man of leisure, laid hold of me for their purposes, every part of our civil government, and almost at the same time, imposing some duty upon me." It seems fair to say here that Franklin's lifelong habits of deferring to the public even in the act of manipulating it has finally exacted its price. Whatever seems left of the private self is now in dutiful servitude to the public role of good citizen with all its physical trappings that Franklin attended to. One consequence of this is that Franklin is often obscured by his material. So abundant is the presence of minutiae that on one occasion he is moved to justify their inclusion; he is talking about his plans for cleaning the Philadelphia streets:

> Some may think these trifling matters not worth minding or relating. But when they consider, that tho' dust blown into the eyes of a single person or into a single shop on a windy day, is but of small importance, yet the great number of instances in a populous city, and its frequent repetitions give it weight and consequence, perhaps they will not censure very severely those who bestow some attention to affairs of this seemingly low nature.

The note of ingratiation is still there, but it is apologetic rather than shrewd; the voice is less lively, more impersonal, now preoccupied not with showing the virtuous self to advantage, but with indurate fact in all its variety. Franklin's concern now is to keep the public eye dust-free rather than directing it toward himself, and in the process, any sense of a private self virtually disappears from his account; the public style has become the man.

The best education may be to imitate good models so well we become them, and, as Peter Gay has argued, the eighteenth century models of civility may have provided that social repression necessary when religious authority weakens. But in the record of Franklin's play with his public masks, we have lost all sight of the private heart. D. H. Lawrence had it right: "Benjamin had no concern, really, with the immortal soul. He was too busy with social man."

In my next lecture I'll talk about Emerson's effort to recover the private heart from its enveloping social masks.

THE EDMUND KEMPER BROADUS LECTURES

Ralph Waldo Emerson: Unsettling Community

Ralph Waldo Emerson was the son and grandson of New England preachers, and even before his own ordination as junior pastor of the Second Church, Boston, in 1829, he diligently prepared himself for the family calling by setting down plans for sermons in his journal. One of these, dated in 1827, strongly reiterates the communal hopes of John Winthrop's *Arbella* sermon:

> When we came up this morning to the house of God, did we come in savage solitude, each from his lonely house, a congregation of hermits to whom society is unwelcome. And when the hour of prayer is past, are we to separate again to sunder these sympathies of devotion. . . . Thank God it is not so. . . . We came up to the house of God in company. We have taken sweet counsel together. We do not live for ourselves; we do not rejoice, we do not weep alone. Our lives are bound up in others. . . . It is delightful to remark the immense addition that is made to the power and the happiness of each by the existence of others.

There is every evidence in Emerson's early writings that he fully meant to accept the communal responsibilities of John Cotton, that he meant to serve his congregation as pastor, counsellor, and guide. But there is also ample evidence that he felt, even more intensely than had John Cotton, the need for direct inspiration so that his preaching might provoke and pierce the private heart. And it was this intensity that hurried his resignation from the Second Church in 1832, in effect his resignation from the traditional social roles of the minister. In June of 1832, he wrote in his journal: "I have sometimes thought that, in order to be a good minister, it was necessary to leave the ministry. . . . In an altered age, we worship in the dead forms of our forefathers." His resignation was finally prompted by the congregation's denial of his request to discontinue his administration of the sacrament of communion, almost the last ritual of collective worship still retained by the Unitarians. In a sermon explaining his reasons, Emerson says:

> I fear it is the effect of this ordinance to clothe Jesus with an authority which he never claimed, and which distracts the mind of the worshipper. . . . I appeal, brethren, to your individual experi-

ence. In the moment that you make the least petition to God, though it be but a silent wish that He may approve you, or add one moment to your life—do you not, in the very act, necessarily exclude all other beings from your thought? In this act, the soul stands alone with God, and Jesus is no more present to your mind than your brother or your child.

Given the extremity of this Protestant position, Emerson's resignation from the pulpit was probably inevitable, for by removing even Jesus Christ as a mediator with God, he necessarily removed this role for the minister as well. Emerson's convictions made the pastoral role, as it had developed within New England's city on the hill, simply obsolete, setting him to wander, in Hooker's phrase, through a solitary desert place alone with his God.

The immediate result of this withdrawal was the vocational crisis suffered by Emerson in the 1830s, a crisis first studied in detail by Henry Nash Smith in 1930. Smith points out that "during the thirties Emerson created, tested, and abandoned a whole company of ... somewhat ghostly characters, such as the Man of Genius, the Seer, the Contemplative Man, the Student, the Transcendentalist," in order to rehearse his plans for both a new vocation and a new public style to serve it. Although Emerson resigned his pulpit, in doing so he gave up only one part of the preacher's profession he shared with John Cotton—the communal responsibility of pastoral guidance. Emerson's later career demonstrates, I think, that whatever title he used to label his sense of vocation, he retained at its centre Cotton's intention to pierce and provoke the heart, an intention best signaled by a remark about preaching in his controversial address to the Harvard Divinity School in 1839: "Truly speaking, it is not instruction, but provocation, that I can receive from another soul." That Emerson resigned his pulpit does not mean that he gave up a social language. Rather, he found a ready-made social language that he adapted to his intentions with great fluency, and, as we shall see, the word "fluency" is even more appropriate for Emerson's social language than its common denotation would suggest. My purpose here is first to describe briefly Emerson's major public style—the style of his addresses and essays—and then to define what he made of it, the ways in which he used it to provoke and pierce the heart.

Emerson himself gives the clue to his major public style in a journal entry of 1839 celebrating the lyceum lecture, the medium by which he made his living for the rest of his life and the medium that made him famous:

> Here is all the true orator will ask, for here is a convertible audience and here are no stiff conventions that prescribe a method, a style, a limited quotation of books, and an exact respect to certain books, persons, or opinions. No, here everything is admissible, philosophy, ethics, divinity, criticism, poetry, humor, fun, mimicry, anecdotes, jokes, ventriloquism. All the breadth and versatility of the most liberal conversation. . . . Here is a pulpit that makes other pulpits tame and ineffectual. . . . Here he may lay himself out utterly, large, enormous, prodigal, on the subject of the hour. Here he may dare to hope for ecstasy and eloquence.

Emerson seems here to be celebrating a form so free of restraints that it has no shape at all, but by summing it up in the phrase "liberal conversation," Emerson is, I think, aligning this public style with the tradition of the familiar and the personal essay—a tradition that began with his beloved Montaigne, flourished in English with the *Spectator* and the *Rambler*, and in contemporary England with the work of Leigh Hunt, De Quincy, Lamb, Hazlitt, and Coleridge. The nineteenth century essayists hardly conform to Johnson's definition of the middle style as exemplified by Addison. They practiced self-revelation more frequently than the *Spectator's* polite familiarity, were more interested in landscape than in the town, and their subjects tended to the philosophical and literary rather than the moral, but like the eighteenth century essayists, they retained the conversation of gentlemen as their model, valuing its conventions of social intimacy, polished ease, and wide accommodation for digression and the other appearances of spontaneity.

That the model had stretched considerably since Addison is indicated by the fact that Emerson could find and approve it *even* in the work of his difficult friend, Carlyle: ". . . how inexhaustible a mine is the language of conversation. . . . [Carlyle] draws strength and mother-wit out of a poetic use of the spoken vocabulary, so that his paragraphs are all a sort of splendid conversation." And, given the differences between the eighteenth and the nineteenth centuries, it is this social language that Emerson shares with Franklin. Yvor Winters (*Maule's Curse*, 1938) alone has recognized this particular connection—recognized it and judged it: "Emerson was the most widely read and most pungent aphorist to appear in America since that other limb of the Devil, Benjamin Franklin." But the only critic to make much of Emerson's affinities with the style of the eighteenth century is Richard Poirier (in *A World Elsewhere* [1966]). He claims that Emerson's ecstatic utterances occur in the stylistic surroundings of the polite essay of a literary and urbane man. Emerson's radical, even subversive, outbursts, like the passage about the "transparent eyeball," have a genteel context, according to Poirier. I agree that Emerson's public style is marked by a warring combination of genteel language and subversive intentions, but because I believe the war is deliberate, I also think that Poirier has misplaced the emphasis. In Emerson's work the radical impulse threatens and subverts the social forms, as it was meant to, far more frequently than those forms modify, muffle, or mute the radical impulse. But despite Emerson's skills in using social language of the everyday world, the substantial stuff of the world tends to evaporate under Emerson's touch. Hawthorne puts it with telling succinctness: "Mr. Emerson is a great searcher for facts; but they seem to melt away and become unsubstantial in his grasp." When we understand that this treatment is the result of a deliberately subversive motive, we may also see another bearing for Winters' cryptic epithets; if Franklin may be called a limb of the devil because of motives concealed behind his contrived social masks, Emerson may be the other because he is so intent on rendering society itself as a mask. Franklin used the social language of gentlemen in order to ingratiate himself; Emerson uses the ingratiating language of society in order to discredit it and finally to dispel it. He made frequent and direct attacks on society's coercive imposition of forms and roles, most substantially in the essay "Self-Reliance." There he describes and then denounces the barriers society erects against self-trust. Emerson insists, for example, that in society,

> we come to wear one cut of face and figure, and acquire by degrees the gentlest asinine expression. There is a mortifying experience in particular, which does not fail to wreak itself also in the general history; I mean 'the foolish face of praise,' the forced smile we put on in company where we do not feel at ease, in answer to conversation which does not interest us. The muscles, not spontaneously moved but moved by a low usurping wilfulness, grow tight about the outline of the face, with the most disagreeable sensation.

But this assault on social forms was even more pervasive and sweeping than his overt pronouncements suggest. It is necessary, then, to trace more carefully Emerson's efforts to free his auditors from the encrusted forms of social coercion—even from social language itself—by deliberately provoking them. At bottom, Emerson is still the preacher, still concerned to use his public style as an instrument for changing his auditors, an instrument preparing them for the regenerating or transforming influx of spirit. One difficulty in the way of understanding how he tried to make this instrument work has been a pervasive misunderstanding, evident among both Emerson's partisans and his detractors, of his conception of the child, a misunderstanding that has done much to obscure the modes of his provocation.

Many critics of Emerson relate him directly to Rousseau's writing on the enlightened education of the child and insist that he stresses and praises the child's view of the world over that of the adult. Although much of Emerson's work is deliberately pedagogic, it never accorded the child's angle of vision any special prestige. In fact the opposite is true. Despite his frequent but always conventional use of images associated with the romantic child, the truth is that Emerson agreed with Rousseau, agreed to the extent that the effort to transform childish modes of perception into more complex and sophisticated ones virtually dictates the shape of his public style.

Those critics who have mistakenly praised Emerson's child have overlooked the case against the child's vision made clearly and directly by Emerson in his book *Nature*, and as clearly in several other places. In chapter six of *Nature*—the chapter titled "Idealism"—Emerson lists the effects of culture—and he uses the word to mean "education"—as a series of experiences which conspire to move the individual from a child's naïve materialism, "this despotism of the senses," to the mature faith of the Idealist. So persuasive does he think these experiences are that he feels it necessary near the end of the chapter to enter a personal disclaimer: "But I own there is something ungrateful in expanding too curiously the particulars of the general proposition, that all culture tends to imbue us with idealism. I have no hostility to nature, but a child's love to it. I expand and live in the warm day like corn and melons." But—and the step is crucial to his argument—this celebratory mood of the child must give way to "the true position of nature in regard to man, wherein to establish man, all right education tends; as the ground which to attain is the object of human life, that is, of man's connexion with nature." The idealist's faith is, then, the aim of all right education, and to achieve it, the wise man gives up—or is induced to give up, however reluctantly, the child's vision. Emerson concludes this paragraph as follows: "Children, it is true, believe in the external world. The belief that it appears only, is an afterthought, but with culture, this faith will as surely arise on the mind as did the first."

The question of just *how* Emerson himself intended to prepare his audience for this mature faith is complicated by his sense of the hierarchy and priority of forces at work in the process. Like John Cotton, Emerson believed Spirit to be the operative force in the regeneration of the individual. He puts it this way in "Self-Reliance": "The inquiry leads us to that source, at once the essence of genius, of virtue, and of life, which we call Spontaneity or Instinct. We denote this primary wisdom as Intuition, whilst all later teachings are tuitions." But while Emerson was resolved to trust intuition, he also recognized limitations in what he called "this flash-of-lightning faith." If intuitions are irresistible, immediately self-evident, and completely authoritative, they are also like seizures, unbidden however welcome, random, momentary, and infrequent. In his book *Nature*, Emerson set out to describe a less direct means of education which, while only a secondary agency finally empowered by Spirit, yet overcomes some of the difficulties of depending upon intuitional seizures. Chapters two through six of *Nature* record a progressive series of steps by which nature conspires with culture to change the individual's perception of itself, conspires in ways which are constant, ubiquitous, and cunningly fitted to draw out and develop the whole range of human powers. And it is this natural process which is largely responsible for emancipating the child from the despotism of his senses, and for moving him towards a mature grasp of those powers of mind and spirit that are naturally and potentially his. But if all this is true, can there be any active role left for the human teacher other than as a recorder or expositor of the educational process? Certainly Emerson played this latter role frequently. But the question of human agency persisted for Emerson; his journals and other writings also show him experimenting with a variety of styles by which he might more directly prepare his audience for the Idealist's faith.

Emerson had addressed the question of human agency directly in the third of a series of lectures first given in 1837–38 under the title "Human Culture." After explaining how nature functions to effect "the Culture of the Intellect," he asked: "What can we do for it? The main thing we can do for it is to stand out of the way, to trust its divine force, to believe that God is in it, and only disencumber and watch its workings." This is less negative advice for the prospective teacher than it might first appear, for if he is enjoined to the passive acts of trusting and observing, he is also urged to the more active work of disencumbering, and this last term becomes one of a set of verbs by which Emerson frequently described the intended force of his own public style. O. W. Firkins (1915), one of the best students of Emerson's prose, has remarked on Emerson's "fondness for the prefix 'dis'. . . ," and Emerson was often in the mood to disabuse, disembody, disillusion, disarrange, dislodge, dismantle, disperse, disturb, disappear, dissolve, and destroy. The violence implicit in these activities took greater urgency for Emerson as he estimated the increasing degree to which his society was conspiring to inhibit or retard what might otherwise be a wholly natural, almost inevitable development from childish modes of perception to Idealist adult ones. In the "Address on Education" first delivered at Providence in June 1837, he defined "this triumph of the senses": "Is there not even at this time, a more than usual torpidity in the high ideal faculties whence always the life, the regeneration of Society proceeds? An immense prosperity—*an immense activity*, that is, of the *senses*, and devotion to the senses, has taken place, without example in history." It is this which demands new and more strenuous efforts as "fosterers of the superior nature of man...."

The first human agent mentioned in *Nature* in the list of the forces which conspire to transform childish dependence upon the senses into the mature idealist's faith is the poet. As Emerson explains it in 1836, the poet's educative role was to disencumber; it was to unsettle, to disturb, and thus finally to dispel naïve, but ingrained impressions of the substantiality of nature. The poet "unfixes the land and the sea, makes them revolve around the axis of his primary thought, and disposes them anew." His target is the sensual man who has unreflectively carried the common sense convictions of childhood into adult life, the sensual man "who conforms thoughts to things." As a corrective "the poet conforms things to his thoughts. The one esteems nature as rooted and fast; the other, as fluid, and impresses his being thereon. To him, the refractory world is ductile and flexible...." The aim of the poet, then, is nothing less than to effect the disillusionment of the sensual man. His principal tool is the plastic power of his imagination to disassemble and rearrange the sensuous impressions made by natural stimuli, "to magnify the small, to micrify the great," and in general "to make free with the most imposing forms and phenomena of the world." Shakespeare provides Emerson's illustrations for "this transfiguration which all material objects undergo through the passion of the poet,—this power which he exerts to dwarf the great, to magnify the small...." Nature's very susceptibility to the poet's extravagant manipulation becomes for Emerson a proof of its insubstantiality. Having already closed off any way of knowing material realities by reference to the impossibility of testing the accuracy of the senses, Emerson is now dealing with nature solely as it is perceived by the senses. When, therefore, the poet boldly plays with sensuous appearances for his own purposes, he is in fact enacting the causal powers which emancipation from naïve materialism brings. Emerson thought the effect of this power on an audience to be particularly persuasive; it produced "a pleasure mixed with awe," and, he goes on, "I may say, a low degree of the sublime is felt from the fact, probably, that a man is thereby apprized, that, whilst the world is a spectacle, something in himself is stable."

We have learned from Henry Nash Smith to be cautious in assigning specific vocations to Emerson, but I will argue that the poet's power of unsettling, as Emerson defined it in *Nature*, is his first extended explanation of the imperatives that governed his own efforts to make his public lyceum style an instrument of right education. In the month before attaining his majority in 1824, Emerson had conducted a vocational self-assessment in his journal. He first recognized that "my reasoning faculty is proportionably weak , nor can I ever hope to write a Butler's Analogy or an Essay of Hume." This would be a serious handicap, especially in Unitarian strongholds, for a career in theology, "which," says Emerson, "is from everlasting to everlasting 'debatable ground.'" But he felt reassured because "the preaching most in vogue at the present day depends chiefly on imagination for its success, and asks those accomplishments which I believe most within my grasp." Emerson's early confidence in his "strong imagination" sustained him even more after he had exchanged his Unitarian pulpit for the lyceum lecture platform; he would use Coleridge's invidious distinctions between the reasoning faculty, labouring servant to the limited functions of the Understanding, and the Imagination, close partner with visionary Intuition, in order to redefine for himself the methods of the preacher.

If the poet-preacher was to be fully successful in emancipating the materialist from the despotism of his senses, Emerson believed that the way to begin was by dislodging language itself from its enfolding social web of customs, forms, and traditional usages. He apparently took this hint from one of his own childhood experiences. He spoke of it first in a letter to Margaret Fuller in 1841: "I know but one solution to my nature and relations, which I find in remembering the joy with which in my boyhood I caught the first hint of the Berkelian philosophy, and which I certainly never lost sight of afterwards." In a journal entry later that year, Emerson explained the nature of that first hint more fully:

> I remember when a child in the pew on Sundays amusing myself with saying over common words as 'black,' 'white,' 'board,' &c. twenty or thirty times, until the word lost all meaning and fixedness, & I began to doubt which was the right name for the thing, when I saw that neither had any natural relation, but all were arbitrary. It was a child's first lesson in Idealism.

And in the letter to Margaret Fuller this manipulation of language in order to unfix the child's impressions provides the core of a graphic description of the ways in which he now conceives his own skills at unfixing. He compares himself to Phineas Quimby, the then celebrated animal magnetist who, says Emerson, gets his living by going about lecturing on electricity and by drawing sparks out of common objects:

> Well I was not an electrician, but an Idealist. I could see that there was a cause behind every stump & clod, & by the help of some fine words could make every old wagon & stone wall oscillate a little & threaten to dance; nay, give me a fair field,—& the selectmen of Concord & the Reverend Doctor Pound-me-down himself began to look unstable and vaporous.

This comparison of his performance with Quimby's is in part a comic deflation, in part a mischievous celebration of his unsettling rhetorical powers, but he immediately turns serious in assuring Miss Fuller that it was these skills that attracted her. "You saw me do my feat—it fell in with your own studies—and you would give me gold & pearls. Now there is this difference between the electrician, . . . and the Idealist, namely, that the spark is to that philosopher a toy, but the dance is to the Idealist terror and beauty, life and light." This letter is dated in March of 1841, and its note of rhetorical violence, however playful in the presence of Miss Fuller, sounds frequently and intensely in the privacy of his journals between May and September of that year. On May 25, he had decided that "People wish to be settled. It is only as far as they are unsettled that there is any hope for them." Three days later he defines what happens in really good conversation: "All that we reckoned settled, shakes now and rattles, and literatures, cities, climates, religions leave their foundations and dance before our eyes," and three days later: "Our weak eyes make goblins and monsters. But man thyself and all things unfix, depart, and flee." In June he again describes what poetry does; it "causes to vibrate the sun and the moon, which dissipate by terrible melody all this iron network of circumstance." This storm of unsettling climaxes in a September entry emphatically underscoring Emerson's own intention to make himself an unsettler. "I unsettle all things. No facts are to me sacred; none are profane; I simply experiment, an endless seeker with no Past at my back."

Emerson worked most of these passages into the essay "Circles," which may be seen both as the extreme terminus and the best example of his more violent experiments in making his public style the means of unsettling his audience; and it is probably for these reasons that "Circles" had attracted more contemporary attention than his other essays. Two of these he seems to have taken special delight in recording: "One 'thought [my lecture] as good as a kaleidoscope.' Another, a good Staten Islander, would go hear, for he had heard that I was 'a rattler.'" And then there is the report of the lady who said that listening to Mr. Emerson was like going to heaven in a swing. Perhaps we should concede that any conscientious effort to track in detail Emerson's affective strategies may require some innovative language of its own. But if we can excuse Emerson's critics for the unsettling ways in which they explain how we are unsettled, we must also see that they have been so tempted by Emerson beyond the traditional restraints of language that they have abandoned the conversation of rational men altogether. They have entered some strange realm where even the basic law of noncontradiction does not hold. This is, of course, Emerson's intention for them; in his poem "Brahma," he even defines a realm where the law of noncontradiction is simply void: "If the red slayer thinks he slay,/ or if the slain thinks he is slain,/ They know not well the subtle ways/ I keep, and pass, and turn again." Insofar as they have noted it, most commentators on the effects of Emerson's unsettling intentions have tended to approve them, generally presuming an upward, edifying direction. Kenneth Burke (1966) is typical. Writing about the book *Nature*, Burke makes Emerson into Dr. Feel-Good: "If only like loving a pleasant dream, love him for his idealistic upsurge. For it reads well, it is medicine." A few, however, have taken a more stringent view of such medicine, and a more skeptical survey of its direction. Santayana (1900), for example, insists that "what seemed, then, to the more earnest and less critical hearers a revelation from above was in truth rather an insurrection from beneath, a shaking loose from convention, a disintegration of the normal categories of reason. . . ." Santayana is quite right, in part because his judgment recognizes Emerson's own deliberate efforts in shaping his public style to unsettle his listeners' hold on the traditional, social counters of discourse and thought.

Santayana is, however, also right because his judgment points to a limitation Emerson himself felt in what he could accomplish as a preacher. In his Divinity School Address to a class of graduating ministers, in the midst of expansive, upsurging advice that the Unitarian establishment was quick to stigmatize as "the latest form of infidelity," Emerson insisted on a limitation that even John Cotton would have recognized as wholly orthodox Calvinism. After celebrating the priest's calling, Emerson adds: "But observe the condition, the spiritual limitation of the office. The spirit only can teach." Like John Cotton, Emerson believed that the spirit most often teaches through the preacher's words, and his own work most often speaks with the assured confidence of the inspired, but, as Perry Miller has suggested, Emerson also retained enough affinities with Calvinist tradition to believe that the spirit, however generously its presence was conceived, cannot be finally compelled or controlled by human agency. At best the poet-preacher must regard his own exertions as preparing the believer for the influx of spirit; by his deliberate efforts he can only make the ground open and fallow, now ready for the seed of regenerating grace.

It has to be seen, then, that Emerson's techniques for unsettling his audience in order to break the encrusted hold of sensuous materialism and its social forms are properly defined as preparation for the influx of grace rather than the event itself. And this is what makes Emerson's style so dangerous for the individual who is unsettled by it. If grace is not, and cannot be assured, such preparation leaves the unsettled soul at great risk. And Emerson cannot promise his audience that grace will come. Emerson's humility in this respect is so infrequently explicit that it is easily overlooked: "Of that ineffable essence which we call Spirit," says Emerson, "he that thinks most, will say least." This statement occurs in the very short chapter seven of *Nature* titled "Spirit," and what makes the remark more than an echo of old pieties is that this chapter sets a limit to his program of unsettling as it had been outlined in the previous chapter. In this chapter Emerson seems fully aware of the dangers of preparing the believer for an influx of grace that might never arrive:

> Idealism is a hypothesis to account for nature by other principles than those of carpentry and chemistry. Yet, if it only deny the existence of matter, it does not satisfy the demands of the spirit. It leaves God out of me. It leaves me in the splendid labyrinth of my perceptions, to wander without end. Then the heart resists it, because it balks the affections in denying substantive being to men and women.

If God does not come, Emerson's program of unsettling brings those for whom it has worked to a perilous brink, for there they must wander in a labyrinth, however splendid, longing for the embrace of spirit while pining for the communal world they have lost. But Emerson can only report his own experience with grace: "Crossing a bare common, in snow puddles, at twilight, under a clouded sky, without having in my thoughts any occurrence of special good fortune, I have enjoyed a perfect exhilaration. I am glad to the brink of fear." And then:

> Standing on the bare ground,—my head bathed by the blithe air and uplifted into infinite space,—all mean egotism vanishes. I become a transparent eyeball; I am nothing; I see all; the currents of the Universal Being circulate through me; I am part or parcel of God. The name of the nearest friend sounds then foreign and acci-

dental: to be brothers, to be acquaintances, master or servant, is then a trifle and a disturbance.

This moment is offered as a triumph, and the loss of the sensuous world, the social world, even identity itself, is a trifle compared with the experience of spirit.

This is, of course, Emerson's most famous testimony of community lost and well lost, but there is later testimony that suggests some second thoughts. In 1879, the Harvard Divinity School made peace with Emerson by inviting him again to address the graduating class, and he chose to deliver remarks entitled "The Preacher." Most of this lecture repeats his familiar optimism, albeit a little worn and tired by this late date, but there is one passage that graphically describes the state of the unsettled soul to whom God's grace has not yet come.

> I see movement, I hear aspirations, but I see not how the great God prepares to satisfy the heart in the new order of things. No Church, no State emerges; and when we have extricated ourselves from all the embarrassments of the social problem, the oracle does not emit any light on the mode of individual life. A thousand negatives it utters, clear and strong on all sides; but the sacred affirmative it hides in the deepest abyss.

And then, "Unlovely, nay, frightful, is the solitude of the soul which is without God in the world." This chilling note may have been Emerson's final realization that his public style, without the advent of God's grace, might work only to isolate the private heart in this frightful solitude.

It is from just such a solitude that Hawthorne works to restore the private heart to community, and that is the subject for my next lecture.

Nathaniel Hawthorne: Restoring Community

Nathaniel Hawthorne often characterized his vocation by somewhat slyly adopting the critical stance of his own Puritan ancestors. The most notable example occurs in "The Custom-House" sketch:

> Doubtless, however, either of these stern and black-browed Puritans would have thought it quite a sufficient retribution for his sins, that, after so long a lapse of years, the old trunk of the family tree, with so much venerable moss upon it, should have borne, as its topmost bough, an idler like myself. No aim, that I have ever cherished, would they recognize as laudable; no success of mine—if my life, beyond its domestic scope, had ever been brightened by success—would they deem otherwise than worthless, if not positively disgraceful. "What is he?" murmurs one gray shadow of my forefathers to the other. "A writer of story-books." What kind of business in life,—what mode of glorifying God, or being serviceable to mankind in his day and generation,—may that be? Why, the degenerate fellow might as well have been a fiddler!" . . . And yet, let them scorn me as they will, strong traits of their nature have intertwined themselves with mine.

A year later, in a preface for a reissue of *Twice-Told Tales*, his first collection, which had originally appeared in 1837, Hawthorne provided one answer to his forefathers' questions about the public use and value of his storytelling. He begins with an ironic claim: "He was, for a good many years, the obscurest man of letters in America." So obscure, Hawthorne goes on, that questions arose whether "the Author could regard himself as addressing the American public, or, indeed, any public at all. He was merely writing to his known or unknown friends." Hawthorne attributes this to a lack of sufficient force in his stories:

> They have the pale tint of flowers that blossomed in too retired a shade,—the coolness of meditative habit, which diffuses itself through the feeling and observation of every sketch. Instead of passion there is sentiment; and even in what purport to be pictures of actual life, we have allegory, not always so warmly dressed in its habiliments of flesh and blood as to be taken into the reader's

mind without a shiver. Whether from lack of power, or an unconquerable reserve, the Author's touches have often an effect of tameness...."

Hawthorne then adds that if his stories lack force, they also lack depth: "The sketches are not, it is hardly necessary to say, profound; but it is rather more remarkable that they so seldom, if ever, show any design on the writer's part to make them so."

So far, Hawthorne sounds as if he has accepted his ancestors' judgment that what he does is simply idle and trifling, but at this point the preface takes an unexpected turn from apology to defence: "They have none of the abstruseness of idea, or obscurity of expression, which mark the written communications of a solitary mind with itself. They never need translation. It is, in fact, the style of a man of society. Every sentence, so far as it embodies thought or sensibility, may be understood and felt by anybody who will give himself the trouble to read it, and will take up the book in a proper mood." Hawthorne then explains the reason for this mixture of deprecation and defence: "This statement of apparently opposite peculiarities leads to a perception of what the sketches truly are. They are not the talk of a secluded man with his own mind and heart, ... but his attempts, and very imperfectly successful ones, to open an intercourse with the world." Hawthorne's modest concessions and qualifications in the preface almost obscure its point, and perhaps this is one reason why it hasn't been taken, as I think it should be taken, as an apt description of his public style. Hawthorne does speak in his best work "in the style of a man of society," and he does so in order to open, for his reader as well as for himself, an intercourse with the world.

The most obvious bearing of this last phrase is biographical, and his first publication of *Twice-Told Tales* is often bracketed with facts like his successful courtship of Sophia Peabody and his summer's participation in the Brook Farm communal experiment as evidence of his deliberate efforts to end his own painful sense of isolation from community. He spoke of that sense in a letter to Longfellow: "I have made a captive of myself, and put me into a dungeon, and now I cannot find the key to let myself out,—and if the door were open, I should be almost afraid to come out.... For the last ten years, I have not lived, but only dreamed of living." We should not, however, regard his attempts to reach a public audience as essentially self-expressive, as a kind of romantic therapy or release. His sketches are not, he insists, the talk of a secluded man with his own mind and heart. Despite the self-revelations of "The Custom-House" sketch, he is careful to point out that he still keeps "the inmost Me behind its veil," the same veil he had mentioned earlier in the long autobiographical preface to *Mosses from an Old Manse*: "I have appealed to no sentiment or sensibilities save such as are diffused among us all. So far as I am a man of really individual attributes I veil my face; nor am I, nor have I ever been, one of those supremely hospitable people who serve up their own hearts, delicately fried, with brain sauce, as a tidbit for their beloved public," a phrase he had originally used in his journal in reference to Lord Byron. Some readers have found Hawthorne's public masks and veils as disconcerting as Franklin's or the Reverend Mr. Hooper's, the character who so conspicuously advertises the fact that he conceals his face in the story of "The Minister's Black Veil." But Hawthorne's own veils are most often and explicitly a means of affirming his personal reserve, or denying that his work is meant as self-display, and this suggests that his intention "to open an intercourse with the world" has a bearing beyond the simply personal.

Hawthorne's major preoccupation is just that difficult relationship between community and the private heart that I've been tracing in these lectures. More than any other writer of his generation, Hawthorne expressed his awareness of the dangerous extent to which the two had become separated in the course of American experience. Newton Arvin made this point at some length in his 1929 biography of Hawthorne: his works "can be called an elaborate study of the centrifugal. They are a dramatization of all those social and psychological forces that lead to disunion, fragmentation, dispersion, incoherence.... the causes and consequences of estrangement is their consistent theme. And numerous as are the forms which estrangement takes in this drama, it is clear that they all have their roots in an error for which there is no better single word than pride." Arvin makes the point in order to claim—and I think correctly claim—for Hawthorne the status of a major writer as measured by the criterion of conveying "fully and directly some central spiritual experience of his people and his time." Certainly Hawthorne regarded his attempts to penetrate the depths of the private heart not as introspection, but as an inquiry into a common human nature. In the preface to *The Snow Image*, he described himself as "a person, who has been burrowing, to his utmost ability, into the depths of our common nature, for the purposes of psychological romance,—and who pursues his researches in that dusky region, as he needs must, as well by the tact of sympathy as by the light of observation." But the desire to make his researches public is only part of what shaped Hawthorne's style.

There is little doubt that Hawthorne's best stories are, in his ancestor's phrase, "serviceable to mankind" as cautionary case studies which display, in some vividly memorable images, the causes and consequences of an individual's separation from community, but to see them only in this way misplaces the emphasis on the private heart, rather than on its true place within community. Such emphasis threatens to overlook what F. O. Matthiessen (1941) called "the human norm" against which we are to understand and to sympathize with "the one-sided and broken figures who throng his most typical pages." Too much emphasis on these figures also leads to the kind of overstatement made by Henry Bamford Parkes (1941) when he says that Hawthorne's world lacks "any sense of society as a kind of organic whole to which the individual belongs and in which he has his appointed place." Hawthorne himself clearly believed that any exposure of the deformities of isolation, unaccompanied by some means of correction, some means of restoring the bond of community, was morally suspect. Always anguished about the propriety of burrowing into the secrets of the private heart, he had formulated the problem and its solution in an early notebook entry: "The Unpardonable Sin might consist in a want of love and reverence for the Human Soul; in consequence of which, the investigator pried into the dark depths, not with a hope or purpose of making it better, but from a cold philosophical curiosity,— content that it should be wicked in whatever kind or degree, and only desiring to study it out." Hawthorne's public style, then, is shaped to avoid this sin. He will study out and make public the causes and consequences of the isolated heart, but he will also attempt to make it better, to end its isolation by opening an intercourse with the world which might restore a bond of community. Hawthorne summarized this purpose in a sketch called "The Procession of Life": "Fixing our attention on such outside shows of similarity or difference, we lose sight of those realities by which nature, fortune, fate, or Providence has constituted for every man a brotherhood, wherein it is one great office of human wisdom to classify him."

It is more than a little unsettling to discover that one of Hawthorne's most direct and eloquent definitions of a bond for community is expressed in the form of a sermon preached by Satan himself. It occurs in the story of "Young Goodman Brown":

> "Welcome, my children," said the dark figure, "to the communion of your race. Ye have found thus young your nature and your destiny. My children, look behind you. . . .
> "There . . . are all whom ye have reverenced from youth. Ye deemed them holier than yourselves and shrank from your own sin, contrasting it with their lives of righteousness and prayerful aspirations heavenward. Yet here are they all in my worshipping assem-

bly. This night it shall be granted to you to know their secret deeds. ... By the sympathy of your human hearts for sin ye shall scent out all the places—whether in church, bed-chamber, street, field, or forest—where crime has been committed, and shall exult to behold the whole earth one stain of guilt, one mighty blood spot. Far more than this. It shall be yours to penetrate, in every bosom, the deep mystery of sin, the fountain of all wicked arts, and which inexhaustibly supplies more evil impulses than human power—than my power at its utmost—can make manifest in deeds. And now my children, look upon each other. . . .
"Depending upon one another's hearts, ye had still hoped that virtue were not all a dream. Now are ye undeceived. Evil is the nature of mankind. Evil must be your only happiness. Welcome again, my children, to the communion of your race."

These promises are offered as the final step in what has become for Goodman Brown a disillusioning process of education during his night journey into the wilderness. Because he has discovered that his teachers, the leaders of his community, his ancestors and parents before him, and even his wife have all taken the same dark journey, he already feels "a loathful brotherhood by the sympathy of all that was wicked in his heart," and he stands ready to be fully initiated into this communion of sinners. But at the last moment, he cries to his wife: "'Look up to heaven, and resist the wicked one.' Whether Faith obeyed he knew not. Hardly had he spoken when he found himself amid calm night and solitude. . . ."

Had Hawthorne stopped here, the story might have been little more than a conventional fable of temptation successfully resisted, but he continues by raising a question about the status of Brown's experience: "Had Goodman Brown fallen asleep in the forest and only dreamed a wild dream of a witch-meeting? Be it so if you will; but alas! it was a dream of evil omen for young Goodman Brown. A stern, a sad, a darkly meditative, a distrustful, if not a desperate man did he become from the night of that fearful dream." Brown thereafter separates himself from his community by his suspicions that his neighbors are the vilest hypocrites, concealing their true depravity behind masks of pious and kindly social lives within the village. "And when he had lived long, and was borne to his grave a hoary corpse, followed by Faith, an aged woman, and children and grandchildren, a goodly procession, besides neighbors not a few, they carved no hopeful verse upon his tombstone, for his dying hour was gloom." Most readers have agreed that "Young Goodman Brown" is one of Hawthorne's most compelling stories, but there has been very little agreement about what it means. This disagreement does, however, help illuminate his public style.

Some critics argue that it makes no difference whether Brown's experience in the forest is reality or dream; Brown believes it to be real and thus he rejects his community. As a consequence, his life is blighted. *Other* critics have suggested that it makes every difference in the world whether the experience is reality or a dream. If the witch's sabbath is real, then the community is in fact composed of depraved hypocrites, and Brown may be morally right in rejecting it even at the expense of his blighted life. But the critics have shied away from this alternative, preferring to see the experience as only a dream in order to make the case that Brown has woefully and wrongfully misjudged his community, his dream a projection of his own evil impulses onto his innocent community, his judgments diseased. Such arguments seem fired by an unstated indignation, even a horror at the prospect that Hawthorne used Satan to voice at least some of his own convictions. The efforts by critics to vindicate the innocence of Brown's community seem designed to vindicate Hawthorne as well from any hint that one of the strong Puritan traits that he shared might be the belief in original sin.

Authors who preached original sin might well seem Satanic in an increasingly enlightened climate of opinion. But the trouble, finally, with the arguments that affirm the community's innocence by making Brown a self-deluded paranoid is that they must ignore the pervasive evidence in Hawthorne's work that he believes the universal communion of sin to be not only real, but finally inescapable. In a sketch called "Fancy's Show Box," after showing the protagonist his sins of intention in an otherwise blameless life, the narrator says: ". . . with the slight fancy work we have framed, some sad and awful truths are interwoven. Man must not disclaim his brotherhood, even with the guiltiest, since, though his hands be clean, his heart has surely been polluted by the flitting phantoms of iniquity." This sad and awful truth serves very well as an explicit moral to be derived from the story of Young Goodman Brown. Brown's life is blighted because he disclaims his brotherhood with the guilty. His education remains incomplete because he fails to acknowledge his own share in the communion of sin. He persists in suspecting others of what he denies in himself, the impulse that took him into the forest in the first place, and he dies in despair. Satan had promised that the initiate would exult in the discovery of the universality of sin, but, as in Brown's case, Hawthorne consistently offers this discovery as an occasion for initial pain and revulsion.

He also shows us, however, other cases, to balance Brown's, in which such discovery prepares the initiate for a redemptive restoration to community. The discovery of the communion of sin, however painful, can become, when properly acknowledged, the source of some good for men. These convictions, as they are dramatized in Hawthorne's stories, edge him close to the doctrine of the fortunate fall. Hester Prynne is initiated by her scarlet letter: "She shuddered to believe, yet could not help believing, that it gave her a sympathetic knowledge of the hidden sin in other hearts. She was terror-stricken by the revelations that were thus made." Yet it is the development of these sympathies that helps Hester overcome her isolating conviction that her sin was special, that "what we did had a consecration of its own." Arthur Dimmesdale's guilt is redoubled by his realization that his hidden sin makes him a better preacher:

> But this very burden it was, that gave him sympathies so intimate with the sinful brotherhood of mankind; so that his hearth vibrated in unison with theirs, and received their pain into itself, and sent its own throb of pain through a thousand other hearts, in gushes of sad persuasive eloquence. Oftenest persuasive, but sometimes terrible! . . . It is inconceivable the agony with which this public veneration tortured him!"

But if it brings him agony, it also educates him to reclaim his true place within community by his public confession of his share in "the sinful brotherhood of mankind." For Hester and Dimmesdale, sympathy overcomes isolation and it is then and only then that they are restored to community, "to the people, whose great heart was thoroughly appalled, yet overflowing with tearful sympathy, as knowing that some deep life-matter—which, if full of sin, was full of anguish and repentance likewise—was now to be laid open to them." As Hawthorne puts it in the story of Ethan Brand, those who have lost "hold of the magnetic chain of humanity" can learn again to be "a brother-man, opening the chambers of the dungeons of our common nature by the key of holy sympathy, which gives them a right to share in all its secrets."

The task, then, that Hawthorne set himself as a storyteller was "to open the chambers or the dungeons of our common nature" in order to restore a bond of community, and the key to his public style, to both its method and its aim, is what he calls "the key of holy sympathy." Some of Hawthorne's early critics were repelled by the enterprise, characterizing such exposures with fantasies of sadism, images probably more appropriate, if finally unfair, to the work of Edgar Allan Poe. Poe's clinical exploitations of psychotic isolation can serve as useful contrasts to the style of Hawthorne's own case studies, but in fact Poe offered better insight into

Hawthorne's style in his review of *Twice-Told Tales*. Poe began by analyzing the tales' effect on Hawthorne's readers and summarized his analysis in this way: "Henceforward there is a bond of sympathy between them—a sympathy which irradiates every subsequent page of the book." Poe then confirms Hawthorne's own definition of his style as that of a man of society by stressing his affinities with the Augustans, particularly in the ease of his "natural style," which Poe defines by reference to its tone "which, at any given moment or upon any given topic, would be the tone of the great mass of humanity." After complaining about Hawthorne's use of allegory, Poe returns to a comparison with the Augustans: "*The Spectator*, Mr. Irving, and Hawthorne have in common that tranquil and subdued manner which I have chosen to denominate *repose*," but Hawthorne's style is to be distinguished from the others because ". . . a strong undercurrent of *suggestion* runs continuously beneath the upper stream of the tranquil thesis. In short, these effusions of Mr. Hawthorne are the product of a truly imaginative intellect, restrained, and in some measure repressed, by fastidiousness of taste, by constitutional melancholy, and by indolence."

Poe's reviews set the terms in which Hawthorne's style has been most often described. It is urbane, reserved, diffident, thoughtful, subdued, judicious, meditative, unobtrusive, quiet, and noncommittal. These choices testify, I think, to a general recognition that Hawthorne was successful in reporting the frequently troubling results of his inquiries, as he said he must, with "the tact of sympathy." No one has been more generous in making the point than Melville: "Such touches . . . argue such a depth of tenderness, such a boundless sympathy with all forms of being, such an omnipresent love, that we must needs say that this Hawthorne is here almost alone in his generation—at least, in the artistic manifestation of these things." But some critics, pondering what Poe touched on as a discrepancy between tranquil manner and disturbing matter have raised questions about whether there is a need also to describe his work as evasive, ambiguous, equivocal, mystifying, and deliberately elusive for an adequate account. Is tranquility the result of sympathy or is it deceptive? Melville warned that some of Hawthorne's stories "are directly calculated to deceive—egregiously deceive, the superficial skimmer of pages," and confessed that he himself had been duped by "Young Goodman Brown": "You would, of course, suppose that it was a simple little tale, intended as a supplement to Goody Two Shoes. Whereas, it is as deep as Dante; nor can you finish it without addressing the author in his own words—'It shall be yours to penetrate, in every bosom, the deep mystery of sin.'" And D. H. Lawrence's warning (in *Studies in Classic American Literature*, 1923) was even more emphatic: "You must look through the surface of

American art, and see the inner diabolism of the symbolic meaning. . . . That blue-eyed darling Nathaniel knew disagreeable things in his inner soul. He was careful to send them out in disguise." Both Melville and Lawrence find in Hawthorne a style that provokes the reader or at least penalizes him for careless reading.

My own view is that Hawthorne's style is less a disguise than an exemplary revelation of the kinds of restraints, reserves, and respectful cautions that embody what we mean by tact and sympathy. One of the sad and awful truths Hawthorne makes us confront is that genuine community may be possible only by our mutual recognition of universally shared flaws, weakness, and limitation—by our mutual acknowledgment of what is worst in us. Such a community is less to be celebrated than tolerated, and it both depends upon and makes difficult those balanced attitudes that can condemn sin even as it is forgiven.

These difficulties may account for the fact that Hawthorne's portraits of actual communities, despite the claims made for their restorative or sustaining powers, are often so uninviting. In *The Scarlet Letter*, Hawthorne can speak in the last chapters of restoration to the great heart of the people, but we shouldn't forget the unflattering choral portraits of those same people in the opening chapters, where the citizens of Boston are exposed as crassly self-righteous, inflexible, and insensitive. Clifford Pyncheon may be following a restorative impulse of sympathy when he wants to rejoin "the great world's movement" passing beneath his window in *The House of Seven Gables*, but the individual men and women who make up that procession are characterized as variations on the string of adjectives Hawthorne uses to describe one of them; they are "hard, vulgar, keen, busy, hackneyed . . . ." Ethan Brand's tragedy is that he has lost hold of "the magnetic chain of humanity," but that chain is represented in the story by a collection of maimed and derelict citizens who hang around the village tavern. So "low and vulgar" are "their modes of thought and feeling" that Brand is moved to doubt whether he had already found the unpardonable sin and only in himself. Hawthorne's claims for the social bond of sin are, then, central to his work, but so qualified with the reserves and cautions of his style that they suggest his uneasy awareness of what A. O. Lovejoy, in his well-known essay on "Milton and the Paradox of the Fortunate Fall" (in *Essays in the History of Ideas*, 1948) calls "some of the moral difficulties and metaphysical pitfalls which lay behind the conception of the *felix culpa*—difficulties and metaphysical pitfalls which Augustine himself cannot be said to have wholly escaped." Hawthorne's awareness of such problems is dramatized most concisely near the conclusion of his last novel, *The Marble Faun*.

The young American sculptor Kenyon is trying to draw a moral for his friend Hilda from what they have witnessed of the effects of sin on Donatello:

> "Sin has educated Donatello and elevated him. Is sin, then,— which we deem such a dreadful blackness in the universe, is it, like sorrow, merely an element of human education, through which we struggle to a higher and purer state than we could otherwise have attained? Did Adam fall, that we might ultimately rise to a far loftier paradise than his?" . . .
>
> "Oh, hush!" cried Hilda. . . . "This is terrible; and I could weep for you, if you indeed believe it. Do not you perceive what a mockery your creed makes, not only of all religious sentiments, but of moral law? and how it annuls and obliterates whatever precepts of Heaven are written deepest within us? You have shocked me beyond words!"
>
> "Forgive me, Hilda!" exclaimed the sculptor, startled by her agitation; "I never did believe it! . . . Were you my guide, my counsellor, my inmost friend, with that white wisdom which clothes you as a celestial garment, all would go well. O Hilda, guide me home."

Kenyon's sudden capitulation here is less a repudiation of the doctrine of the fortunate fall than it may first seem. The doctrine has already been fully articulated and accepted by other characters as a true description of Donatello's story. Hilda does have the last word, but because it contains little more than the transcendental commonplaces that Hawthorne had already satirically rejected in the sketch called "The Celestial Railroad," it hardly seems means as refutation. And the full record of his previous work remains, work frequently and clearly informed by evidence of the value of community, especially its value as a deterrent to isolating pride, for those who through sympathy learn to confess or to otherwise acknowledge their share in the community of sin.

But Kenyon's capitulation does provide a final clue to Hawthorne's conception of community. Kenyon too easily gives up his views in order to please the woman he loves. He abandons his speculations among metaphysical pitfalls in the interests of domestic felicity, and in this he may reflect Hawthorne's own inclinations. Hawthorne realized that his communal portraits were often unsubstantial and the communities uninviting. Most often he attributed this either to his own inabilities or to the paucity of social materials in the American scene. But it may also be true that his own troubled sense of a community based on the mutual awareness of sin inhibited his attempts to imagine and to show exactly how such a community would work. In any event, he often took Kenyon's way out. Kenyon joins Hawthorne's gallery of satisfied husbands who find fulfillment, not in the community at large, but within the circle of the domestic hearth. At one extreme, such portraits represent a retreat from community; as one character puts it in the story of "The Ambitious Guest": "It is better to sit here by the fire . . . and be comfortable and contented, though nobody thinks about us."

Insofar as Hawthorne gives voice to this impulse, he represents in his fiction what Alexis de Tocqueville, in his early study of *Democracy in America*, defined as the peculiar form of American individualism: "Individualism is a mature and calm feeling, which disposes each member of the community to sever himself from the mass of his fellows and to draw apart with his family and his friends, so that after he has thus formed a little circle of his own, he willingly leaves society at large to itself." It must finally be said, however, that Hawthorne's portraits of domestic felicity are less often a retreat from community than an attempt to show a balance or a correlation between the communal recognition of shared sin and the warmth of family affections. In the preface to *The Snow Image*, he said that he would need both "the tact of sympathy" and "the light of observation" in order to conduct his inquiries into the depths of our common nature. In "The Custom-House" sketch, in his famous image of "a neutral territory," an imaginative middle-ground for the artist, he specified the mixture of light necessary for observation. One sort is moonlight by means of which details "are so spiritualized that they seem to lose their actual substance, and become things of intellect." But this kind of light, the light of Kenyon's speculations, must be mixed with light from the domestic hearthfire: "This warmer light mingles itself with the cold spirituality of the moonbeams, and communicates, as it were, a heart and sensibilities of human tenderness to the forms which fancy summons up." And in the sketch called "Fire Worship," it is the hearth-fire which illuminates the individual's place within a larger community, and "which gives the human spirit so deep an insight into its fellows and melts all humanity into one cordial heart of hearts." What saves Hawthorne's celebrations of domestic felicity both from de Tocqueville's isolating individualism and from sentimentality is that its affections both sustain and are tempered by an awareness of and a willingness to enter the community of shared sin. The young bridal couple in the story of "The Canterbury Pilgrims" chose to leave the artificial isolation of the Shaker community, and "with chastened hopes, but more confiding affections, went on to mingle in an untried life." Even before their encounter with the stern

Puritans in the story of "The Maypole of Merry Mount," the young Lord and Lady of the May become aware of what one speaks of as "the mystery in my heart": "From the moment that they truly loved, they had subjected themselves to earth's doom of care and sorrow, and troubled joy, and had no more a home at Merry Mount."

There is a pair of remarkable chapters in *Moby-Dick* which may be taken, I think, as a commentary on the contrast I've tried to draw between the public styles of Emerson and Hawthorne. Chapter 93 is called "The Castaway" and tells the story of little Pip the cabin-boy, the least important member of the crew but the only person on board the *Pequod* who experiences a direct union with God. Pip is stranded alone in the ocean after having jumped from a whale boat during a chase:

> The sea had jeeringly kept his finite body up, but drowned the infinite of his soul. Not drowned entirely, though. Rather carried down alive to wondrous depths, where strange shapes of the unwarped primal world glided to and fro before his passive eyes. . . . He saw God's foot upon the treadle of the loom, and spoke it; and therefore his shipmates called him mad. So man's insanity is heaven's sense; and wandering from all mortal reason, man comes at last to that celestial thought, which, to reason, is absurd and frantic; and weal or woe, feels then uncompromised, indifferent as his God.

It is sorely tempting to see this as an image of what awaits those successfully unsettled by Emerson's public style, but it is even more tempting to see the chapter that immediately follows this one as a description of Hawthorne's enterprise. Chapter 94 is called "A Squeeze of the Hand," and there Ishmael describes the task of preparing the spermaceti taken from the whale's head. He is seated with his shipmates around the sperm tub.

> I squeezed that sperm till a strange sort of insanity came over me; and I found myself unwittingly squeezing my co-laborers' hands in it, mistaking their hands for the gentle globules. Such an abounding, affectionate, friendly, loving feeling did this avocation beget; that at last I was continually squeezing their hands, and looking up into their eyes sentimentally; as much to say,—Oh! my dear fellow beings, why should we longer cherish any social acerbities, or know the slightest ill-humor of envy! Come; let us squeeze hands all round; nay, let us all squeeze ourselves into each other; let us squeeze ourselves universally into the very milk and sperm of kindness.

Would that I could keep squeezing that sperm for ever! For now, since by many prolonged, repeated experiences, I have perceived that in all cases man must eventually lower, or at least shift, his conceit of attainable felicity; not placing it anywhere in the intellect or the fancy; but in the wife, the heart, the bed, the table, the saddle, the fire-side, the country; now that I have perceived all this, I am ready to squeeze case eternally.

Hawthorne once called Mr. Emerson "that ever lasting rejector of all that is, and seeker for he knows not what." Like Ahab's, Emerson's quest may be courageous and heroic, but like Pip's experience it may end in madness and a cosmic indifference to the values of community. Like Ishmael, Hawthorne lowers "his conceit of attainable felicity." He settles for less, but his public style is nonetheless heroic as it attempts to restore that difficult relationship, so often threatened in America, between community and the private heart.

American Essays
Pedagogy, Provocation, and Preaching

Poor Richard and *Playboy*: Brothers under the Flesh

Mr. Hugh Hefner, editor-publisher of *Playboy* magazine, is now famous and affluent enough to have been explained by a number of interesting names. The less pejorative include "moral benefactor," "liberator," "theologian," "oracle," and "prophet." Even this small collection of wowsers means that whatever Mr. Hefner *qua* Hefner really is, he has become, like kosher pizza and the late Clara Bow, a cultural phenomenon. Whether Mr. Hefner welcomes this status is literally, of course, his business; whether it can be here and properly explained is mine. And the way to begin is to insist that labels like the above are shamefully inadequate. The truth is simply that Hefner as cultural phenomenon is the twentieth-century avatar of Benjamin Franklin. To know Hefner, then, we must begin with Ben.

Dr. Franklin's attendance at the birth of so many other American institutions may obscure his services as obstetrician for the nation's capitalism, but it's true that even before Hamilton and his colleagues could deliver infant capitalism to the new Republic, Franklin had provided prenatal care by creating necessary habits in the public mind. The problem of a people seeking economic as well as political independence is to create its own capital, and the least dependent method is simple abstinence. Franklin was the colonies' most vocal champion of the abstemious or squirrel virtues, industry and frugality. By practicing industry, he tirelessly insisted, the amount produced could be increased. By practicing frugality, one could refrain from consuming some of the increased production, thereby creating even more capital.

Franklin did not, of course, invent the Protestant Ethic; his unique contribution to this lovely marriage of money and morals was to publish its banns. His media were those snappy maxims, now part of folklore, spread to the tradesmen and farmers of his day in the pages of *Poor Richard's Almanack* appearing between 1733 and 1758. Franklin described the *Almanack* in his *Autobiography* as "a proper vehicle for conveying instruction among the common people, who bought scarcely any other books," and explained his choice of proverbial sentences as "chiefly such as inculcated industry and frugality, as a means of procuring wealth and thereby securing virtue."

The economic essence of Poor Richard was distilled in Franklin's famous sermon *The Way to Wealth*, so enduringly popular that it has since appeared in more than seventy English editions and has been translated into at least sixteen languages, including such exotic script as Catalan and phonetic writing. Father Abraham, another of Ben's avatars, there delivers himself of some choice Poor Richardisms: "We may make the times better, if we bestir ourselves. There are no gains without pains, then help hands for I have no land. . . . A fat kitchen makes a lean will, as Poor Richard says. If you would be wealthy, think of saving as well as getting." Such is the stuff of capitalism's folklore; for us the verbal vestiges of the institution's past.

But the infant institution nursed by Franklin has aged, and its mature needs are far different from, indeed the reverse of, those of its swaddling days. The change has made Ben's once good advice at worst obsolete, at best embarrassing. Franklin had to assume an economy of scarcity; we must assume an economy of abundance. Franklin demanded abstention from consumption in order to create capital; we must consume mightily in order to further multiply capital. In short Franklin's ethics of production served an infant capitalism; we now need an ethics of consumption to maintain a mature one. And it is just here, of course, that Mr. Hefner, as cultural phenomenon, was born; or rather it is just here that Dr. Franklin refreshes himself with an avatar.

This simple fact would have been recognized long ago had not the dazzling flesh of Hefner's *Playboy* hidden the Poor Richard within. Hefner himself has been coy as a belly dancer's navel about acknowledging his debt, allowing only the slyest confessions as on the occasion when his editors finally granted Franklin the title of "that respected playboy of the past." But usually two hundred years of improvements in the arts of making magazines amply enfold the old gentleman in the new fashions.

Properly exposed, however, the Franklin pit in Hefner's peach is revealing in more ways than one. For instance, it tends to exonerate Hefner from one of the more frivolous charges brought against him. Those who fulminate against the naked cuties in his magazine must understand that the girl on the gatefold is only the shill to get the marks into the tent. Once here the citizen is subject to a proselytizing much more severe than easy invitations to lust. A new, now swinging Father Abraham takes over and his message—the essence of *Playboy*—is simply Franklin's prudential ethics, differing from the original only because of a slight temporal adjustment. As a *Playboy* editor once mused: "Every time we're told that a penny saved is a penny earned, we find ourselves wishing there were some governmental bureau to adjust proverbs—like price supports or vital statistics—to take into account the advance of civilization." The man was badly misled; no need to look to the government when his own free-enterprising employer has done the job. Ben urges us to be frugal; Hefner implores us to be prodigal. Ben counsels us to productive industry; Hefner enjoins us to strenuous leisure. As *Playboy* says, "chaste makes waste." And while it's true that the original maxims for active abstinence have given way to those for active indulgence because the institution their preacher serves has matured, all else is the same. The economic moralist is in business at the same old stand. As Marx inverted Hegel, so Hefner has turned Franklin outside in, but in the process of reembodying the old essence, he has retained enough of Franklin's manner to make it a dead giveaway.

Hefner repeatedly describes himself as a man with a deep sense of mission, on one occasion as "a rather dedicated and one-way kind of guy." And he has been candid about the mission, carefully explaining that "our editorial emphasis is on entertainment and leisure-time activity rather than on the ways in which man earns his daily bread" and yet the articles, on the creature comforts and the infinite variety of man's more elegant, leisure-time possessions, clearly stress that these are the prizes available in our society in return for honest endeavor and hard work. The prudential virtues recommended by Franklin are, then, by no means their own reward. Once they have accomplished the accumulation of capital, they quite naturally become their opposites, indulgence and prodigality, now enjoying the prizes which Franklin implicitly promised and which Hefner graphically displays.

The essential identity of these two economic moralists is further established by certain shared habits. There is, for example, their aggressive candour in discussing the uses of venery, or the fact that both, having early arrived at fame and fortune, devote their declining years to good works, then the Philadelphia charities, now the chartered, nonprofit Playboy Foundation. Note also the emphatic protest of Franklin-Hefner against harsh and repressive sex laws. It was in the course of such a protest, as a matter of fact, that Franklin anticipated his modern avatar by inventing the playmate bunny. Striking at the law of Puritan Massachusetts, Franklin imagined the plea of one Polly Baker, early swinger, to her judge. She argues that it is wrong to punish her for doing her duty, "the duty of the first and great command of nature, and of nature's God, *increase and multiply.* A duty, from the steady performance of which, nothing has been able to deter me; but for its sake, I have hazarded the loss of the publick esteem, . . . and therefore ought, in my humble opinion, instead of a whipping, to have a statue erected to my memory." In at least a symbolic sense, Hefner's cottontail legions are Polly's true memorial.

Such parallels are, however, minor when compared with the rather startling truth that Hefner was seemingly compelled to adapt the entire format of his magazine from that of *Poor Richard's Almanack*. Compare, for example, this advertisement for the first issue of the *Almanack* with the table of contents in any *Playboy*. In addition to Lunations and Eclipses, retained by Hefner as the Bunny Calendar, Richard Saunders' first offering included "many pleasant and witty verses, jests and sayings, author's motive of writing, Moon no Cuckold, Batchelor's Folly, New Fashions, Games for Kisses, Katherine's Love, Conjugal Debate, Men and Melons, Breakfast in Bed." *Playboy's* gustatory adventures find models in Poor Richard's often exotic receipts, one for "Dauphiny Soup, which in Turkey is call [sic] Trouble." "International Datebook" is the economy jet set's version of Poor Richard's listings of the annual fairs and Quaker general meetings. Poor Richard's homely counsels on when to plant "pease" are extended by the Playboy advisor who is knowledgeable on such anxiety-producing matters as whether the pleats of the cummerbund should be worn opening upward or downward, or who should mount the tandem bicycle first, boy or girl. The point is simply that despite the gaudy new exterior, the old American come-on and know-how remain unmistakably the same.

Perhaps the most direct hints that we are in the presence of Poor Richard when we read *Playboy* are the ruminations of J. Paul Getty, self-made billionaire and the magazine's contributing editor for finance and business. Getty frequently out-Franklins Franklin. For instance, in an essay in the April 1965 issue called "Force of Habit," Getty perhaps unwittingly illustrates his title as he revives one of Ben's maxims: "That ancient adage 'Time is money' has always been valid and it is more valid today than ever before." Getty continues at some length to make the familiar case for the habit of thrift and its related virtues, the old prudential ethics thus nesting comfortably amid its modern brothers in *Playboy*. Getty's essays for the magazine have been collected and published by the Playboy Press as *How to be Rich*, a title making it the obvious sequel for those generations who have arrived via Franklin's *The Way to Wealth*.

For those who remain unconvinced that Hefner is Franklin's avatar, the final argument is of course that neither of these economic moralists quite practices what he preaches. In Franklin's career, this discrepancy is revealed in his *Autobiography*, justly celebrated as the first American success story. In form the work is a classic comedy, charting the protagonist's rise in fortune "from the poverty and obscurity in which I was born and bred, to a state of affluence and some degree of reputation in the world." This ascending curve displays his career as an exemplum demonstrating that the assiduous practice of the prudential virtues would, in fact, lead to capitalistic success.

Yet read the story carefully and it reveals Ben as being less interested in being industrious and frugal than in appearing so. The reason is simply that the money which gave him his start did *not* come from capital accumulated through personal industry and frugality; it came instead from wealthy patrons who saw him as a good risk, amiably conned by their protégé's skill in projecting the image of industry and frugality. "In order to secure my credit and character as a tradesman, I took care not only to be in *reality* industrious and frugal, but to avoid all *appearances* of the contrary."

The record is rich in further evidence of Franklin's skill with appearances. For example, "to show that I was not above my business, I sometimes brought home the paper I purchas'd at the stories, thro' the streets on a wheelbarrow. Thus being esteemed an industrious thriving young man, . . . I went on swimmingly." Even Franklin's lapses from prudence are done with an eye to public response. "A book, indeed, sometimes debauch'd me from my work; but that was seldom, snug, and gave no scandal." As Franklin later says of his attempt to practice humility: "I cannot boast of much success in acquiring the *reality* of this virtue; but I had a good deal with regard to the *appearance* of it." Much the same can be said for his performance of the capital-producing virtues he so ardently thrusts upon us.

Mr. Hefner has not yet written his autobiography, although the cinema version has been long announced, but his technicolour rise to affluence and celebrity, a curve repeating Franklin's, has prompted several reportorial glimpses into his private life, among them Bill Davidson in *Saturday Evening Post*, Diana Lurie in *Life*, and Richard Gehman in *Fact*. Their approach, by now seemingly definitive, has been to offer two Hefners, the public Playboy and the one I now must insist is the private Franklin. Out front, of course, Hefner is suave, urbane, London-tailored, Escoffier-fed, potable-loaded, and given to tasting every delight from Abelard to Zucchini-Flambeau. The insiders tell us he is driven, boyish, habitually pajamaed, short-order fed, Pepsi-filled, and happiest when consumed by his enterprise—in short, a most careless consumer.

In fact probings of Hefner's private life have given the impression that he lives in a cork-lined closet in the bowels of his mansion, spinning the gaudy world of *Playboy* out of the constantly strained resources of his personal industry and frugality. This tension between public and private Hefner displays the man as what a longer-lived Franklin might have been. In the old days, Franklin took pains to be publicly industrious and frugal, debauching only in the snugness of his closet where it gave no scandal. Today Hefner must spectacularly debauch in public, and only in the snugness of *his* closet can he be, without scandal, industrious and abstemious.

It would be base to accuse these economic moralists of deliberate hypocrisy. That the demands of their role force them into behaviour at variance with their personal inclinations might, for all we know, be the price of success. Their common inability, however, to meet the demands of the virtuous life which they lay on others does suggest that while the prophetic spirit of capitalist morality that sustains them both is forever willing, the flesh they share with us is weak.

Thoreau and Mailer: The Mission of the Rooster

Although Norman Mailer is quick to climb into the ring with literary contenders, he has given only the back of his hand to "academics who wolfed down a modern literature with an anxiety to find your classification, your identity, your similarity, your common theme, your corporate literary earnings, each reference to yourself as individual as a carloading of homogenized words." Anxious, insensitive, author-devouring—thus the academic, and presumably Mailer has teeth marks to prove it. Knocking the processors, however, does not exempt him from the process of classification, identification, and comparison with other writers. Because Mailer has taken full advantage of having been forced early into celebrity, we know abundantly who he is. We need means other than his self-advertisement to know what he has achieved, and the truth is that many of the things Mailer has done, Henry David Thoreau did before him, including banging on academics. Mailer's work prior to *Advertisements for Myself* (1959) has been best characterized by Diana Trilling and Norman Podhoretz. I will classify, however rudely, a newer Mailer by reference to Thoreau, for Mailer now shares with him at least three defining concerns: a prophetic demand for life awakened into the immediate present, a preoccupation with self as the necessary symbol for that life, and the effort to write a prose protean enough to record the awakened self.

One of Mailer's best stories, "The Man Who Studied Yoga," may be compared to *Walden* if only because the two works are sustained by the same simple mission, to awaken the reader. This task of the rooster is announced in the epigraph of *Walden*: "I do not propose to write an ode to dejection, but to brag as lustily as chanticleer in the morning . . . if only to wake my readers up." In Mailer's story, the narrator is hinted to be Sergius O'Shaugnessy, the rooster of *Deer Park* and "The Time of Her Time." O'Shaugnessy introduces the story's slumbering protagonist by insisting "It is fit to describe him now, for like most humans he prefers sleeping to not sleeping," and then relentlessly details "the flat and familiar dispirit" of Sam Slovoda throughout a contemporary urban Sunday. In order to heal Sam as he struggles again into sleep, O'Shaugnessy voices a formula to arouse life: "destroy time, and chaos may be ordered." Sam repeats it, but "in desperation to seek his coma, mutters back, 'I do not feel my nose, my nose is numb, my eyes are heavy, my eyes are heavy.'" At this aborted climax, Mailer's narrator, like Thoreau, must crow away tedium by shattering the habits which enforce it, by destroying the routines that define time. Thoreau glossed the point perfectly in *Walden*: "By closing the eyes and slumbering, and consenting to be deceived by shows, men establish and confirm their daily life of routine and habit everywhere, which still is built on purely illusory foundations." Part of the coil in the prose of both writers is their barely sympathetic contempt for the lot of most men. Sam Slovoda's flat dispirit is labeled "familiar" perhaps because it was first identified in America by Thoreau as quiet desperation (Mailer borrows the phrase in "The White Negro"). And although Mailer's portrait gallery of walking sleepers is larger and more graphically detailed than Thoreau's, his descriptions add nothing essential to Thoreau's image of the ladies of the land "weaving toilet cushions against the last day, not to betray too green an interest in their fates."

The consciousness Thoreau and Mailer would awake in others, they seek themselves in the most alert apprehension of the present moment. The central purpose of Thoreau's elaborately justified enterprise at Walden Pond is to capture and savour just that experience which resides at the intersection of past and future: "In any weather, at any hour of the day or night, I have been anxious to improve the nick of time, . . . to stand on the meeting of two eternities, the past and future, which is precisely the present moment." This is also Mailer's demand, most explicitly stated in "The White Negro." There he defines the American existentialist who "exists in the present, in that enormous present which is without past or future, memory or planned intention, the life where a man must go until he is beat. . . ." Such a man is or becomes a psychic outlaw, and Mailer's term is accurate here because although he and Thoreau occasionally pose as criminals challenging the structures of tradition and prudential planning, their essential quarrel is with the psychic equivalents of these institutions, anxious memory and anticipation. Freedom from institutional restraints is, for both, important, but meaningless without the psychic autonomy which they claim as possible for the fully awakened consciousness. James Russell Lowell was the first to notice in Thoreau what Norman Podhoretz later discovered in Mailer. Lowell, with no love lost on his sometime Concord neighbour, insisted it was a defect in character which made Thoreau think "everything a discovery of his own, from moonlight to the planting of acorns and nuts by squirrels," but grudgingly conceded this as one of his "chief charms" as a writer. Podhoretz judges the same trait in Mailer to be healthy: "He must always work everything out for himself and by himself, as though it were up to him to create the world anew over and over again in his own experience."

To make only this point about what the two writers have in common would confirm Mailer's original complaint against academics, for it dumps both into a carload capacious enough to hold any number of other romantics and near-romantics. Diana Trilling, for example, has linked Mailer with D. H. Lawrence, "his predecessor in the line of literary minds dedicated to the renovation of society by means of a revolution in the individual consciousness." Of course she is right; Thoreau is only a more remote predecessor in dedication to what Mailer says he learned from Lawrence: "be true to the logic of each moment." Thoreau and Mailer are uncommonly good at doing just this. Yet they are not, like Emerson, poet-priests of beatific vision; neither are they therapists who train the faculties of vision. They are, like roosters, agents of the awakening by speaking as vivid examples of the awakened. Like roosters, their function as alarm clock is ancillary to a concerned delight in their own voices. And, like roosters, their characteristic voice is extravagant, rambunctious, and exuberant.

No one in American letters since Thoreau has insisted as much on literary egocentricity as Mailer. In the process the core of self created in his prose has unmistakably repeated the image left by Thoreau—cocky as hell, full of Chanticleer's pride and strut in surveying mimic empires, for Thoreau the environs of Concord, for Mailer any contemporary arena smelling of power. Thoreau's ant battle in *Walden* and Mailer's three sets of presidential conventions since 1960, lordly captures of the minute and the mutable, testify to the skill they share in reporting what other men overlook. One qualification seems necessary here. Mailer's skill in fixing the moment with even its smallest fact—present everywhere in his reports of actual events—is as notable for its absence in at least two novels. In *An American Dream* and *Why Are We in Vietnam?* action, reaction, consciousness itself seem deliberately unfixed from the controlling stimuli offered by the world. Too often the moment becomes purely cerebral, as in Nojack's habit of sending psychic missiles against his enemies, or purely rhetorical, as in D. J.'s early verbal acrobatics. This may suggest that, free from the obligation to report actual events, Mailer finds the value of the moment less in those contours of the world's body it exposes than in the quality of consciousness excited by it. This is at least what Thoreau meant when he wrote: "My work is writing, and I do not hesitate, though I know that no subject is too trivial for me, tried by ordinary standards; for, ye fools, the theme is nothing, the life is everything. All that interests the reader is the depth and intensity of the life excited." Both writers, quick to reject the tyrannies of past and future, seem, then, equally capable of resenting the coercive potential, the recalcitrant facts of the present moment. Their expressions of such resentment are, however, infrequent, and seem to result from an acute, and therefore painful, awareness of how many demands and disciplines are required by a genuine awakening.

Ideally the excited consciousness of the writer is omni-attentive; its discipline, however difficult, promises at least the possibility of simultaneously apprehending everything offered by the present moment in order to capture its essence. Thoreau "wanted to live deep and suck out all the marrow of life, . . . to cut a broad swath and shave close. . . ." And Mailer in a similar mood wants "to see and to see hard, to smell, even to touch, yes to capture that nerve of Being which may include all of us. . . ." Given such demands, it seems inevitable that both writers deliberately cultivate what we timid men call egotism. The Self—rather than Nature or Society—is the locus for what they consider the only genuine connection in time, the intercourse of perceiver and perceived circumscribed by the moment. The ability to record this self—to know it through language—is one test of whether or not genuine connection, so actually elusive in its passing, has taken place. Mailer makes this point, for example, in "Prologue to a Long Novel" with which he concludes *Advertisements for Myself*, by a dialogue between "a tall dignified Negress with a velvet sensuality" and a square physicist. Cara Beauchamp says: "Like Time is when you connect." The physicist translates: "'Time rests as potential?' he asked, excitement in his dry sad voice, 'rests there until the gap is jumped to Time dynamic.'" Cara's response to this is a capsule description of the way in which Mailer believes awakened consciousness and language interact to create the self. "For the rest of her life she had two new words, and what words they were. Through all her unconscious were flexings of cellular pleasure—so much of her experience was rushing to the higher plateau of more precise language." Cara's experience is comparable to one Thoreau reports: "I want nothing better than a good word. The name of a thing may easily be more than the thing itself to me. Inexpressibly beautiful appears the recognition by man of the least natural fact, and the allying his life to it."

This notion of the self moved to new definition by the nominal properties of the moment raises several problems, one of which is illustrated by a maneuver in Emerson's essay "Self-Reliance." In scourging a concern for consistency as a barrier to self-reliance, Emerson raised the possibility of self so responsive to the unique demands of the present that its identity might be destroyed, fragmented into myriad selves, each discrete because called forth by peculiar, although successive moments. But Emerson is quick to assure us that proper reliance on Self actually insures its consistency, at least in written record: "Let me record day by day my honest thought without prospect or retrospect, and, I cannot doubt, it will be found symmetrical, though I mean it not and see it not." For both Thoreau and Mailer, the self is a stage made endlessly flexible as it is styled by the language of moments, but because the stage is contained within the theatre of character, a rough coherence in performance seems assured. In "First Advertisement for Myself," Mailer worries the difficulty for a writer when he "begins to jiggle his Self for a style which will have some relation to him." What happens to consistency? "To write about myself is to send my style through a circus of variations and postures, a fireworks of virtuosity designed to achieve . . . I do not even know what. Leave it that I become an actor, a quick-change artist, as if I believe I can trap the Prince of Truth in the act of switching a style." In a *Paris Review* interview, Mailer turned to the actor capable of all such performances: "A really good style comes only when a man has become as good as he can be. Style is character." This echoes a remark by Thoreau: "The best you can write will be the best you are. Every sentence is the result of a long probation. The author's character is read from title-page to end."

Sustained by a faith in the coherence promised by good character, both tend to regard writing as the discovery of new styles, styles which will connect the awakened self and the awakening moment. For this reason, I think, both focus attention on the sentence rather than on the function or the development or the cohesion of such sentences within larger patterns and forms. The mission of the rooster seems to require a prophetic style comprised of loosely related aphorisms. The arrangement of such aphorisms of immediate conception into larger units must be described as loose because, at least in the cases of Thoreau and Mailer, it is governed by the unpredictable shapes to which the succession of moments urges the exfoliation of self. Mailer's most elaborate definition of form suggests that he, like Thoreau, prefers organic metaphors for the process of literary composition. In one of his self-interviews in *Cannibals and Christians*, he defines form as "the record of a relationship," that persistent residue which survives an abrasive encounter between contending forces. Mailer uses the forms of driftwood to illustrate his definition. It is pointless to classify the shapes of driftwood; it seems equally pointless to assign the works of these writers to established genres. Mailer resists his public's celebration of his "journalism" by insisting he is still a novelist, but such categories are as irrelevant for appreciating the power he shares with Thoreau as the question of whether *Walden* is an anthology of essays, a poem of the seasons, a naturalist's report, or an autobiography. What is important is an understanding of the reasons why their sentences are so consistently tonic, an enterprise made difficult because the protean self assumes so many styles. Tracking Thoreau's prose habits, for instance, from early Transcendental abstraction, through the precision of Linnaean classification, to the tangy colloquialisms borrowed from friends like farmer Minot, hints poorly at his resources. Similarly, Mailer learned, in part from Dwight Macdonald as he reports in *The Armies of the Night*, that "the clue to discovery was not in the substance of one's ideas, but in what was learned from the style of one's attack." His projects have sharpened enough variety in attack to leave behind everything from the serviceable tones of *The Naked and the Dead* to the tumescent prose of "Prologue to a Long Novel" and the flat-out invective of *Why Are We in Vietnam?* Yet, despite the fact that both writers scorn styles that can be imitated, there are at least two characteristics common to their sentences: the first is a quality that Thoreau spoke of as "vascular," the second a special kind of balance.

For Thoreau, the act of writing involved the whole man, the whole of a man in a literal way which, had he been less inhibited, would have sorely offended the decorums around him. As it was, he only anticipated the inevitable shock shortly to come from Whitman by advising: "We cannot write well or truly but what we write with gusto. The body, the senses, must conspire with the mind. Expression is the act of the whole man, that our speech may be vascular. The intellect is powerless to express thought without the aid of the heart and liver and of every member." Mailer's styles obey these injunctions more easily than Thoreau's and, in fact, Thoreau more accurately predicted the experience of Mailer's readers: "They must have the essence or oils of himself, tried out of the fat of his experience and joy." Mailer's styles are not only oleic, they are visceral, lymphatic, corpuscular, and gallinaceous to boot. What distinguishes his accounts of political conventions from those of other reports is exactly this crackling of liver and lights with which he flavours his objectivity. The following examples are from "Miami Beach and Chicago," an essay which exudes the odors of Mailer's personal try works in a way to rival the rich stinks he found near the Chicago stockyards. There are "the first freshets of his brooding," "the root of his nerve," his "orator's muscle," and "the sleeping festering hair of his outrage" to remind us that Mailer is present, rendering "the orgiastic fats of the liberal center," Bill Miller's "political oils," and "the suet at the center of his [Humphrey's] seat." Mailer reveals Nixon "stretching the subtle rubber of his own credibility," notes that "at different heats, the oils of separate psyches were loosened," and discovers "the tender germ in the living plasma of the party." Here, under "Lyndon's volcanic breath," policemen burst like boils, "quivering jowls beamed bad cess to puffed-out paunches," and, over all, "that high smoke of action carried from night to night in the electrified cool of the blood." At times

Mailer can sound like Nathanael West: he describes McCarthy's epigrams as "hard and sanctified little goat turds," politicians have "jaws like amputated knees," and Mailer is among his captors "jostling like jockstrap mystics on a collective web of isometric exercises." For Thoreau, "a fact stated barely is dry.... It must be warm, moist, incarnated,—have been breathed on at least." Thoreau's chief resources for doing so were botanic; he could describe good sentences as verdurous, transferred to the page with dirt still clinging to the roots. Mailer takes the next step; his political conventions are drawn by a physiologist in high heat. Use of the body's infracostal regions has in fact become the craftmark of Mailer's recent prose—work still warm, moist, incarnated, but now with human chemistry rather than the quiet generations of plants and animals at Walden. Mailer neatly, even if obscurely, phrased this mark in "Prologue to a Long Novel": "for if I am the creature of relationship, I must be not so much consciousness as corporeal, containing a blastopore whose nucleic proteins limn a signature."

The principle which tends to control the transformation of such diction into the metaphors and syntax of Mailer's sentences is a special kind of balance he shares with Thoreau. Commenting on Sir Walter Raleigh's style, Thoreau wrote that "the most attractive sentences are not perhaps the wisest, but the surest and soundest.... They were spoken in the nick of time." This deemphasis of wisdom, of learning sanctioned by endurance, combined with the notion of assurance at a critical moment, aptly describes the excitement caused by a reader's sense of precariously maintained linguistic balance. For this reason, it is tempting to call their prose sure-footed—a cock-of-the-walk amble over rough terrain—but this is too clumsy to identify properly in their prose a habitual dexterity with constructions balanced between formal rigors on the one hand and obscurity, contortion, or simple nonsense on the other. Both writers seem prompted to aspire to such balance by their preoccupations with the shifting relationships between self and the present moment, preoccupations in turn shared with the baroque prose masters of the late sixteenth and seventeenth centuries (to whom Thoreau frequently acknowledged his debt). The concern of these early moderns for process rather than perfected form, for the acts of thinking and imagining rather than the polished results of thought and imagination, led them to challenge the rules of Ciceronian ease in order to simulate in prose the dust and heat of minds at work. Such baroque features as the exploded period and syntactical asymmetry are signals that attention was being transferred from classical repose to the energies of a modern immersion in time. This sense of release apparently allowed the baroque writer new adventures in walking the line between order and excess, the line at which order may be present in excess and yet endangered by it. And this seems exactly the line both Thoreau and Mailer want to walk in their prose. In *Walden* Thoreau disdains the conventional expectations of his reader: "It is a ridiculous demand which England and America make, that you shall speak so that they can understand you. . . . I fear chiefly lest my expression may not be *extravagant* enough. . . . I desire to speak somewhere *without* bounds; like a man in a waking moment, to men in their waking moments; for I am convinced that I cannot exaggerate enough even to lay the foundation of a true expression." Mailer makes much the same point in "The White Negro" by describing the language of Hip as a language of energy, extravagant, without bounds because the hipsters "do not have the protection of a position or a class to rely on when they have overextended themselves." In this language, a few words serve many functions within a "dialectic of the instantaneous differentials of existence in which one is forever moving forward into more or retreated into less." By grafting the energies of Hip to his own startling and enormous vocabulary, Mailer frequently creates an extravagance in which balance comes off as a hard-won achievement. In the sentences of both Thoreau and Mailer, balance calls attention to itself not as a result of measure and restraint, but rather as the result of risks taken and tensions resolved, however temporarily.

This linguistic poise reflects the interests of both writers in expressing selves which are frequently defined as a balance of contending opposites. Mailer has called the artist's personality "an incredible balance of opposites and incompatibles," and has often spoken of his own as a satisfying mixture of the wild man and the Harvard man: "The reporter had gone for years on the premise that one must balance every moment between the angel in oneself and the swine." And Thoreau, also a Harvard man: "I found in myself and still find, an instinct toward a higher, or, as it is named, spiritual life, as do most men, and another toward a primitive rank, and savage one, and I reverence them both. I love the wild not less than the good." These sentiments indicate a large, but hardly unusual hospitality for all the vagaries of experience—a desire to integrate disparate elements in one personality. More significantly, both writers have felt this duality as the need for a careful balance between the awakened self and its reflective recorder. Mailer confesses himself "an egotist of the most startling misproportions, outrageously and often unhappily self-assertive, yet in command of a detachment classic in severity. . . . Such egotism being two-headed, thrusting itself forward the better to study itself. . . ." And Thoreau in *Walden* explained that he was "sensible of a certain doubleness by which I can stand as remote from myself as from another.

However intense my experience, I am conscious of the presence and criticism of a part of me, which . . . is not part of me, but spectator, sharing no experience, but taking note of it. . . ." This double vision is not uncommon among American writers—F. Scott Fitzgerald for one was frequently eloquent about his. But Thoreau and Mailer, unlike Fitzgerald, share the ability to close the interval between participant and reporter, until, in their best moments, in their best prose, the two roles seem one.

Mention of Fitzgerald admits again that Mailer is shirt-tail kin to many writers, and therefore justly resents being confused with any of them. With equal justice, it must be said that the major force of his prose, particularly of his nonfiction prose, isn't really new; it was felt first and strongly in Thoreau. Thoreau's lines continue to be read because they can still awaken perceptions, moments, that seem at once alert, sensuous, and principled. Mailer is now widely read for the same good and bad topical reasons. He merits comparison with Thoreau because his recent work also performs successfully the mission of the rooster. It is true that Mailer can awaken us from slumbers unknown to Thoreau, the lassitudes and confusions created by what he has helped sort out as totalitarian glut. But then he has help unknown to Thoreau—the experience of war, Hip, Lawrence, Marx, Freud. What he shares with Thoreau is the ability to write sentences which convey a tonic effect rare in American prose, an effect which Thoreau described fully after hearing a cock crow:

> That sound commonly reminds us that we are growing rusty and antique in our employments and habits of thought. . . . There is something suggested by it that is a newer testament,—the gospel according to this moment. He has not fallen astern; he has got up early and kept up early, and to be where he is is to be in season, in the foremost rank of time. It is an expression of the health and soundness of Nature, a brag for all the world,—healthiness as of a spring burst forth, a new fountain of the Muses, to celebrate this last instant of time.

Moby-Dick As an Education

The increase in the number of interpretations of *Moby-Dick* is by now only a modest index to the layers of pedagogical help which await the reader who first comes to the book. One unfortunate result of this diverting abundance has been to obscure the very level upon which the first reader most directly encounters the novel, its own pedagogic level. I wish to uncover this "little lower layer" in order to argue that a proper appreciation of the novel begins with the unmediated experience of its remarkably intricate play of pedagogy.

Melville began by assuming a reader who, as Ishmael says of himself before he signed on the *Pequod*, "was wholly ignorant of the mysteries of whaling." If the whale itself is to exist for this initiate as something more than its name, information which will dispel "the profound ignorance which, . . . to this present day still reigns in all but some few scientific retreats and whale-ports" must become common property. The first necessity is, then, that the landlubber be made to acquire at least a provisional expertise about matters cetological and the affairs of the nineteenth-century whale fishery. After a certain amount of casual information in the first thirty-one chapters, Ishmael begins the reader's formal instruction with the chapter titled "Cetology" (Ch. 32):

> at the outset it is but well to attend to a matter almost indispensable to a thorough appreciative understanding of the more special leviathanic revelations and allusions of all sorts which are to follow.
>
> It is some systematized exhibition of the whale in his broad genera, that I would now fain put before you. Yet is it no easy task. The classification of the constituents of a chaos, nothing less is here essayed.

These remarks introduce Ishmael's own bibliographic taxonomy of the whale, but the key phrase also describes the method of the reader's most elementary training in the most grandiose terms. It will be nothing less than the classification of the constituents of a chaos, clearly, as Ishmael insists, no easy task; indeed, at bottom, an impossible one. Yet the phrase does indicate both the shape and the magnitude of the undertaking. Melville will create an intelligible world out of the original chaos of an esoteric subject. This world must be literally constituted for our attention, first anatomized by simply naming out its virtually numberless constituents, then fixed and particularized by definition, and then reconstituted by modes of organization which range well beyond conventional taxonomy. Yet even naming the sequence of tasks required points Melville's complaint that the traditional means are cumbersome and mechanical. The chapter titled "Cetology," for instance, is as much about the difficulties and limitations of systematic taxonomy as it is a vivid description of whales, and, as Ishmael carefully explains at the end of it, any such enterprise cannot hope to be complete. What is important for the reader's initial education is that it seem exhaustive—that the reader believe both that all available information has been here assembled for him and that the definitive limits of such information have been brought into view. Melville promotes this belief by frequent reminders of the scope of Ishmael's labors, such reminders credibly supported by the sheer wealth of data, but also slyly raising the bounds of such data by exaggerating the effort to reach them. Consider, for example, the description of the "Extracts" which begin the book as "whatever random allusions to whale he could anyways find in any book whatsoever, sacred or profane" and Ishmael's remarks in the last of the cetological chapters: "Since I have undertaken to manhandle this Leviathan, it behooves me to approve myself omnisciently exhaustive in the enterprise; not overlooking the minutest seminal germs of his blood, and spinning him out to the uttermost coil of his bowels. Having already described him in most of his present habitatory and anatomical peculiarities, it now remains to magnify him in an archaeological, fossiliferous, and antediluvian point of view" (Ch. 104).

But anything like the possibility of a magnified, thorough understanding with which to dispel the "mysteries of whaling" is of course finally collaborative, depending not only on Ishmael's labors in marshalling matters of fact, but on the reader's willingness to be informed, and here the testimony indicates a clear division among readers. Some of the early reviewers, anxious to do their own classification of this strange book, celebrated it as encyclopedic, and they were pleased to respond with their own inventories of what Melville had done for the whale. Here, for example, is the London *Examiner*: "It contains more about the whale, its habits, manners, morals, oil, blubber, feeding, swimming, mode of chasing, capturing, harpooning, cutting up, . . . than we should have supposed possible. . . ." Among comparable modern testimony, none is more amusing than from that band of readers, usually academics, who have extended their enthusiasm for what the book has taught them into an appetite for any additional detail about the whale, spreading their expertise over the pages of the "Melville Society Newsletter," and ornamenting their offices with anatomical models and pictures of whales, sailors' scrimshaw, and even, on occasion, an antique harpoon in the umbrella stand. This eagerness to be instructed in cetological lore is not, however, universal. Somerset Maugham, for instance, produced a version of *Moby-Dick* published in 1949 which simply leaves out the troublesome cetological chapters. To read this version is to be made to feel how essential the missing material is to Melville's original enterprise, for the experience is a peculiarly desiccating one; left with only the scraped backbone, one longs for the rich flesh of the original.

But to speak of *Moby-Dick* as an experience is already to move beyond consideration of the book's instruction in matters of fact. The reader's receptivity to information about whales and whaling is necessary for the novel's purposes, but possession of the facts themselves can yield little more than the genuine, but still minimal satisfactions one might get from reading the forgotten craft manuals of the 1850s—say, for example, Mr. M. Quinly's *Mysteries of Bee-Keeping Explained; Being a Complete Analysis of the Whole Subject* published two years after *Moby-Dick*. The assiduous student could acquire a comparable basic training in whaling from the extant logs of whaling ships, the standard histories on the subject, and the personal narratives of those who have been a whaling—from the same sources in fact that Melville used to supplement his own experience. In commenting on the illustrations in one such source, Captain William Scoresby's *An Account of the Arctic Regions*, a book he had found particularly useful, Melville yet indicates that bare outlines and inventories of fact are, however accurate, too often pedantic, ludicrously random, and finally inert:

> Even Scoresby, ... after giving us a stiff full length of the Greenland whale, and three or four delicate miniatures of narwhales and porpoises, treats us to a series of classical engravings of boat hooks, chopping knives, and grapnels, and with the microscopic diligence of a Leuwenhoek submits to the inspection of a shivering world ninety-six facsimiles of magnified Arctic snow crystals. ... in so important a matter it was certainly an oversight not to have procured for every crystal a sworn affidavit taken before a Greenland Justice of the Peace. (Ch. 56)

Although Ishmael assembles his own data with the occasionally comic diligence of that "mere painstaking burrower and grubworm," the sub-sublibrarian, he avoids the excess he mocks by insistently investing the language of their presentation with the full force of his subjectivity, and thus he animates mere facts, transforming them from discrete items in objective inventory into the play of stimuli within specific human experience. It is Ishmael, rather than Ahab or the Whale, which provides the novel's dynamic principle. *Moby-Dick* is the register of an individual's experience, but again the first reader must pay attention to Ishmael's frequent and wholly pragmatic insistence that experience itself is at once both the most reliable source of knowledge and its most operative form. Captain Peleg understands Ishmael's motives for signing on the *Pequod* as including the intention "to find out by experience what whaling is" (Ch. 16), and thereafter Ishmael often claims the authority derived from his personal experience: "But I have swam through libraries and sailed through oceans; I have had to do with whales with these visible hands" (Ch. 32).

Ishmael's manipulation of his whaling facts is, then, only a preliminary step in conveying what he calls "the real living experience of living men" (Ch. 41). Melville is of course aware that his reader's share in such experience must remain vicarious, at one point reminding us that "the only mode in which you can derive even a tolerable idea of [the whale's] living contour, is by going a whaling yourself" (Ch. 55), but it is significant that he later contradicts this exclusive generalization by offering another such mode, submission to the artist's illusions. He articulates this second mode in pictorial terms. In Chapter 56 Ishmael considers "the less erroneous pictures of whales and the true pictures of whaling scenes," using the opportunity to celebrate the few artists who have gone beyond simple outlines to create full-rigged whaling scenes. They are to be praised "because it is by such pictures only, when at all well done, that you can derive anything like a truthful idea of the living whale as seen by his living hunters." Ishmael is particularly struck by "two large French engravings, well executed, and taken from paintings by one Garneray," and goes on to say: "Who Garneray the painter is, or was, I know not. But my life for it he was either practically conversant with his subject, or else marvellously tutored by some experienced whaleman." This last phrase is of special interest because it accurately describes Ishmael's own relationship with the reader; he is the experienced whaleman who marvellously tutors us not simply in the facts about, but in the experience of whaling and the whale.

But the remarks cited above are misleading if they suggest that the chief and most marvellous method of Ishmael's tutelage is pictorial. While it would be foolish to deny that the texture of impressions from the novel ranges the entire sensuous spectrum, it is also true that the pattern of imagery which most immediately conduces to a strong illusion of personal experience is the kinetic. And it is our kinesthetic response to these complex evocations of movement which makes the novel—to borrow Ishmael's phrase for Starbuck's life—"a telling pantomime of action, and not a tame chapter of sounds" (Ch. 26). One might wish for a rigorous image count or a behaviourist's psychogalvanometer to support this point; if one lacks them, the testimony of sensitive readers will serve as well to report with great clarity the peculiar quality of the experience shaped by *Moby-Dick* and to be shared by those who read it. I wish only to add emphasis for the educative function of these kinetic appeals, the part they play in creating for us the illusion of experiential knowledge.

Such appeals are of course to our sixth sense, our kinesthetic sense, and among the kinds of sensual responses stimulated by language, this is perhaps the least understood. The term itself was coined in 1880 by a German anthropologist in order to distinguish the sensations of movement, effort, or strain that accompany a voluntary motion of the body. Later research has enlarged the understanding of the kinesthetic mechanisms; it has, for example, isolated and named the proprioceptors, the internal receptors for physical stimuli located in the skin, in the muscles, and in the tendons. In combination with organs like the statocyst, the body's contrivance for locating the pull of gravity, these sensors not only help perform such workaday tasks as keeping us upright and allowing our hands to find each other behind our backs, but they are also the agencies by which complex bodily skills are acquired and retained. Like the other senses, they may also be exercised in vicarious experience. The art most dependent upon kinesthetic sensation is the dance. In its most formal manifestations, it is spectacle, and its impact is visual, but even here the effect may excite the spectator's kinesthetic response so that muscles necessarily tense and relax in imitation of the dancer's movements. But if dance is the most kinetic of the arts, language is the most flexible, incorporating most of the sensuous provocations of the others. By its verbs, its rhythms, even by the strain necessary to vocalize an awkward string of consonants, language continuously engages and plays upon our kinesthetic awareness. Students of Melville's style have done much to analyze the practice of his kinetic appeals, but they have also recognized the great difficulties in explaining exactly how they work. But an understanding of the technical means by which Melville works to engage our kinesthetic participation is less important here than a recognition of the crucial function such engagement serves in the reader's education.

The most primitive effect of these appeals is to move the reader's kinesthetic imagination through a complex sequence of physical posturings which replicate the specific experiences of the whaling voyage.

"Though most men have some vague flitting ideas of the general perils of the grand fishery, yet they have nothing like a fixed, vivid conception of those perils, and the frequency with which they recur" (Ch. 45). One extended example of Ishmael's effort to fix such vivid conceptions is contained in the last three paragraphs of Chapter 60. Here Ishmael incites us to discover what it is to be obliged to row strenuously while seated "amid the hempen intricacies" of the line which folds the whaleboat "in its complicated coils, twisting and writing around it in almost every direction." By the equally intricate maneuvers of his imagery, Ishmael induces a very particular muscular sense of the utmost physical exertion conducted within a cramped and constantly changing margin of safety, that margin exactly, if unpredictably measured by the whizzings of the line. And in the degree to which we can feel this, we also learn to appreciate the skills required to survive for "only by a certain self-adjusting buoyancy and simultaneousness of volition and action, can you escape being made a Mazeppa of, and run away with where the all-seeing sun himself could never pierce you out" (Ch. 60). Out of context the phrase might strike one as vague or excessive, but conditioned by the tightly meshed dynamics of the entire passage, it seems perfectly apt. And this practice of grounding experience in kinesthetic sensations of the vectors, momentums, and stresses of movement is everywhere present in *Moby-Dick*. It is most often felt as dexterity under pressure, a precarious poise or balance in the act of being challenged or threatened. We learn to mistrust the dreamy elevation of standing the masthead by the sudden vertigo of "Descartian vortices." We measure the joyful transports of squeezing sperm by the undeniably strange but liberating sensation in fingers which begin "to serpentine and spiralize." We enact the ties of comradeship by gingerly hefting Queequeg as he works at the end of the monkey-rope, and we are moved to Ishmael's doubt of Ahab's quest by sharing the disorientation of reversing a proper stance at the helm. By a thousand such empathic exercises, the whaling facts which have been borne upon us are gathered into what can only be called a growing sense of competence so that, in recounting the final scenes, Ishmael need only allude to "that wild simultaneousness of a thousand concreted perils" (Ch. 134) to prompt our recall of intimate acquaintance with the specific dangers he has, as we now have, in mind. To be sure, this competence is appreciative rather than active, the skill of the *aficionado* rather than of the *torero*, but it is nonetheless true that when Ishmael explicitly names the whaleman's "wondrous habitude of unconscious skill" (Ch. 48), he is also adumbrating something very like the awareness his efforts should have tutored in the reader. It is important to note further that this awareness conditions, directs, even dictates certain functional attitudes within the reader. It stimulates, for example, a familiar respect for the crew of the *Pequod* which genuinely vindicates and elevates them—a respect which the elaborate, but facetious arguments of the chapter called "The Advocate" (Ch. 24) can only halfheartedly demand. In the opening passage of the chapter titled "Cetology" (Ch. 32), Ishmael had hoped for an understanding from the reader qualified as both thorough and appreciative; it is the peculiarly sensuous, specifically kinesthetic dimension of his thoroughness which does most to inculcate the appropriate quality of appreciation. When Ishmael names one component of that appreciation as "the peculiar congenialities arising from a common pursuit and mutually shared privations and perils" (Ch. 53), he has already made us feel it.

At the centre of this increasing illusion of experiential knowledge is a sensuous apprehension of the great whale, and its major aim is an acute perception of the whale's enormous power. "I would have you investigate it now with the sole view of forming to yourself some unexaggerated, intelligent estimate of whatever battering-ram power may be lodged there" (Ch. 76). Again, the preliminary steps toward such an estimate require the painstaking accumulation of detail about size, appearance, and structure. Ishmael takes us on a guided tour of the whale; it is almost literally that—asking us to measure mass by pacing around and over it, inviting us to finger textures, and urging us to descend into and move about in interior spaces. But at most this physiologist's and anatomist's training can disclose only the capacities for power, only energy latent or potential. It is again by subtly engaging our kinesthetic responses that Ishmael attempts to make us register the measure of that power frighteningly, yet magnificently active. It is Ishmael's own impulse to strike for the essence which prompts him to end the chapter with a confession: "The more I consider this mighty tail, the more do I deplore my inability to express it. At times there are gestures in it, which, though they would well grace the hand of a man, remain wholly inexplicable." Ishmael's characteristic insistence on human inability to decipher nature's essential meanings further prompts him to call the power concentrated in the tail "measureless," yet this grand superlative is finally misleading; the tail's power *is* measured for the reader, not on the meters of physics or in its absolute form, but by its fine contour of seismic shocks on the sensibility. Consider, for example, this phrase dropped casually into another scene of the chase: "the strength of a thousand thighs in his tail" (Ch. 81). The image is oddly, potently sexual and its peculiar ergs of psychic energy contribute to the reader's achievement of the erotic experiential knowledge which is not debased by labeling it as carnal. Melville moves us from documentation through acts in an approach to essence. The novel's instruction begins by an accumulation of available empirical evidence which then guides and informs the reader's participation in action perceived and felt as dynamic, interacting exertions of force. It is, however, in their approach to essence that these specifically pedagogical strategies shade into the questionably rhetorical.

It is a curious fact about the novel that while Ishmael expends every effort to initiate us into his whaling world, the intended result is clearly not the security of certain knowledge. Ishmael would transform us from initiates originally and "wholly ignorant of the mysteries of whaling" into adepts who are now wholly cognizant of those mysteries, chiefly the mysteries of the great whale. The curious potential in the phrase "the mysteries of whaling" is borne out by Ishmael's method, for, while working to strengthen our sense of vicarious competence, he takes every opportunity to increase our insecurity by mystifying us. In short he both clarifies and obscures his subject. The narrative procedures required by each remain strikingly opposed.

If the book's instruction is designed largely to specify, its mystification reverses this aim, being intended to despecify, to gesture toward that which cannot or will not be particularized. Instruction demands elaborate exposition; by contrast mystification depends largely upon the power of certain words and phrases to unfix and dissipate concrete impressions—to position or distance that which is to elude our understanding, the nameless, measureless, ungraspable, boundless, unfathomable, illimitable, resistless. Such adjectives function as spatial or physical superlatives which magnify their subjects by the curious process of denying the possibility of any kinesthetic response from the reader. Thus they broach that which is beyond experiential or rational knowledge in a way perhaps best expressed in the famous phrase from the chapter titled "The Lee Shore": "in landlessness alone resides the highest truth, shoreless, indefinite as God . . ." (Ch. 23). These terms hint at the outer limits of the chaos which Ishmael otherwise seeks to constitute, classify, and delimit; they hint by positing the presence of superior knowledge beyond the reach of that common understanding which may be achieved through education. But they can only hint. One further clue to this tactic and its own limits is another frequent choice, the word "portentous," used first, for example, in Chapter 1 as Ishmael explains his motives for going to sea: "Chief among these motives was the overwhelming idea of the great whale himself. Such a portentous and mysterious monster roused all my curiosity." And the word is used again twice to describe the mysterious mass at the centre of the picture in the Spouter Inn, a picture "that fairly froze you to it, till you involuntarily took an oath with yourself to find out what that marvelous painting meant" (Ch. 3). "Portentous" accurately describes the specific nature of the lure felt by Ishmael and intended to enlist a comparable suspense and curiosity from the reader. The word's root denotes the physical action of stretching forth, and the meaning has enlarged to suggest a stretching forward in time and imagination under the stimulus of a foreboding expectation. The whale is thus early established as a portent, a sign of that which has yet to be understood and thus, in effect, a promise of something yet to be revealed.

It is, however, a promise that is not, and cannot be kept. As the voyage of the *Pequod* proves, to become an adept of the mysteries of whaling is only to discern yet deeper mysteries of the whale; if this is to be so, the portentous qualities of the whale must be sustained and increased, not fulfilled. And it is here, I think, that Ishmael's education of our understanding gives way to his techniques for mystifying it, for making it insecure and uneasily aware of its many limitations. "Truly speaking," said Emerson in the Divinity School "Address" of the effort to convey genuine truth to another, "it is not instruction, but provocation." And while one might agree that such provocation is necessary to enhance the reader's willingness to trust intuitions more than tuition, there is yet something suspicious in the provocative high rhetoric of the measureless, unfathomable, and resistless. One should remember Ahab's mystifying performances on the stage of the quarterdeck, half satanic magician and half P. T. Barnum, as he exploits the superstitious ignorance of his crew, and one can hear an unpleasant petulance in Ishmael's occasional denigration of his pedagogical tasks: "yet Ahab's larger, darker, deeper part remains unhinged. But vain to popularize profundities, and all truth is profound" (Ch. 42). This rhetoric of mystification is more than occasionally wearing, provoking not intuitions of meaning beyond the reach of understanding, but the distaste which Ishmael himself feels for Elijah's "ambiguous, half-hinting, half-revealing, shrouded sort of talk" (Ch. 19). Mysteries so insistently, yet so vaguely invoked thereby run the risk of meriting another of Ishmael's judgments of Elijah: "a humbug, trying to be a bugbear," and the Gothic theatricality of the devices for invoking them are as likely to call up skepticism as they are credence—skepticism of the kind that moved Melville to write to Hawthorne: "we incline to think that the Problem of the Universe is like the Freemason's mighty secret, so terrible to all children. It turns out, at last, to consist in a triangle, a mallet, and an apron,—nothing more!" Finally, then, it must be said that the methods of mystification, depending as they do largely on high rhetoric, contribute to the reader's education by causing a vague, but persistent ringing in the ears, perhaps alerting us to the inferential source of sound, but only by noise which obscures and removes it from us.

But fortunately Melville has means for directing the reader's appreciation of any significance to be derived from whaling experience that are more convincing and reliable than mystification. One can grasp this by considering Ishmael's statement that "only in the heart of quickest perils; only when within the eddyings of his angry flukes; only on the profound unbounded sea, can the fully invested whale be truly and livingly found out" (Ch. 103). The third phrase here too quickly generalizes toward the nether limits of that immediate investment of experiential knowledge promised by the first two. Although, as I have conceded, the reader's attention for profundities lurking in such investiture is kept nervously alert by such reminders and their accompanying surmises, speculations, and inferences, it is the firm illusion of experiential knowledge itself which transforms general attention into specific and functional attitudes. As Ishmael says in the chapter titled "Moby Dick," "even stripped of these supernatural surmisings, there was enough in the earthy make and incontestable character of the monster to strike the imagination with unwonted power" (Ch. 41). I have tried to demonstrate how Ishmael's instruction in whaling lore and his vigorous manipulation of our kinesthetic responses conspire to create a growing sense of competence, of performed bodily skills felt and rather precisely measured against the specific perils of the chase and the powers of the whale. It is by the agency of this competence that we learn most thoroughly the whale's "earthy make" and feel its "incontestable character" with a firmness of grasp that gives this last adjective its force. I have further argued that this competence dictates certain appreciative attitudes in the reader. If, for example, we learn respect for the crew of the *Pequod* because of perils vicariously shared and adroitly survived, we also learn awe of the whale because we have thus been schooled in the full measures of his power. And Melville is clearly convinced that his reader's capacity for the awesome needs training. Not only has man "lost that sense of the full awfulness of the sea which aboriginally belongs to it" (Ch. 58), but "so ignorant are most landsmen of some of the plainest and more palpable wonders of the world, that without some hints touching the plain facts, historical and otherwise, of the fishery, they might scout at Moby Dick as a monstrous fable, or still worse and more detestable, a hideous and intolerable allegory" (Ch. 45). My argument has been intended in part to rescue the considerable literal force of this last passage from the emphasis on its possible ironies which it has frequently received. By not taking his reader's sense of the awesome for granted, Melville binds himself to educe the wonderful from the sensuously palpable; this is of course the very reverse of that easier route by which the merely palpable is lent significance by association with the resonant abstractions which generate traditional allegory.

Just as the mastery of a subject through more conventional courses of education may be said to culminate in the assumption of appropriate attitudes by the student, so the controlled education offered by *Moby-Dick* is virtually completed when the reader is led toward a genuine experience of awe in the imaged presence of the whale. Yet to recognize that Ishmael is training us toward this complex reaction is also to concede that the novel may make it easier to experience than to define. Conventional definitions of the term as denoting an uncertain mixture of fear, wonder, and reverence increase the problem, yet one way through is to understand the capacity for awe as the end of the novel's instruction in a double sense, at once both its aim and its limit. Ishmael insists early in the novel that "ignorance is the parent of fear" (Ch. 3); the knowledge he works to impart is, by extension, the parent of awe. If ignorant fear, like modern anxiety, has no real focus and therefore no discernible bounds, the feeling it names is correspondingly diffuse and vague. By contrast, awe is inspired and pointed by an object the knowledge of which is disconcerting because that knowledge so clearly contains and is confined by its own limits. We can be told that the whale is terrible and magnificent, but we learn to feel terror and respect for the whale as a locus of powerful curbs successfully resisting human efforts to master it. We can be told that the whale is wonderful, but we apprehend its wonders by the sustained illusion of performing to the fine tolerances of what is possible "in the heart of quickest perils, in the eddyings of his angry flukes." We can be assured by Ishmael that the sight of the whale's brow inspires the same reverence we may be accustomed to give to deity, but we experience it in dread as featureless, inscrutable, impenetrable, as "the dead blind wall butts all inquiring heads at last" (Ch. 125).

But finally the problem of defining awe touches the very heart of *Moby-Dick* because the central question raised in the novel—and left for us to answer—is precisely how that definition should be made. What the novel's dramatic spectacle, as distinct from its pedagogical program, invites us to do is observe and make judgments about the several forms which this emotion takes in other men who have confronted the whale. And it is just this invitation for which Ishmael's patient tutoring has prepared us. In the degree to which we have genuinely experienced the whale as awe-inspiring, our empathic yet critical concern with the various ways in which this common root emotion flowers—or is blighted—in the novel's characters is both compelled and informed. So engaged, we are moved to compare and evaluate these differences in such a way that we find ourselves, I believe, considering the question of just which manifestation of awe toward the whale constitutes right worship. In Chapter 10, Ishmael raises the question and answers it from the easy security of his newly found comradeship with the pagan Queequeg: "But what is worship?—to do the will of God—*that* is worship. And what is the will of God?—to do to my fellow man what I would have my fellow man to do to me—*that* is the will of God." But the force of this answer, so reminiscent of Benjamin Franklin's enlightened confidence, dissipates as it becomes only one in the dramatic series of alternate answers embodied in the actions, attitudes, and speech of the other characters—a series ranging from Father Mapple's orthodoxy to Ishmael's own speculations on the whiteness of the whale, "a colorless, all color of atheism from which we shrink" (Ch. 42), from Flask's inability to feel awe "so utterly lost was he to all sense of reverence for the many marvels of their majestic bulk and mystic ways" (Ch. 26), to Ahab's terrible prayer in the chapter called "The Candles": "I now know thee, thou clear spirit, and I now know that thy right worship is defiance" (Ch. 119). To understand and rightly assess this range of feeling is the challenge of the novel, a challenge which puts it squarely within the American nineteenth-century debate about the organizing modes of religious feeling which began with the Transcendental reaction to Unitarianism and may be said to conclude with William James's *The Varieties of Religious Experience* (1901–1902). It is beyond the purpose of this essay to enter such debate; strictly speaking, it is a debate invited by rather than conducted within *Moby-Dick*—an issue dramatized rather than decided by Melville.

Much that is valuable in the commentary on the book seeks to engage the reader on just this issue—as does, to cite only one example, Marius Bewley's fine chapter on Melville in *The Eccentric Design*. My point is that, before we can find such debate compelling, meaningful, or even very interesting, we must be prepared by something other than the convictions we might originally bring to the book—my argument has been that we are so prepared by the novel's deliberate program of education, an education which frames the question of right worship and makes it not only credible, but vital for us," so that when I shall hereafter detail to you all the specialities and concentrations of potency everywhere lurking in this expansive monster; when I shall show you some of his more inconsiderable braining feats; I trust you will have renounced all ignorant incredulity. . . . For unless you own the whale, you are but a provincial and sentimentalist in Truth" (Ch. 76). The pun is apt; we must own the whale by being educated to possess him in particular degree and limit before we can either acknowledge him or assess the forms in which he is acknowledged by others.

Walt Whitman and the Limits of Embarrassment

If American authors compose a family, then Walt Whitman is its belching, unbuttoned uncle, for the simple truth is that almost all his readers have found both his prose and his poetry embarrassing. Randall Jarrell has submitted the appropriate epitaph; it is to read: "WALT WHITMAN: HE HAD HIS NERVE." And the evidence is enormous that generations have shared this sentiment. The first edition of *Leaves of Grass* was immediately greeted by the scandalized outcries of the establishment. The Boston *Intelligencer* cried: "Bombast, egotism, vulgarity, and nonsense!" The *Christian Examiner* cried: "Impious libidinousness" and "Ithyphallic audacity!" and Wendell Phillips observed dryly: "Here seem to be all sorts of leaves except fig leaves." Yet despite these provocative advertisements, the first edition did badly at the bookstores. To help sales, Whitman wrote for the press at least three anonymous, and very favourable reviews. In one such review, he virtually predicts what has been the response to his work from the beginning. "Very devilish to some, and very divine to some, will appear the poet of these new poems, the *Leaves of Grass*; an attempt, as they are, of a naïve, masculine, affectionate, contemplative, sensual, imperious person, to cast into literature not only his own grit and arrogance, but his own flesh and form, undraped, regardless of models, regardless of modesty or law...."

Most critics since have sweated over deciding whether the undraped Whitman is devil or divine. Most have evaded the problem by declaring him an uncertain mixture of both. John Jay Chapman, after calling him "the mare's nest of 'American Literature,'" concludes that in his poems "the elemental parts of a man's mind and the fragments of imperfect education may be seen merging together, floating and sinking in a sea of insensate egotism and rhapsody, repellent, divine, disgusting, extraordinary." Swinburne found Whitman "a writer of something occasionally like English, and a man of something occasionally like genius." Gerard Manley Hopkins once said: "I always knew in my heart Walt Whitman's mind to be more like my own than any other man's living. As he is a very great scoundrel this is not a very pleasant confession."

The record of this awkward attempt to do justice to Whitman by embracing his extremes could be continued indefinitely. Indeed the mission of modern criticism for Whitman has been likened to a continuous tightrope act—an agonized effort to rescue him from parody on the one hand and from idolatry on the other. Perhaps the only way to test this peculiar challenge of his poetry is to chart the bumps raised on one's sensibility by a speaker who describes himself as "hankering, gross, mystical, nude"; who discovers "no sweeter fat than sticks to my own bones," who announces that he is "delicate around the bowels," and that "the scent of these armpits aroma finer than prayer." Even the most emancipated sophistication cannot completely dampen the shock of a voice which insists, after these confessions, that "I dote on myself, there is that lot of me and all so luscious."

The primitive power of such lines is generated because they affront so directly folkways even stronger now than in 1855. They assault the conventional barriers against immodesty, brag, personal conceit, and the thousand forms of self-advertisement. Homer's heroes, and their romantic descendants, might loudly vaunt their prowess; our modern heroes, to please us, must toe-scrape. The impact of Whitman's affront to these conventions is not lessened by our awareness that it is calculated and deliberate. In "Song of Myself," he announces that:

I know perfectly well my own egotism,
Know my omnivorous lines and must not write any less,
And would fetch you whoever you are flush with myself.

Not words of routine this song of mine,
But abruptly to question, to leap beyond yet nearer bring.

"Embarrassment" may be defined, I think, as the reaction to an assault on any familiar and expected convention; our awareness that the convention is threatened prompts those physiological ties by which our uneasiness at such a threat is partially released. Whitman deliberately provokes this reaction and he does so under license of his exalted notions about the function of the poet. Most of these notions he derived from Emerson, who had attempted to dignify the office by restoring to the poet his lost roles as bard, prophet, and seer. For both Emerson and Whitman, the poet was a liberating god, and it is to fill this high office that Whitman undertakes to free his readers from restrictive social conventions—in this case the restraints of modesty and self-effacement. "I chant the chant of dilation and pride,/We have had ducking and deprecating about enough."

Whitman's self-imposed prophetic mission was designed to ensure the success of the American experiment. For him, the basic requirement for a successful democracy was suitable personnel—the creation of what he called more than once "fine and healthy persons." To create such persons, he would inspire complete self-confidence. "I will effuse egotism and show it underlying all, and I will be the bard of personality." But the method of this bardic effusion is very much akin to electrical shock therapy. By exposing in extravagant terms his self-love, he hoped to force the reader—through the mechanisms of embarrassed shame—beyond his own meeching inhibitions.

Actually Whitman's method is very little different from that adopted by Thoreau in *Walden*, published the year before the first edition of *Leaves of Grass*. In the book's epigraph, Thoreau had boldly announced: "I do not propose to write an ode to dejection, but to brag as lustily as chanticleer in the morning, standing on his roost, if only to wake my neighbors up." And Thoreau explained the reason for the method he shared with Whitman much more succinctly than the poet ever did. "If I seem to boast more than is becoming, my excuse is that I brag for humanity rather than myself." So Whitman. In celebrating himself, he hopes to persuade others to celebrate, instead of to deprecate self. Critics who castigate Whitman's brag by quoting the first line of "Song of Myself"—"I celebrate myself, and sing myself"—often distort his intention by failing to quote the next two lines—"And what I assume you shall assume,/For every atom belonging to me as good belongs to you." What Whitman was trying to accomplish with his embarrassing exhibition of self is perhaps best summed up in these lines from "Song of Myself":

You there, impotent, loose in the knees,
Open your scarf'd chops till I blow grit within you,
Spread your palms and lift the flaps of your pockets,
I am not to be denied, I compel, I have stores plenty and to spare.
And anything I have I bestow.

It must be said, I think, that Whitman's defiant assault on the usual conventions which shape sensibility sometimes succeeds. Sustained immersion in his immodesty can release us and give us the joy, as Chapman puts it, "of being disreputable and unashamed." His immodesty, once this mood has captured the reader, can be magnificent.

I find I incorporate gneiss, coal, long-threaded moss, fruits, grains, esculent roots,
And am stucco'd with quadrupeds and birds all over.

Quite simply, it takes guts to utter lines like these, but once uttered, they offer a peculiar elation.

But what is most interesting about Whitman's eagerness to blow grit into his reader—to therapeutically inspire him with self-respect—is that it forced him to probe the very limits of embarrassment. One of the most touching aspects of *Leaves of Grass* is the spectacle of Whitman straining to break through cold print and somehow overwhelm the reader with his own hard-breathing, direct embrace. "From throat and tongue—(My life's hot pulsing blood,/The personal urge and form for me—not merely paper, automatic type and ink,)." Such impulses occasionally result in his impatience with the limits imposed by the written, or even the spoken word. In "A Song of the Rolling Earth," he writes:

I swear I begin to see little or nothing in audible words,
. . .
I swear I see what is better than to tell the best,
It is always to leave the best untold.

When I undertake to tell the best I find I cannot,
My tongue is ineffectual on its pivots,
My breath will not be obedient to its organs,
I become a dumb man.

Given such distrust of words, Whitman seems occasionally to feel that the very lines and images through which he so defiantly displays himself might also serve to mask or hide him from the reader. He expressed such a doubt most directly in the poem called "As I Ebb'd with the Ocean of Life":

O baffled, balk'd, bent to the very earth,
Oppress'd with myself that I have dared to open my mouth,
Aware now that amid all the blab whose echoes recoil upon me, I
    have not once had the least idea who or what I am,
But that before all my arrogant poems the real Me stands yet
    untouch'd, untold, altogether unreach'd,
Withdrawn far, mocking me with mock-congratulatory signs and
    bows,
With peals of distant ironical laughter at every word I have writ-
    ten.

But these explicit doubts are rare. Usually Whitman overcomes them by simply ignoring the fact that he communicates with his reader only through words and the printed pages. In the poem which terminated

Leaves of Grass proper, titled "So Long," he makes a final effort to imaginatively leap the gap which separates him from his reader:

> My songs cease, I abandon them,
> From behind the screen where I hid I advance personally solely to you.
>
> Camerado, this is no book,
> Who touches this touches a man,
> (Is it night? are we here together alone?)
> It is I you hold and who holds you,
> I spring from the pages into your arms—decease calls me forth.
>
> . . .
> Remember my words, I may again return,
> I love you, I depart from materials,
> I am as one disembodied, triumphant, dead.

It must be seen that Whitman's poetry of egotism has a very primitive, thoroughly intimate power to embarrass us. He deliberately invites responses which, as conditioned social beings, we might prefer to withhold. And in so doing Whitman seems to me to be playing a dangerous poetic game. It's quite true that the shock of such lavish immodesty might, and occasionally does disarm us and make possible a new taste of the joys of self. But the mechanisms of embarrassment work not only to raise the barriers preventing such joys, they also serve to protect the self. The mechanisms of embarrassment, once stimulated, might well have an effect opposite to the one intended by the poet. Alarmed by the intimacy of Whitman's efforts to blow grit into us, to clasp us in his direct embrace, we might react by reaffirming the sense of privacy which he would brush aside. Instead of being inspired to return his eagerly offered embrace, we might be moved to resent it, saying in effect—"You, whoever *you* are, keep your hands and your ego to yourself."

But the problem of assessing Whitman's self-advertisement is easy compared with that of properly judging his celebrations of sexual love. Most modern readers think themselves emancipated from the polite restrictions which hedged sex as a topic for our grandfathers. And it's probably true that we are more permissive even than the few English readers who surprised a reviewer by buying copies of *Leaves of Grass* in an age and country where "piano-legs wear frilled trousers, where slices are cut from turkeys' bosoms, and where the male of the gallinaceous tribe is called a rooster." In this modern mood of large tolerance, we are apt to hail Whitman as a pioneer, liberating American poetry from the stuffy remains of Puritanism and courageously experimenting with erotic imagery.

> I believe in you my soul, the other I am must not abase itself to you,
> And you must not be abased to the other.
> . . .
> I mind how once we lay such a transparent summer morning,
> How you settled your head athwart my hips and gently turn'd over upon me.
> And parted the shirt from my bosom-bone, and plunged your tongue to my bare-stript heart,
> And reach'd till you felt my beard, and reach'd till you held my feet.

There is nothing in this easy eroticism that should embarrass us, especially when we recognize that the imagery of erotic play is here used in part to dramatize a harmonious relationship between the speaker's body and his soul. Whitman's occasional use of erotic imagery throughout *Leaves of Grass* is in fact one source of its great vitality, as Whitman himself obliquely noted when he wrote: "To the lack of an avowed, empowered, unabashed development of sex, . . . and to the fact of speakers and writers fraudulently assuming as always dead what everyone knows to be always alive, is attributable to the remarkable nonpersonality and indistinctness of modern production in books." Aside from its incredible syntax, not only is such a statement *not* embarrassing today, it isn't even very interesting.

But it is one thing to approve of Whitman's incidental eroticism and another to actually read or hear his overt celebrations of procreative love. Such celebrations form the second major section of *Leaves of Grass*, and are collectively titled "Children of Adam." This section was first included in the third edition in 1860 and is meant to chant what Whitman calls "Amativeness," a term derived from phrenology meaning the sexual union of man and woman.

> From my own voice resonant, singing the phallus,
> Singing the song of procreation,
> Singing the need of superb children and therein superb grown people,

Singing the muscular urge and the blending,
Singing the bedfellow's song, . . .

Whitman's resonance creates "the Body Electric": "This is the female form,/A divine nimbus exhales from it from head to foot,/It attracts with fierce undeniable attraction"; and again: "This is the nucleus—after the child is born of woman, man is born of woman,/This is the bath of birth, this the merge of small and large, and the outlet again."

Such poetry, let me assure you, is a burden to read aloud—a burden not because the subject matter should be excluded from polite company, but rather because Whitman's treatment of sex has transformed it into something peculiarly embarrassing. It's clear that Whitman was not content to treat physical love simply and directly. In "Song of Myself," he had announced that his purpose was to give voice to what had erroneously been considered obscene:

Through me forbidden voices,
Voices of sexes and lusts, voices veil'd and I remove the veil,
Voices indecent by me clarified and transfigur'd.

Had he simply removed the veil and clarified his subject, he might have written some genuine love poetry. Instead, driven by his impulse to correct social error, he sought to transfigure sex, but in the process, he makes even the simplest gesture of love into something monstrous and grotesque. The body correlative, the body electric, the divine nimbus, the bath of birth constitute a flourish of tubas. Our response to such poetry can only be the embarrassed awe felt by Melville's Ishmael as he views the young Leviathans' amours in the Malaysian deeps.

Perhaps the most cruel and yet the most apt judgment of Whitman's love poetry was made by D. H. Lawrence in his *Studies in Classic American Literature.* There Lawrence likens the voice "that aches with amorous love" to a locomotive under forty million foot-pounds of steam pressure. Lawrence is, of course, right about Whitman; his love poetry is superhuman and mechanical. And the reason is simply that, for Whitman, heterosexual love is a plank in his poetic platform for democracy rather than a closely observed or deeply felt human concern. In "Children of Adam," sex becomes a force, like that of electricity or waterpower, because it is productive—because it creates an abundance of healthy citizens for the utopian democracy of which he had made himself the prophet. To find these chants of sex erotic is as absurd as being aroused by a hydroelectric installation. Henry Adams, himself interested in the relationship between the Virgin and the dynamo, found Whitman unique, the only American artist "who had ever insisted on the power of sex, as every classic had always done." Adams meant this as a compliment, but in fact he exposes the weakness in Whitman's love poetry. Whitman "transfigures" sexual love into a force that can only be registered on the meters and gauges of physics—not on the more sensitive instruments of genuine human feeling. The result is poetry that should and does embarrass us, *not* because it unveils sex, but rather because it changes the mysteries of sexual love into a public utility, detached, disembodied, and contrary to Whitman's intentions, dehumanized.

In his treatment of both self-love and reproductive sex, Whitman deliberately transgressed the conventional limits of embarrassment. He was convinced that traditional taboos inhibited a healthy respect for self and for sex. To remove these inhibitions, he provokes our embarrassment in the hope of exorcizing it. But in his urgency and in his eagerness, he has adopted strategies which can only erect for us uneasy barriers a bit further beyond the conventional ones. The final embarrassment present in Whitman's poetry is not, however, one which it provokes in the reader. It is one which the poet discovers within himself, and, curiously, this discovery made him a better poet.

The most difficult poems in *Leaves of Grass* to properly assess are those in the section titled "Calamus." So difficult are they that most critics have simply passed over them. "Calamus" is the third major section and was first included in the 1860 edition as the companion for "Children of Adam." As the Children of Adam poems celebrate "Amativeness," so the Calamus poems celebrate "Adhesiveness," the phrenological term for love between comrades, between man and man. Within the scheme of Whitman's prophetic mission, the Calamus section had a definite programmatic function. Here Whitman addresses himself to the problem which has constantly plagued theorists of democracy—the problem of reconciling individual freedom with social order. His solution calls for the cultivation of the respect, love, and sympathy which one man can feel for another. This adhesiveness—this shared comradeship—is to be the social cement which binds free individuals together into an orderly and harmonious group. The theoretical basis for this section is best expressed in "For You O Democracy":

Come, I will make the continent indissoluble,
I will make the most splendid race the sun ever shone upon,
I will make divine magnetic lands,
With the love of comrades,
With the life-long love of comrades.

But this bravado, so consistent with the celebratory tone of the first two sections of the book, is not characteristic of the "Calamus" section as a whole. And the reason is that this time Whitman could not shoulder aside embarrassment—could not so confidently violate a taboo which he feels as strongly as his readers. The poems in "Calamus" actually reveal that Whitman was as Victorian as any man in his reluctance to explore the implications of male comradeship in print. Compare, for example, these lines from "Calamus" with the passage above:

> In paths untrodden,
> In the growth by margins of pond-waters,
> Escaped from the life that exhibits itself,
> From all the standards hitherto publish'd, from the pleasures, profits, conformities,
> Which too long I was offering to feed my soul,
> Clear to me now standards not yet publish'd, clear to me that my soul,
> That the soul of the man I speak for rejoices in comrades,
> Here by myself away from the clank of the world,
> Tallying and talk'd to here by tongues aromatic,
> No longer abash'd, (for in this secluded spot I can respond as I would not dare elsewhere,)
> Strong upon me the life that does not exhibit itself, yet contains all the rest,
> Resolv'd to sing no songs to-day but those of manly attachment.

The self-declamatory confidence of "Song of Myself" is gone; the speaker here is timid, hesitant as he picks his way along paths untrodden. So treacherous is the subject he explores that Whitman must abandon the reckless invitations he had scattered elsewhere in *Leaves of Grass*:

> Whoever you are holding me now in hand,
> Without one thing all will be useless,
> I give you fair warning before you attempt me further,
> I am not what you supposed, but far different.
> . . .
> The way is suspicious, the result uncertain, perhaps destructive.

The warning of this last line is an honest one. Unlike the poems of ecstatic celebration in the earlier sections, the Calamus poems are permeated with melancholy. Responding to the leaves of the Calamus plant, associated in folklore with the phallus, Whitman writes:

> Yet you are beautiful to me you faint tinged roots, you make me think of death
> Death is beautiful from you, (what indeed is finally beautiful except death and love?)
> O I think it is not for life I am chanting here my chant of lovers, I think it must be for death,
> For how calm, how solemn it grows to ascend to the atmosphere of lovers.

Why, given Whitman's poetic program, does he associate the symbol of male love with death? If the love between man and woman celebrated in "Children of Adam" is to be valued because it is fertile, reproductive, life-giving, then the love of comrades, which does not produce offspring, is by contrast sterile, barren, and death-dealing. These and similar imaginative implications of Whitman's concern for comradeship in fact threaten the whole prophetic mission which he had earlier embraced. If the poet is to be the liberating god, the health-bringer, he cannot give way to self-doubts about his own liberation, his own health. As Whitman himself phrased it in one of his own reviews of the book: "If health were not his distinguishing attribute, this poet would be the very harlot of persons." There is some evidence that the combination of Whitman's fascination with and yet embarrassment about the subject of comradeship convinced him that he might better abandon his self-imposed poetic mission completely. In the 1860 Calamus section, he included an untitled poem removed from all later editions:

> And then, to enclose all, it came to me to strike up the songs of the New World—And then I believed my life must be spent in singing;
> But now take notice, land of the prairies, land of the south savannas, Ohio's land,
> Take notice, you Kanuck woods—and you Lake Huron—and all that with you roll toward Niagara—and you Niagara also,
> And you, California mountains—That you each and all find some body else to be your singer of sings,
> For I can be your singer of songs no longer—One who loves me is jealous of me, and withdraws me from all but love,
> With the rest I dispense—I sever from what I thought would suffice me, for it does not—it is now empty and tasteless to me.

Whitman did not, of course, abandon his poetic enterprise; instead, he made poetry out of his temptation to do so.

The Calamus poems have been called the only genuine love poetry in *Leaves of Grass*. I can't agree, largely because I find better love poetry in "Song of Myself." If Whitman loved anything, he loved himself. But I also believe that the Calamus poems are among the best contained in *Leaves of Grass*. And my reason is that instead of demanding our embarrassment, they solicit our sympathy. These poems display a personality in credible and dramatic conflict with itself, eager to express, yet reluctant to explore its own depths.

> Here the frailest leaves of me and yet my strongest lasting,
> Here I shade and hide my thoughts, I myself do not expose them,
> And yet they expose me more than all my other poems.

The Calamus poems do expose something important about Whitman as a poet. Elsewhere he flourishes embarrassment as a flaming sword in his prophetic cause. Here, he is himself the victim of that sword, and it is only here that he can make genuinely moving poetry from the limits of human embarrassment.

Bill Gorton, the Preacher in
The Sun Also Rises

When *The Sun Also Rises* was published in 1926, many critics found it a thoroughly immoral book. *Now* everyone agrees that it is a very moral book indeed. There is, however, little agreement about the proper definition of its morality. Hemingway's policy of deliberate understatement is usually taken to mean that any identification of the moral system which informs the action must be painstakingly supplied by inference and abstraction from that action. Some critics have searched out the book's "moral centre," most often appointing a character or characters to embody the standards by which behaviour is to be assessed. Others have erected the book's rituals—social, sporting, or religious—into moral measures. And others have concentrated on deciding whether such implicit standards should be classed as counsels of despair or as saving affirmations, particularly as they are ranked against more traditional moral systems. The result of this enterprise is a bewildering variety of generalizations from the critics, most offering to state what the book allegedly does not. The truth is that while the novel does understate most of the impressions it conveys, it is full to overflowing with deliberate, explicit injunctions as to how one ought to behave. The problem, then, in defining the book's morality is not to supply what is only implied, but rather to sort out what is so explicitly and abundantly present.

No one has yet noted that perhaps the most characteristic utterance of the characters in this novel takes the imperative form. The members of the expatriate community command each other to behave in a certain way with almost the same frequency with which they invite each other—again in the form of commands—to have a drink. Consider, for example, the first occasions Brett and Jake find to speak to each other privately, detailed in the last part of Chapter Three and in Chapter Four: three brief exchanges, the first while they are dancing, the second in a taxi, and the third later that evening in Jake's apartment. In the sparse dialogue allotted them, Brett still has time to command Jake to behave as follows: "Don't talk about it," "Don't talk like a fool," "Don't touch me," "You mustn't," "You must know," "Please understand," "Don't be silly," "Don't be cross," "Don't try and make me drunk," "Don't look like that" (she says this twice), "Don't be an ass." Jake, in his turn, commands Brett: "Don't talk like a fool," "Let's shut up about it," "Kiss me," "Try and be there," "Don't be sentimental," and "You don't have to go." Such listings can't of course suggest the gradations in tone and intention established by context—inviting, pleading, kidding, wishing, demanding—but they do suggest that the two lovers share a rhetoric which casts all of these intentions as imperatives and, for the most part, negative imperatives. Such evidence further suggests that the more intense the emotion being felt by the character, the more likely he is to resort to commands. Consider, for example, the exchange between Jake and Cohn after Jake is angered by his younger friend's persistent idealization of Lady Brett. Occupying only a single page at the end of Chapter Five, the course of Jake's anger is expressed by a sequence of nine of his commands to Cohn: "don't ask me a lot of fool questions if you don't like the answers," "go to hell," "Sit down," "Don't be a fool," "cut out the prep-school stuff," "don't go to hell," "Stick around," "Forget what I said," and "Let's get something to eat." If this imperative habit were exclusively Brett's or Jake's, it might be understood as the display of a particularizing trait, but in fact the habit is shared by virtually every character in the novel. One clue to this is the almost continuous barrage of commands to amend or alter his behaviour directed at Robert Cohn—commands from Jake, but also from Francis Clyne, Harvey Stone, and every one of his companions at Pamplona. If Cohn behaves badly, it is not because he lacks direction from others.

Most often these imperatives are immediate judgments passed upon a previous remark or action; they forcefully express the speaker's preference for a style or quality of behaviour and discourse which has not been adhered to by his auditor. The most frequently repeated commands in the novel are "don't talk like a fool," "don't be a fool," "don't be silly," "don't be an ass," but it doesn't really help much to infer that the novel's moral standard should therefore be defined as the prohibition of action or speech which is foolish, silly, or asinine. Perhaps the most that can be derived from the imperative habit of the novel's speakers is the generous collection it provides of examples by which we may grasp just exactly what styles the characters find it necessary to demand of each other. But Hemingway doesn't leave us with this barely manageable collection of particulars. He provides a means for organizing these examples because he goes beyond display of this pervasive habit to make explicit a code which most of the imperatives assume, making it difficult in a way which surprisingly has been overlooked by those who have tried to define the famous Hemingway "code."

The voice of Hemingway's code in *The Sun Also Rises* is Bill Gorton. Gorton is in fact the novel's preacher, and the clues to this function are some significant differences between the other characters' imperative habits and his own. The other characters tend to be captious in their commands, particularly in their negative ones, using them to express personal offense taken at a specific breach of expatriate proprieties. Strictly speaking, then, these imperatives function as sanctions for a code rather than direct definitions of the code itself. As such they are immediate retaliations for a particular act or remark; the intention is to swiftly judge and control behaviour through the implicit promise of punishment or rewards. Robert Cohn, for example, on at least three occasions, responds to Jake's irascible commands with "don't be sore, Jake," a wistful plea to withhold what he understands as Jake's implicit threat to respect him less. Despite our understanding that the withdrawal or grant of personal respect is perhaps the only meaningful sanction left to Jake and his friends, it can't be denied that the expatriate group is a touchy and censorious lot. Indeed such remarks as "don't be silly" and "don't be an ass" are repeated so frequently, and in such a variety of contexts, that they come to seem little more than habitual expletives of displeasure, and it is therefore easy to lose sight of the characters' persistent intent to express definite checks or goads to the behaviour of others.

By contrast Bill Gorton gives voice to a series of imperatives which are very different in nature and in effect, imperatives which in fact have the force of commandments. Consider the following, which together can be understood as a statement of a code which is only being implied by the irascible commands of the others. "Never be daunted," "Work for the good of all," "Show irony and pity," "We should not question," "Let us rejoice in our blessings. Let us utilize the fowls of the air. Let us utilize the product of the vine." Unlike the characteristic imperatives of the others—commands which are most often negative judgments of particular acts, which are prompted by irritation or anger, and which implicitly promise sanctions—Bill's remarks are general, largely disinterested, and instructive rather than censorious. Rather than being cut to fit specific situations, they are offered as universal guides to action, although they are not in the novel, and cannot be, laws of the kind which Moses brought from Mount Sinai. Bill's comic tones qualify his Biblical diction and phrasing and thus provide only a wry echo of the absolute and unconditional injunctions of Exodus and Leviticus. The context further suggests that Bill is less akin to Moses than to Koheleth, the preacher of Ecclesiastes. That Bill's commandments should be delivered in traditional homiletic modes is of course no accident; he is, particularly in the fishing scenes at Burguete, deliberately parodying preacherly rhetoric, but the parodic intent bears less on the wisdom of his commandments than it does on the spirit in which they are delivered, the nearly despairing, slightly cynical, worldly-wise spirit of Ecclesiastes.

Bill's other roles in the novel seem intended to reinforce his function as preacher of the code. Because Bill is the only major character not Jake's rival for Brett, he can serve as Jake's confessor, even as a physician to Jake's wounded spirit. The boyish persiflage of their exchanges, meant by Hemingway to express their manly lack of sentimentality, only thinly disguises Bill's real affection and solicitude for his friend. Bill's commandments are directed first to Jake, and they are shaped in part by his recognition that the traditional sources of spiritual guidance have failed for his companion. Bill's advice to Jake is less specifically important than his comforting presence, and because of his undemanding good nature, his ability to enhance Jake's simplest pleasures, and his capacity to see the world as "wonderful," yet be keenly aware of its failings, he earns much of the respect that some critics have already sought for him. Bill is no saint: he bets foolishly when angered, he baits Jews, and he adds to the violence at Pamplona by his drunken intention to "festa" the Biarritz swine, but yet he remains the voice of wisdom in the novel. This is indicated by the frequency with which his remarks convey a thematic resonance beyond the narrow limits of what Hemingway later referred to as "the bloody first person" point of view. Hemingway consistently charged Bill's words with a significance beyond their immediate context. Indeed Bill's inclination to summarize and generally comment upon his experience offers the very few occasions in the novel when general or even universal implications are deliberately evoked. Of his tour of European cities, he says—"Injustice everywhere"; on the anxieties of lovers—"What bloody-fool things people do"; on human nature—"Sex explains it all"; and on the need for imagination—"You ought to dream." Bill's penchant for summary expression further allows Hemingway to squeeze out what verbal benedictions are available to the expatriates: on the climactic evening at Pamplona—"What a night!" on the whole experience of the fiesta—"It's like a wonderful nightmare"; on Romero's courage—"That's quite a kid"; and finally on the disgraced and departed Cohn—"I feel sorry about Cohn.... He had an awful time."

But, to repeat, Bill's major function in the novel is as preacher of its code. His five commandments, although scattered throughout the text, together become a firm measure against which we can judge the characters. Let me rearrange the order in which the five occur so that I may briefly analyze them: "Utilize a little," "Never be daunted," "Work for the good of all," "Show irony and pity," and "Do not question." The first two are guides to inner conduct, the second two demand a particular social behaviour, and the last suggests the proper attitude toward the problem of what justifies, of what authorizes such commandments.

Part of Bill's mock sermon to Jake at Burguete is a direct echo of Ecclesiastes. Bill says: "Let us rejoice in our blessings. Let us utilize the fowls of the air. Let us utilize the product of the vine. Will you utilize a little, brother?" The Old Testament Preacher repeats this advice several times: since all men, rich or poor, wise or foolish, must die, and since all *is* vanity, "There is nothing better for a man that he should eat and drink, and that he should make his soul enjoy good in his labor." And the Biblical text continues: "This also, I say, that it was from the hand of God." Bill can invoke divine sources only to parody them. His advice is authorized not by God, but by Hemingway's celebration of the earth. Hemingway once wrote to Maxwell Perkins that the real hero of *The Sun Also Rises* is the abiding earth, and there is truth in his remark. The novel is impressive because of its convincing display of earth's bounty, particularly as Hemingway skillfully captures the small joys and savours of immediate sensation: the taste of wild strawberries, the sheen of a newly gutted trout bedded in ferns, the raw smell of garlic stew, or the tang of stream-cooled wine. These simple pleasures are etched so sharply that we are prepared to approve those who have the sensitivity and restraint necessary to appreciate them. It is this capacity which saves Jake from being a completely burnt out case; conversely, Hemingway manipulates, in order to demean, Cohn's incapacity to savour the immediate sensation. The third sentence of the novel tells us that Cohn dislikes the boxing he is so good at; Cohn is sick of Paris and restlessly longs for adventure in South America; Cohn sleeps through the trip over the Spanish earth which moves Bill to the Hemingwayesque exclamation, "This is country"; and Cohn gets sick and passes out during the first and most genial party at Pamplona. In another context, Cohn's failures to utilize might have been simply pathetic, but in the postwar world of diminished possibilities, Hemingway is clearly edging us toward seeing them as immoral. At least Cohn's failures go far in confirming the wisdom of Bill's commandment in the novel's world.

But if the novel's abiding earth provides opportunities for appreciation with precision and restraint, the social world of the lost generation does the opposite by promoting alcoholic excess as a means of escape. The specific motive for Bill's command that one never be daunted is his awareness that he is drunk in the extreme, but his choice of verb phrase is significant. To daunt means to tame or subdue, to make afraid or to intimidate, or to dishearten, and Bill's command never to be the victim of or submit to such threats is a counsel of courageous resistance. The only character in the novel who consistently meets this demand is Pedro Romero, and the often-quoted phrase "the holding of his purity of line through the maximum of exposure" is an apt description of the style required, but it is Bill's deliberate phrasing that carries the command. It is important to see that Bill's code actually demands action much less heroic than Romero's. As Jake says, "Nobody lives their life all the way up except bull-fighters." Cohn replies, "I'm not interested in bull-fighters. That's an abnormal life." For once, Cohn is right. The novel does invite the reader to be less interested in Romero, exemplar of stylish courage, than in the novel's more normal characters—and the reason is that to be normal in this postwar world is to be particularly vulnerable to its ability to tame, to subdue, to make afraid, to intimidate, and to dishearten. Bill's ethics recognize this; he modifies his commandment to Jake by explaining: "Secret of my success. Never been daunted. Never been daunted in public," and then, "If I begin to feel daunted I'll go off by myself. I'm like a cat that way." Here Bill's unqualified demand for inner courage and resistance gives way to a recognition of one's responsibility to others when those qualities weaken and fail. And here we remember that Jake's intense anguish breaks through only in the solitude of his own bedroom. Like Jake, Cohn is normal because he is daunted; he approaches immorality by being daunted in public. Because of Cohn's romantic obsession with Lady Brett, he irritates, embarrasses, and finally injures his friends, all in a completely childish and ineffectual way. While he may be forgiven for being daunted, to be so in public is to become one who daunts, one who threatens the already precarious restraints on the disabling anguish of others.

Bill's third command, "Work for the good of all," is perhaps the most ironic of his injunctions. In the specific context, he makes the remark to commend Jake's early-morning energy in digging for their fishing worms while he himself remains in bed—a comic repudiation of altruism. And this repudiation echoes the situation of the expatriates; they have deliberately withdrawn from the large community in whose name they had been willing to sacrifice personal for public good during the World War. Because of this, they are charged by their critics with evading social responsibility, indeed with not working at all. Bill defines New York's view of the expatriate life: "You don't work. One group claims women support you. Another group claims you're impotent." This last remark is unintended and Bill worries that he may have hurt Jake, but his point is well taken. Impotent because of his participation in the struggle to work for the good of all, Jake's capacities for altruism have been seriously diminished. As he must now say: "I try and play it along and just not make trouble for people." The community to which he now makes himself responsible is that small group that can be recognized as survivors. Hemingway simply assumes that the social virtue of his survivors—their painful sacrifice for the public good—will be attested to by what they now suffer.

Their social debts paid, the one remaining obligation to the good of all is a negative one—to avoid making trouble for each other. The temptation of course is to make their suffering into an excuse for being troublesome. Alone in his room at Pamplona, Jake comes close to ranking his friends according to their ability to resist this temptation: "I wished Mike would not behave so terribly to Cohn, though. Mike was a bad drunk. Brett was a good drunk. Bill was a good drunk. Cohen was never drunk." Jake's own ordeal comes when the rivalry over Brett explodes. In order to calm his friends, Jake must assume the appearance of a stability he can't really feel. Hemingway uses an image from the corrida to make vivid the difficulty of Jake's position. Jake explains to Bill why steers are put in the corrals to receive the fighting bulls: "To quiet down the bulls and keep them from breaking their horns against the stone walls, or goring each other." Bill replies: "Must be swell being a steer." Jake, like the steers, must continue to suffer in order to work for the good of all—must suffer to quiet the outbreaks of his bull-male friends as they quarrel over his beloved Brett.

Bill's next commandment defines a second way in which to serve others. "'Work for the good of all.' ... 'Show irony and pity.'" Bill is recommending that Jake display a complex attitude in which irony and pity mutually qualify each other. But the novel demonstrates that such an attitude is more easily commanded than achieved. Distrusting high rhetoric, Hemingway is obviously hoping that the pathos evoked by his characters' situations will be saved from sentimentality because of its intermixture with ironic distance and humour. But quite simply, his characters lack the wit for this balancing act. As we've already seen, the most typical utterance of the characters is the captious, irritable command, and not the ironic quips whose sting has been softened by their pity. Indeed Bill is the only character whose speech seems even remotely informed by this conjunction of irony and pity. One need think only of his remark just quoted: "Must be swell being a steer." His command serves, then, as a reminder of how frequently the characters fail to balance irony with pity. Hemingway may have hoped that the phrase would function much as do such musical terms as "allegro," or "con brio," that is, as a direction indicating how a passage is to be read. In this connection, consider the final exchange between Brett and Jake, the exact tone of which several critics have worried. "'Oh, Jake,' Brett said, 'we could have had such a damned good time together.' ... 'Yes,' I said, 'isn't it pretty to think so?'" The irony here is clear, but it hardly seems softened by pity, for although we must assume Jake's continuing love for Brett, his speech is a bitter and self-affirming rejection of her romantic might-have-been. The difficulty of constructing statements that can simultaneously and in balance show both pity and irony raises in fact the question of just how Bill's commandments are to be taken. And this question can be answered in part by a consideration of Bill's fifth commandment.

While eating their lunch of chicken and hard-boiled eggs, Jake plays along with Bill's jokes and wonders "what day God created the chicken?" Bill replies: "We should not question. Our stay on earth is not for long." And then,

> "Let us not doubt, brother. Let us not pry into the holy mysteries of the hen-coop with simian fingers. Let us accept on faith and simply say—I want you to join me in saying—What shall we say, brother?" He pointed the drunkstick at me and went on. "Let me tell you. We will say, and I for one am proud to say—and I want you to say with me, on your knees, brother. Let no man be ashamed to kneel here in the great out-of-doors. Remember the woods were God's first temples. Let us kneel and say: 'Don't eat that, Lady—that's Mencken.'"

This anticlimax is more than comic irreverence. The invocation of Mencken, the period's most raucous skeptic, is wholly appropriate here and characterizes Bill's status as a preacher. He must offer his code with tongue in cheek because it is not based on the secure foundation of divine authority. Bill's code cannot be offered with the confident assurance that it is justified by God's revelation of truth for men; the code is instead, as Melville said of Ecclesiastes, "The fine hammered steel of woe." For this reason, Bill's commandments must be curbed and hedged with humorous irony, for they are based only on meagre and bitter experience. His last commandment, a prohibition against inquiring into the metaphysical grounds that might justify a code, reflects Hemingway's own skepticism about the possibility of ever attaining that certain knowledge which is the traditional authority for ethical commands. And this skepticism is in the spirit of Ecclesiastes: "And I gave my heart to know wisdom, and to know madness and folly: I perceived that this also is vexation of spirit. For in much wisdom is much grief: and he that increaseth knowledge increaseth sorrow." Jake Barnes is forced to this same conclusion in the novel. Alone with his misery, vexed in spirit, Jake attempts to seek solace in moral philosophy. He considers for a moment, among others, the principle that you paid for everything that was good. But then he says: "It seemed like a fine philosophy. In five years, I thought, it will seem just as silly as all the other philosophies I've had." And finally he must say: "I did not care what it was all about. All I wanted to know was how to live in it. Maybe if you found out how to live in it, you learned from that what it was all about." Bill articulates a code that advises how to live in it, but can't presume to explain what it was all about.

The code that Bill Gorton preaches is fully conditioned by the world of the novel. Just as the world in which the characters act has been diminished in its possibilities and resources, the standards which govern their conduct have been reduced from the certain moral grandeur of virtue and righteousness to the tenuous status of style. Strictly speaking, Bill's code is not a moral code at all; it is a code of manners. It is justified not by divine authority, but by the principle of group propriety which enforces simple patterns of decency and decorum under stress. Nowhere in the novel do Jake and his talk-weary friends debate, argue, or attempt to justify the rules which only Bill articulates, and by which most of them, with varying success, try to live. Nowhere do they enjoy the luxury of securely condemning or sanctifying others by the authority of those rules. There can be no sinners here; Robert Cohn is only, as Brett says, "a poor devil." The novel demonstrates, then, that Hemingway's moral vision is a negative one. It anticipates no success, expects no victories, claims no great rewards. It endorses guides appropriate to the aftermath of battle, rather than to the preparations for it. But the point is that these guides are fully explicit in the novel, and Bill Gorton is their preacher. I wish to claim for Gorton the function which the pious compiler of Ecclesiastes concludes by attributing to the preacher of Ecclesiastes: "Vanity of Vanity, saith the Preacher, all is vanity. And moreover, because the Preacher was wise, he still taught the people knowledge; yes, he gave good heed, and sought out, and set in order many proverbs."

A Memorial Note for Ralph Ellison

Ralph Ellison will be best remembered for his novel, *Invisible Man*, which was published in 1952, became a bestseller, and in 1953 won the American National Book Award for Fiction. The novel also had staying power: in 1965, a poll of two hundred critics and editors named it as "the most distinguished work" published in the last twenty years. *Invisible Man* is the story of the education of a young black man whose name the reader never learns who narrates his own experience.

Like the protagonist, the reader learns that he is invisible because of the racial stereotypes, definitions, and roles forced or imposed upon him by the expectations of those around him. To the northern liberals who support the southern college he attends, he must play the humble and grateful recipient of charity, but he's baffled to discover that one of his white benefactors attributes to him extraordinary sexual prowess and expects him to behave like an uninhibited animal. Expelled from college, he migrates north to Harlem in New York City and there discovers that his stereotypic identities are multiplied. Communist organizers try to make him an example of the downtrodden black proletariat, and others in Harlem see him variously as a scam artist, a disciple of the black militant known as Ras the Destroyer, a jazz horn-player, and a spineless Uncle Tom. The last chapter is set during the race riots in Harlem in 1943, which the protagonist's tormentors, both white and black, use as cover to come after him. He escapes to a hole and in the end the invisible man has become the underground man, safe for the moment and free to reflect on what his disillusioning experiences have taught him about himself.

Invisible Man is a genuine achievement. It quickly became clear that while Ellison shared the intense moral outrage that had animated Richard Wright, his most distinguished predecessor in American black fiction, he had also found ways to transcend the limits of Wright's bleakly naturalistic novels. *Invisible Man* is a complex blend of both comic and tragic invention laced with the rich rhetorical traditions and folk cultures of Ellison's heritage. There are examples of revival sermons, funeral orations, political speech-making, Harlem street talk like the rhyming slang that anticipates rap, doing the dozens, the languages of the numbers racket, jazz riffs, voodoo, and the blues. In Richard Wright's novel, *Native Son*, the chief character is finally destroyed by impersonal forces over which he has no control. By contrast, *Invisible Man* ends with the hope that the protagonist will survive because, however disillusioning his education has been, he has become more conscious of his personal, cultural, and national history, the ingredients of a firm identity. The protagonist gets lots of advice from people in the course of the novel, but the advice he ponders at the end comes from a character known only as the vet: "Now is the time for offering fatherly advice," he said, "but I'll have to spare you that—since I guess I'm nobody's father except my own. Perhaps that's the advice to give you: Be your own father, young man. And remember the world is possibility if only you'll discover it."

Ellison's novel is in part autobiographical. Born in Oklahoma City in 1914, his family named him for the most famous American optimist, Ralph Waldo Emerson. He received a music scholarship to study at the famous Tuskegee Institute, now Tuskegee University in Alabama, which became the model for the college in the novel. He studied there from 1933 to 1936 and then moved to New York City where, with the exception of service in the Merchant Marine during World War II and two years in Rome on a Fellowship, he lived until his death. While in New York he worked with Richard Wright on the Federal Writers Project and became associated with several left-wing journals and newspapers.

I met Ellison in 1959 when I was a graduate student at the University of Iowa. *Esquire* Magazine sponsored a symposium on American fiction and had invited four writers, Norman Mailer and Ralph Ellison among them. There was a formal evening session, and a wild party after that, which went on well into the morning hours. Mailer had just published his in-your-face collection called *Advertisements for Myself,* and dominated the party by casting himself as the provocateur. My fellow students crowded around Mailer, giving me the opportunity for some quiet talk with Ellison. Like Sam Selvon, Ellison was both handsome and dignified. I remember him as remarkably courteous and patient, answering what seem to me now my naïve questions with clarity and in detail. He seemed to me unflappable, but the next day, I caught one glimpse of the pressures being put on him by the American literary intellectuals that Mailer seemed to be speaking for. At the final session of the symposium, Mailer made a not-so-subtle dig at Ellison for not following up the success of *Invisible Man* with more politically relevant fiction. It had been, after all, seven years since that book had been published. And for a moment, Ellison almost lost his cool. He turned to Mailer and in a very carefully enunciated voice said: "I'm Ralph Ellison, Norman; I *know* who I am." It dawned on me that Mailer was doing to Ellison what the characters in *Invisible Man* did to the protagonist . . . imposing a role on him, in this case, expectations, even demands, that Ellison live up to his promise as a spokesman in fiction for the black American community. Ellison clearly had to resist these ideological expectations in order to retain his freedom both as an artist and as a human being. And he became in later years increasingly concerned to make the reasons for his resistance clear. In a 1974 interview, for instance, he said this:

> The ideology changes, but the human experience, the joy and the pain, the anger and the exultation which should go into art remains.... It isn't yours; it's a group thing which you share in and which you communicate.... If you *do* that, then it seems to me a far more important thing than being ideologically committed. The novel is a form which attempts to deal with the contradictions of life and ambivalence and ambiguities of value. It isn't easy for ideologues to deal with it. They don't trust it because the form itself insists upon a certain kind of truth, a certain kind of objectivity.

Ellison's critics have in fact argued that he spent so much time resisting the ideological expectations of others that he dried up as a novelist. The more sympathetic of these critics find it something of a tragedy that he never completed a second novel. Such judgments ignore the fact that Ellison continued to write carefully crafted short stories, essays, and reviews throughout the rest of his life, resulting in two collections, *Shadow and Act* in 1964, and *Going to the Territory* in 1986. And in his later years Ellison *was* working on a second novel, interrupted at one point by the accidental burning of its manuscript in a house fire. But the truth is that although Ellison may go down in American literary annals as a one-book man, it is a superb book, and the world is lucky to have it.

In June 1975 Ellison attended the opening of a new library in Oklahoma City to be named the Ralph Ellison Public Library. The new library represented, he said, a communal victory. It is appropriate, I think, that together we do homage to his memory in a public library, an occasion sponsored by the Alberta Black Heritage Studies Association, a shared heritage his one novel did much to revive, enrich, and perpetuate.

Western Canadian Literature

What Do You Know about Canadian Literature? Shame On You!

My title contains two assumptions that are themselves presumptuous; the first is that Americans' answer to the question: "What do you know about Canadian literature?" will be something like "next to nothing." The second is that this ignorance, insofar as it exists, deserves something like the parliamentary cry of "Shame, Sir, Shame."

My first assumption is not all that firmly grounded. It comes largely from my experience, over a long period of revisiting the States, of Americans' almost total unawareness of any department of Canadian life. For instance, I've made it a habit to ask Americans I meet a simple question of fact: "How many provinces are there in Canada?" The answers I've received so far range from two to fifty-six. (The correct answer is ten; my first answer to the question was nine because when I studied grade-school geography, there were only nine.) Or, try another quizzing question: "Who is the current prime minister of Canada?"

I can't really expect, then, in the face of such general ignorance, that most Americans will have an acquaintance with Canadian letters, but I do concede that American students and teachers of literature may have the same kind of scatter-gun and very nodding knowledge of Canadian writers that I had when I first moved to Canada in 1968. I knew that Bliss Carman was Canadian, but saw him only as an imitator of Walt Whitman; as an adolescent, I read and enjoyed Stephen Leacock, and had later placed him somewhere between Booth Tarkington and Mark Twain; I knew about Morley Callaghan because he had hung around with the expatriates in Paris during the twenties; and I had a warm if wispy memory from my childhood of *Anne of Green Gables*, although I was never able to remember the author's name (Lucy Maud Montgomery).

Had I remained in the United States instead of coming to Canada in 1968, I would surely have picked up some hints, however random, of the remarkable productivity of Canadian writers since that date. I might have come to know the short stories of Mavis Gallant or Alice Munro, which appear frequently in the *New Yorker*. I would likely have read Marian Engel's novel called *Bear*, about a librarian who has an affair with the title character, or novels by Margaret Atwood, or Margaret Laurence, or Robertson Davies. I would have encountered poems by Earle Birney, Margaret Avison, and Michael Ondaatje, because they are the three Canadians represented in the *Norton Anthology of Poetry* (not in the big edition, which excludes Canadians altogether, but in the shorter edition, revised). And I would certainly have known the lyrics of Leonard Cohen, Canada's answer to Bob Dylan. What is even more likely is that, had I become acquainted with any of these writers, I would have had no special awareness of them as Canadians, and, from their point of view, perhaps this is all to the good. Insofar as they have been incorporated into the mainstream of literature in English, they have arrived, and their national origin or present citizenship is probably irrelevant. It is, however, just as likely that American readers who have come to know these writers simply assume that they belong somewhere below the forty-ninth parallel, and thus we conspire to ignore the Canadianness of Canadian writing. E. K. Brown, one of the best critics of Canadian literature (and one who spent most of his academic life in American universities), puts it this way: "To the reader outside Canada, such works . . . have *not* been important as reflections of phases in a national culture; the interest in the work has *not* spread to become an interest in the movements and the traditions in the national life from which the work emerged. Canadian books may occasionally have had a mild impact outside Canada; Canadian literature has had none." Professor Brown made these remarks in 1943, but they still describe the case. Brown gracefully excused the foreign reader by suggesting that the failure of Canadian literature to make an international impact was due to its comparative youth—it was still potential, still emerging. But about 1967 something happened to change this condition. In that year the celebrations of the one hundredth anniversary of Canada's Confederation—its creation as a separate nation—focused and released an enormous amount of national energy; one result was that the Canadians themselves discovered that they already had a body of indigenous work of considerable range and interest. This discovery further encouraged both established writers and newcomers and, during the twelve years since the centennial, they have made impressive additions to what is now a mature, if still young, body of work. In short, Canadian literature now seems substantial enough—and of such quality—that it deserves the international attention it has hitherto been denied; certainly it deserves the interest and attention of Americans.

What I want to do with the rest of my time is to speculate first about one reason why Canadian literature has not been given an appropriate place within the English curricula offered to American students, and then to hazard a reason in support of my contention that it deserves such a place.

My perspective on this matter comes from being, since 1968, an expatriate in Canada, with the job—naïve cultural imperialist that I am—of teaching American literature to students at the University of Alberta. As the man who not only came to dinner, but who tried to persuade his host to sample the food he brought with him, I've also tried to be a proper guest. I have, for example, taken an interest in the host's library. At first this was a dutiful task; it has long since become a pleasure, and although my familiarity with Canadian books remains an amateur's, it is nonetheless affectionate and respectful. But learning a certain amount about Canada has also involved forgetting a certain amount about the United States.

When I left the States in the summer of 1968, it was going through something that looked very much like a revolution—certainly the key public events were traumatic enough; it was, you'll remember, in the spring of 1968 that Martin Luther King and Robert Kennedy were assassinated. In subsequent years I kept a nervous eye on the course of events at home, but inevitably I lost track, and in the midseventies, I was suddenly brought up short by an MLA talk given by Leslie Fiedler. Fiedler assured us that there had been a revolution in the United States in the sixties, that it was now over, and that it had been successful. His proof was characteristically Fiedlerian. He told the story of his return to the State University of New York at Buffalo after a leave that had to do with his getting busted on a pot charge. (Campus cops: "Welcome back, prof; missed you; as for marrywanna, everyone uses it; why, the pioneers used it; and how do you think them Apaches got their FEE/Nominal vision?") "When I heard that," said Fiedler, "I knew the revolution was over." I had my doubts that there had been a true revolution, in part because as an undergraduate history major, I had stared for four years at a sentence which my major professor had had permanently painted on his blackboard: "History is an evolutionary process with no abrupt breaks or changes." But when I began to think about what I might say, it occurred to me that I had lost track, not only of the course of American events, but of what had happened with the teaching of literature in my native land—could it be that while my back was turned, there may have been a revolution in there somewhere?

There are probably any number of better ways to find out what had happened, but I decided to go through the intervening eleven years of *College English* to see what I'd missed. The experience, let me assure you, was a salutary one, although in reading all those essays, I began to doubt my ability to distinguish between academic satire or parody and the straight stuff. But I did conclude, at least from the record offered by *College English*, that there had been a revolution of sorts in the teaching of literature to American students—and that revolution was within the curriculum I was most interested in—the classic canon of American works I had studied and professed in the fifties and early sixties and that I continued to profess in Canada. What I discovered was that that canon had finally exploded. Clearly this once-sanctioned group of works and writers was now regarded as the enemy, to be pejoratively described and decried. It was now seen as the literary expression of the dominant WASP culture, or of the bourgeois, imperialist civilization that the States had become. And I knew enough about the origins of this canon to know that there was some truth in these attacks. Until the 1880s, the proponents of American literature weren't all that concerned about a national canon; they were still preoccupied with seeking houseroom for American works in England. But in the late 1880s and 1890s, largely in response to the enormous wave of immigrants from southern and eastern European countries, a certain sort of American work gained approval, in part as a means of facilitating the assimilation of these immigrants into the national fabric. These works were almost exclusively by writers who were white, Anglo-Saxon in origin, Protestant in religion, and born in New England. This is the period in which the mass-produced steel engravings of bearded New England bards looked down at pupils from the walls of new urban schools named Longfellow Primary or Emerson High. The texts in these schoolrooms were sure to include Houghton Mifflin's Riverside editions, cheap reprints of the glossy collected works of the New England heavies. Horace Scudder said of the Riverside editions in 1894 that they would be "for a generation to come, the mightiest force that can be reckoned with for the nationalization of the American people." Aside from some additions and deletions by the liberal academics and critics of the twenties and thirties, this canon was to remain entrenched until the middle-sixties, so much so that even Leslie Fiedler had difficulty altering it. In 1967, Fiedler permitted himself, in a retrospective essay about his *Love and Death in the American Novel*, to boast a bit about the ways he had, he thought, succeeded in enlarging the nineteenth-century American canon, succeeded by drawing attention to the novels of Charles Brockden Brown, the less-read fiction of Cooper, Poe's Gordon Pym, and even George Lippard's *The Monks of Monk Hall*. I leave it to you to decide how far Fiedler was successful in promoting these works, but again his target was clear, WASP "good taste."

In 1967 Fiedler was certainly right about the beleaguered state of the old canon. The sons and daughters of the minority groups which the establishment of a corpus of approved American works had been designed to assimilate were now rebelling, were now rediscovering their own unassimilated identities, and were now demanding a literature which would reflect them. *College English* in the late sixties and seventies was full of plans for new courses and the revision of old ones to include works by and about Blacks, Jews, Chicanos, native American Indians, followed closely by other groups hitherto submerged in the dominant tradition—women, homosexuals, folklorists, regionalists, science-fiction fans, and students of popular culture. Indeed the proliferation of curricular proposals for change which appear in *College English* suggests that the very notion of a commonly approved body of work to be offered to students was now seen not only as repressive, but as finally and wholly obsolete. Even those who undertook to defend the old canon didn't seem to have their hearts in it. Some even took up the defence, claiming WASPism itself was merely another subculture, even though it was America's. The issue seemed closed, though later defenders of the old canon were in a mood not to lick the revolution but to join it. Every indication was, then, that by 1973, the old American canon—and even the stars and stripes it was originally meant to serve—had undergone such change as to amount to a revolution. The old "Red, White, and Blue" had become black, brown, red, yellow, and white, only a tiny bit of WASP true blue.

All this is no news, and you may well be wondering why I belabour the point in remarks intended to get some hearing for Canadian literature in the United States. In the face of such curricular explosion it may be simply impractical to urge yet another set of additions to sophomore literature courses. I realized this first when speaking with an old friend during a conference of the Western Literature Association at which a section on the Canadian West had been invited. She said to me, with one of the deeper and more heartfelt sighs I'd ever heard: "O dear, I suppose they'll want us to teach some CANLIT now; I've got enough trouble fitting in all the new American stuff."

I'm sympathetic, but I still think there is both room and reason for including some Canadian literature in surveys in U.S. universities. I discovered further reasons for believing this, again from reading *College English*. The truth is that *CE* reveals that the revolution of which I've been speaking is not yet complete. It is true that most of the boundaries and barriers that excluded one or another kind of literary work from the main stream of literature offered to American students—most of these barriers have been breached—so much so, indeed, that the mainstream is now, like the Platt River, a mile wide. But there is one boundary not yet crossed, one barrier that not only remains intact, but is frequently invoked with pride, at least in the pages of *College English*. It is of course the boundary of American nationalism itself. In the whole preceding run of *College English*, I found only one comment that could be said to challenge the boundary imposed by nationalism, and this was tucked well away in a book review in 1970. The reviewer complains about the book he is reviewing that it exemplifies the insistence on the American-ness of everything. I did a random check of ten anthologies, rhetorical readers, and so on, of the kind used in sophomore literature courses and published by American companies. As was to be expected, over sixty percent of the material included was American in origin; what was even less surprising was that, although there were some pretty exotic foreign entries, out of those hundreds of selections, only one was Canadian, and that was an essay by Northrop Frye. The eleven-year run of *College English* is a covert record of an unexamined chauvinism, a chauvinism which simply endorses one of the more artificial boundaries—to be specific, the arbitrary, if now time-honoured boundary—the so-called longest undefended border—that separates the United States from Canada.

One might have thought that the momentum of the revolution which permitted entry into the curriculum of literary work hitherto excluded might have continued, but there is evidence to suggest that the sense of a national boundary was working to impede that revolution at every stage. What began with an attack on the old WASP canon had a limit. The voices of minorities would now be heard, but heard within the firmly bounded national theatre—these are our blacks, our Chicanos, our homosexuals, our women. For this reason, then, one wonders finally if anything essential had really changed in the teaching of literature in the United States. In 1826, Noah Webster, perhaps the first American literary nationalist, wrote: ". . . I desired to see my countrymen disposed to give a due preference to all their native productions, to promote all efforts to exalt the literary character of their country, and to disengage themselves from the thraldom of an overweening reverence for foreign opinions and authors—a species of slavery that hangs like a millstone about the neck of all literary enterprise in the United States." Webster's comment would have been at home anyplace in the recent run of *College English*, except that the enemy had ceased to be foreign opinions and authors, and had become the old domestic canon itself.

Let me be clear; I am not here complaining about American nationalism itself. What I mean to object to is the unthinking, unexamined nature of that nationalism—in a word, its chauvinism—especially as it is allowed to dictate choices about what should be read and studied by American students. And it is just on these grounds that I recommend American teachers' becoming better acquainted with Canadian literature because it can be an important means of tempering, if not eradicating their share of such chauvinism as they select and guide their students' reading.

There are of course several grounds upon which Canadian literature can be recommended to Americans. One could use the argument of quality because there is a certain number of Canadian works in every genre that equal if not exceed the quality of all but the greatest works produced by Americans. I'm hoping that Americans will have the pleasure of discovering these works. Or one could use arguments of simple propinquity, or of simple justice; after all Americans share the continent not only with Mexico, but with Canada (and their share is something less than half the land mass even though they have ten times the population of Canada). In 1931, E. K. Brown published an essay called "The Neglect of American Literature" in which he made a plea to his fellow Canadians for proper attention to American letters: "Apart from the absolute value of the major works of its greatest writers, American literature has a special value for Canadians, as the literature of the highest rank which is morally and socially nearest their own experience." I would insist that this special value is or should be reciprocal. Or consider simple justice. Living in Canada has shown me that American imperialism—particularly cultural imperialism—begins very close to home. In 1968, an Alberta publisher asked prominent Canadian writers to offer their candid opinions of the United States, which he brought out under the catchy title *The New Romans*. What was most interesting to me about this collection was that over a third of the essays contained a personification of Canada as a woman— either a virgin being raped by Uncle Sam or a whore selling it to him. One way for Americans to resist exploitation of this lady's body is to cultivate some respect for the integrity of her mind.

There are, then, some good and sufficient reasons why Americans should read Canadian literature, but I want to return to what seems to me to be the most relevant one for our purposes here: that is, Canadian literature can be a means of tempering if not eradicating the force of American chauvinism as Canadian teachers select and guide their students' reading. And the reason for this is that Canadian literature is the record of a collective experience which, because of its comparatively reduced scale and range, rather more graphically reveals both the painful tensions and the often equally painful rewards of an attempt at national articulation on the North American continent. There are enough differences from comparable attempts in the United States to be dramatically instructive; there are enough similarities to promote a kind of embarrassing self-recognition.

The most dramatic difference is of course the fact of French Canada. Those aware of nothing else about contemporary Canada have certainly heard news of the success in Quebec of the Parti Québécois, which proposes that Quebec should separate from the national Confederation. This program represents, I think, the practical failure of the nation's efforts to be genuinely bicultural. Although for years the federal government has made bilingualism its official policy, the net effect in Alberta, for example, is little more than cereal boxes that snap, crackle, and pop in two languages. Yet even though the nation is not yet bilingual, Quebec and its French culture remain a fact in Canada, and most Canadians seem to want it to continue to remain a fact. Closely associated with questions of the two major languages, particularly in the west, are problems usually discussed under the heading of multiculturalism. Canada has been, and continues to be, a nation of immigrants to an extent now far greater than the United States—and these immigrants have shown a remarkable resistance to assimilation by the dominant cultural heritage of English Canada—so much so that the metaphor of a mosaic has been traditionally used in contrasting Canada with America's melting pot. While the temperature under that pot has been reduced considerably in recent years, it may still be true that the pressures for cultural homogeneity are more intense in the United States than in Canada. By contrast with American literature, the corpus of Canadian literature illustrates some success, however modest, in accommodating works from several cultures—particularly the French—within its loosely unified framework, and it can, to that extent, stand as a model for what should be America's efforts to incorporate literary diversity without melting down its distinctive parts by an insistent nationalism.

Another potentially useful fact about Canadian nationalism is that in its more vigorous forms, it is a very recent phenomenon and both its vigour and its youth combine to offer object lessons for Americans from a national consciousness that is very self-conscious indeed. Because Canada originated as an alternative to the revolutionary United States, that is, as a more or less deliberate choice to remain dependent on the British crown, the colonial mentality strongly persisted until well into the twentieth century. It was only in the sixties and then largely in reaction to a growing sense of the threat from American imperialism, as epitomized by Vietnam, that aggressive Canadian nationalism became a much debated public and nationwide issue. One result of that debate was an airing of the nooks and corners, the advantages and disadvantages of nationalism in a way not present in contemporary America, or at least not in the pages of *College English*.

Brian Stock *summarized* much of this debate in an essay reporting the vicissitudes of nationalism in Canada to the British in *TLS* in 1976.

Canadian nationalism, despite its benign intentions, has given rise to all the predictable abnormalities. It has given weaklings a flag to hide behind. It has offered up an obvious victim to the scapegoat theory of history. It has acted as a cover for personal gain at the expense of the public good. It has erected false boundaries and enforced false sanctions. It has legitimized mediocrity and admitted a double standard for culture. It has placed an ideological veil in front of many of Canada's real problems—its economic planning, regional disparities, and endemic political instability. In many ways it has made the country smaller, not larger. Yet, despite its many failings, the national movement has one overriding virtue: it is the only universalizing force in the country. Without it, Canada would probably undergo psychological disintegration. All the positive accomplishments of the past generation would be dissolved by particularism.

If these things are true of Canadian nationalism, they seem equally true of American nationalism. Stock's essay would have been appropriate, it seems to me, in the pages of *College English* at any time during the preceding eleven years, but you won't find anything like it there; failing that, Americans might look to Canadian literature for some clear-sighted, forthright, and balanced examination of the tensions and paradoxes of national expression.

Finally, then, let me urge Americans to become better acquainted with Canadian literature. Canadian literature can help Americans enlarge the circumference of their reality as it is measured by—and limited by—the American border. One thing, for example, which I've learned from my Canadian hosts is a very *un*American caution of the kind illustrated by the difference between the two nations' patriotic bumper stickers: In the States, they read: "America: Love it or Leave it." In Canada, they read: "Canada: show some affection or consider emigrating." My feeling remains that the first attitude must be tempered by the second.

The Canonization of *As For Me and My House*: A Case Study

"Time and again *As For Me and My House* has been called a minor Canadian classic. Surely it is time, and we have achieved sufficient maturity and good taste, for the delimiting adjectives to be dropped." John Moss, in his *Patterns of Isolation* (1974), thus secedes from one consensus in order to sponsor the elevation of Sinclair Ross's novel into the canon of major, international classics. Moss's hardihood invites inquiry into both the development and the nature of consensus about the novel. Moss has insisted that it is "probably the most thoroughly analyzed of Canadian novels, with the possible exception of *The Double Hook*...."[1] This analysis, the chief means by which its critics have been sending Ross's novel through an ascending succession of canons, is therefore itself worth scrutiny. The result may be a useful case study of criticism in Canada.

The book's initial reception suggested that, if there was to be any consensus, it would be negative. First published in 1941, the novel, as Ross himself has said, "fell flat on its face."[2] Those who cared about it despaired of its survival. In his original edition of *The Canadian West in Fiction* in 1949, Edward McCourt had lamented that "in Sinclair Ross we may, through indifference and neglect, have permitted a fine artist to perish."[3] But between 1949 and 1970, when McCourt revised his study, something had happened. In the new edition, McCourt altered his conclusion: "Until recently there was reason to feel that Ross was a distinguished artist without honour in his own country, but within the last few years *As For Me and My House* has been recognized as a novel of superior merit and it is now preserved—one hesitates to say embalmed—in the Can. Lit reading lists of our universities."[4] What happened in the interval was that, in 1957, the novel was republished in paperback by McClelland and Stewart's New Canadian Library with an introduction by Roy Daniells. And that this edition has indeed become a staple of reading lists is suggested by the fact that it has so far been reprinted in 1960, 1961, 1964, 1966, 1967, 1969, and 1970 (the latest copies have ceased to include the reprinting dates). Before 1957, the novel was the subject only of a few brief reviews and scattered remarks in commentary on Canadian literature; since that date it has been discussed in public print, in depth and at length, at least ten times. McCourt's pleasure in the novel's recent recognition is a shade darkened

---

*Since this essay is a review of critical reception, references have been documented.

by his worry about academic formaldehyde. The course of the novel's treatment since 1957 suggests some reason to worry.

Both the early reviewers and the first commentators, occupied with such serviceable and scholarly duties as simply bringing the novel's existence to public attention, describing it, and cataloguing it with respect to the range of Canadian letters, were nonetheless willing to pass direct and critical judgments, crisply asserting its merits and its flaws, even if only in passing. By contrast, the post-1957 essayists, now with the leisure for reflection, have tended to convert the flaws originally alleged against it into elaborate techniques for enhancing its virtues. The tendency itself is not necessarily illegitimate; it may well be inevitable as reflective attention develops through time, but the strategies it employs are revealing and disturbing.

Let me illustrate the effects of this change by first tracing the fate of one problem with the novel, raised as an issue by E. K. Brown in the best of the initial reviews—still the most balanced, subtle, and succinct judgment of *As For Me and My House*. Brown recommends the novel, in part on formal grounds. He asserts that Ross avoided most of "the weaknesses and dangers of the diary-form," notably self-pity and discursiveness. He then adds:

> But the major danger, repetition, has not been circumvented: The rain streams down through the roof and drips into the pail in the living room much too often; on too many evenings of summer the moths circle the lamp, and get singed or killed; the boniness of the hero's frame is felt through his coat almost every day. Mr. Ross might reply that his repetitions serve to convey the oppressive narrow monotony of the life in the small mid-western town he paints so cruelly. They do; but in the end they deaden the reader's sensitiveness to the tragedy, and even take away from the human reality of the central pair.[5]

This workmanlike passage would be otherwise unremarkable except in the light of the later critical essays. What needs to be stressed here is that Brown performs a complicated critical task with economy, clarity, and a tactful concern for his reader's own response to Ross's work. He defines the problem by articulating opposing contentions, concedes the force of one, then counters it with his own judgment, in both appealing to the effect of technique on a commonly shared sensibility, as, for example, by the opening trio of details—very specific invitations to compare our reaction with his. The issue, once defined, is then resolved, perhaps too easily, by transforming what was originally offered as an opposition into a continuum in which enough repetition is advantageous and too much is self-defeating. Brown evades the hard part—at exactly what point or degree, and why, does the well-done become overdone—and one could wish for more evidence in support of his concluding judgment, even within the limits of a brief review. But that the problem he addressed is genuine and the terms in which he phrased it persuasive is indicated by the fact that in 1949, McCourt's testimony, although he does not mention his predecessor's review, provided direct corroboration of Brown's concluding criticism, particularly the judgment that too much repetition inhibits the reader's empathy with the characters.

> Phillip [sic] himself is a curiously wooden character. He is seen by the reader so many times in one characteristic action, that of stalking, white-lipped and silent, into his study and shutting the door against the world . . . that after a while he becomes a kind of automaton going with mechanical precision through a limited series of movements.[6]

Brown's point was thus slowly emerging as one focus of consensus about the novel; this is further indicated in the next substantial comment, Roy Daniells' 1957 introduction. Daniells, again without mentioning Brown, seems in complete agreement with him, accepting both his terms for the issue and his specific means of resolving it.

> There is an inescapable monotony contingent upon our seeing everything through Mrs. Bentley's eyes. The reiteration which results is on the one hand brilliantly exploited and made essential to the plot, for if this monotony and reiteration did not exist half the *raison d'être* of the piece would disappear. On the other hand, we must fairly admit that it is overdone, especially in detail; we must accept the repetitive round of life in Horizon and the eternal *obbligato* of the prairie wind: indeed both are felt as essential. It is when Philip goes white for the twentieth time, or once again his study door closes, . . . that our suspension of disbelief becomes a little less than willing.[7]

But, having made the point, Daniells immediately qualified its importance by adding: "Perhaps this is no more than to admit that there are ups and downs of credibility and convincingness, as one would expect." Daniells' remark signals that a recognition of overdone repetition in the novel had become, by 1957, something of a critical commonplace; in fairness one conceded the flaw, perhaps an inevitable one, but also insisted that it not be allowed to overweigh the book's real virtues. Consensus even that the flaw was a flaw was not yet complete; Guy Sylvestre's *Canadian Writers: A Biographical Dictionary* (1964) flatly affirmed that "the general tone of monotony and reiteration, which is the author's intention, greatly increases the novel's effectiveness."[8] But the next year the Brown-McCourt-Daniells view became a quasiofficial one encapsulated by Hugo McPherson in the *Literary History of Canada*: "Ross does not always escape the trap of a reiteration that is merely reflex, yet in technique his book remains one of the most finished works that Canada has yet produced."[9]

This initial consensus is marked by its central concern for the craft of fiction—for both the potentialities and the limits imposed by the choice of specific forms and techniques. If such concern is strict about failures, it also demonstrates an appreciative, even a fraternal sympathy with the artist as he encounters formal problems. Ross's failure to avoid monotonous repetition can be further measured against an aesthetic law first formulated by Yvor Winters as the fallacy of expressive, or imitative, form.[10] This principle holds that a writer fails when he imitates closely in form or expression that state of feeling or being he means to communicate, as, for example, in the attempt to express a state of uncertainty by uncertainty of expression, in writing chaotically in order to express chaos, or in using monotonous forms to convey monotony. Brown's reference to the weaknesses inherent in the diary form and Daniells' hint that Ross's difficulty in sustaining full credibility may be inevitable are consistent with Winters' effort to understand the dynamics governing literary forms, and thus anticipate one means by which Ross's craftsmanship may be more closely assessed. The recent critics, however, have neither refuted this point of the initial consensus nor agreed with it; they have simply dismissed it. Ostensibly the intent may be to free the novel from such formal strictures, but the effect has been to inhibit and reduce any recognition of Ross's control over his material. The result is not sympathetic concern for Ross's problems as an artist, but rather an invitation to the reader to replace, or at least rival, his creativity.

The new direction is illustrated by Laurence Ricou; in *Vertical Man/Horizontal World* (1973) he rejects, somewhat imperiously, the consensus I have been sketching: "The overpowering monotony of the novel remains, however, a problem for the characters and does not become, as Daniells suggests, boring in itself."[11] Ricou doesn't explain why this is so, but one implication of his judgment is probably more telling than the reasons for it. It should first be noted that Ricou's judgment dismisses Brown's worry that the novel's techniques may have damaged its reader's capacity for empathy with the characters. For Ricou it is the characters alone who are overpowered by monotony; the reader, somehow, is exempt. Ricou here adumbrates a strategy which pervades the recent criticism. Whereas earlier commentators tended to assume that the novel's force was dependent upon the reader's identification with the characters, and thus upon his share in their experience, the new view requires that he be detached from them so as to second-guess them. This trend in recent criticism, the core of a new consensus, can be called the debunking of Mrs. Bentley.

In 1957 Roy Daniells both summarized and exceeded the early critics' generally sympathetic view of the novel's narrator: "Mrs. Bentley, in whose words the whole is recounted, through whose eyes, by whose sensibility, all is seen and realized, she it is who engrosses the reader's interest and regard.... She is pure gold and wholly credible." Daniells apparently realized his position was extreme; he prefaced this judgment with a warning: "About the characters there is room for some friendly critical disagreement."[12] The disagreement that was coming was friendly enough to Daniells, but hardly so to Mrs. Bentley. Wilfred Cude, in 1973, joined issue with Daniells directly: "Professor Daniells is not correct when he claims Mrs. Bentley 'sees . . . the whole situation with exquisite and painful clarity'; on the contrary, she is often surprised and shocked by contingencies she did not anticipate and cannot really follow."[13] This new stress on the narrator's limited vision has taken the form of searching out faults in her character. The list compiled by Cude and others is now impressive; she is arrogant, obtuse, stubborn, hypocritical, manipulative, smug, dowdy, petty, deceptive, self-indulgent, jealous, mean, bitchy, self-dramatizing, bitter, subject to delusions, fussy, morose—such disesteem reaching a most excruciating point in what must surely be a Freudian misprint by David Stouck: "—so, towards the end, her power to castrate is still sharply voiced. . . ."[14] So thorough has such denigration become that John Moss feels it necessary to enter an apology: "She is an unfortunate creature, with more strength than weakness, more love than animosity, more compassion, more intelligence and imagination, more insight, more integrity than my argument, perhaps, has given her credit for."[15] He should have omitted the "perhaps," but his belated effort to remind us of her good qualities does suggest that Mrs. Bentley's moral character has become an almost incidental victim of her critics' attack on the real target, her role as narrator; what seems like calumny is actually designed to expose her as a most untrustworthy narrator.

It is remarkable, I think, that each of the four essays from the early seventies[16] on *As For Me and My House* is a scenario of what *really* happens in the novel, in each case licensed by an argument that Mrs. Bentley is unreliable because imperceptive, fallible, limited, or contradictory. One suspects that Wayne C. Booth's study of narrative point of view in *The Rhetoric of Fiction* (1961), which first gave wide currency to implications attending the concept of the unreliable narrator, was the immediate stimulus here. None of the four mention Booth, nor do they heed his warnings against the temptations opened by the private ingenuity needed to substitute a correct vision for the narrator's faulty one. One consequence is that the new consensus does *not* include any agreement about what the correct vision is. It also seems clear now why Ricou denies that the novel is boring; certainly not for any reader alerted to the heady possibilities.

There is evidence that this new consensus facilitates the canonization of *As For Me and My House* more than did the one initiated by Brown. The best illustration is Wilfred Cude's argument that Daniells' view of the book is too confining. Limited as Daniells is, says Cude, by his complete faith in Mrs. Bentley's credibility, it is no wonder he finds her narration monotonous. The result is that the novel "thereby emerges, in Professor Daniells' estimation, as an interesting minor work."[17] Once, however, we discard Mrs. Bentley as the trusted reporter whose authority creates the novel's world, we can see the novel as "a Canadian work so finely structured that it invites comparison with fiction in the first rank of English literature."[18] Cude makes the claim, but not the case for the novel's fine structure; his effort is largely expended in pointing out Mrs. Bentley's limitations, yet his instinct for what could be celebrated seems right. Once we agree that Ross deliberately sacrificed the control of a reliable narrator, it would follow that we need to articulate the techniques and structures, presumably much more oblique and subtle ones, by means of which he might continue to shape and guide his readers' perception and understanding. Without the restraints imposed by such means, the reader would of course be left to his own devices, free to imagine and speculate endlessly about the import of what Mrs. Bentley doesn't say and of what she doesn't see.

A full location and description of such structures in the novel remains to be done. Indeed, for reasons which I hope to make clear, the recent critics seem reluctant to do the job, although a few have taken some tentative steps in that direction. One example, an argument offered by John Moss, permits our return to the specific issue originally framed by E. K. Brown and shows how the new consensus allows flaws to be transformed into virtues. Moss's argument, as I understand it, is an attempt to defend Ross's frequent repetitions as the major way in which the objective world of the novel is established by Ross in counterpoint to Mrs. Bentley's more subjective, and therefore more dubious, perceptions.

> Ross orchestrates a relatively limited number of facts into tight, almost brittle, variations which move his novel toward completion.... Each immediately suggests a number of separate contexts and also the residual impact of its repeated appearance in the narrative.... They have been arranged in the text in a sequence of reflexively associated patterns which explore their individual and interrelated potential as objects of response in the limited world of Mrs. Bentley's perception.[19]

Any concern for the wearing effects of repetition has here been replaced with claims for the skilled intricacy with which it is used. The argument is, insofar as I follow it, an interesting one, but the language in which it is expressed is even more remarkable; it betrays a tendency in the recent criticism which itself approaches the fallacy of imitative form in trying to convey the novel's complexity by writing complexly. This complexity, liberally employing the familiar clichés of the New Criticism, is finally so taxing that it raises questions about the critic's conception of his service to a reader. At the very least it argues a militant pedagogic intent, by which the critic cudgels a reader accustomed to the artist's direction into strenuous and independent effort. Brown assumed a working community of feeling and interest; Moss sends the reader out on his own. Moss goes on:

> Ambiguity in Ross's novel, however, is a function of irony. It is not the cause. The external facts are operative on a single plane of reality. Their impact is simple, subtle, and cumulative. It is because of the response they arouse in the recording consciousness of his narrator that they achieve complexity, ambiguity, that their implicit irony is compounds to pathos and tragic ambivalence.[20]

This passage is opaque, but the feeling Moss seems here to demand of the reader is even more awesomely mysterious. We are asked to apprehend the initially simple impact of external fact as compounded, by what Moss believes should be our response to her response, into a force which, like the Puritan God, is inferred from its attributes rather than directly known, a force not named but shadowed forth as complex, ambiguous, tragically ambivalent, pathetic, implicitly ironic. Donald Stephens, in his essay (1965) on the novel, itself a brilliant burlesque of uncurbed criticism, anticipated this exfoliation of critical demands. After explaining paradoxically that "environment plays a strong role in the story, an environment that is at once uncluttered and cluttered," Stephens' persona multiplies the ambiguous paradoxes with abandon.

> Into a treacherous atmosphere like this Ross introduces his main characters. He does not immerse them totally, but rather just dips them into this sheep-dip of futility and sets them into a corner to let the bitter juices seep into their absorbent beings. Perhaps he has not dipped them for long enough, or again, too much, for none of the characters seem to rise out of the story as individuals of total belief. They are at once types and individuals, yet never really discernible as one or the other. Despite this vagueness, the characters can be analyzed; unfortunately with varying degrees of accuracy.[21]

Hilarious, but Stephens' persona also demonstrates how quickly the unleashed critic can reduce a serious novel to farce.

> Mrs. Bentley explains his [her husband's] faults by saying that he expected too much, and when it was not forthcoming he was caught with his moral and intellectual fibres around his ankles.[22]

Yet despite Stephens' cautionary model, "paradox," "tension," "irony," and "ambiguity" persist as the vocabulary by which the new consensus would canonize *As For Me and My House*. The result is odd, even misleading. Again one might expect that such terms would be used to name devices by which Ross, having given up the authority of a reliable narrator, yet retains an artist's control over his reader's response. The subtlety and skill with which he solved the difficult problem posed by the loss of his narrator's reliability would then be a matter for legitimate congratulation. Instead, such terms are more often employed to limn Ross's forfeiture of control, to name devices permitting the reader maximum freedom in competing with Mrs. Bentley. As Wilfred Cude puts it: ". . . once the author invites you to go beyond the narrator's views, you are playing an entirely new game with words."[23] Or, to paraphrase a remark by Northrop Frye, the novel becomes a picnic to which the author brings the words and the reader the meaning. This celebration of control yielded by invitation to the reader has taken two closely related forms, each illustrating a slightly different strategy in the process of canonization. These are the recommendation of complexity as a value in itself, particularly the sense of complexity generated and contributed by the reader, and the deregionalization of the novel.

Daniells had insisted in 1957 that "simplicity is the keynote of Ross's artistic achievement, the frankest simplicity of setting, of plot, of characterization, as of theme and style."[24] The new consensus disagrees. The usual means of this disagreement is to point to the complicating maneuvers required of the reader when he accepts the invitation to track, evaluate, and correct Mrs. Bentley's judgments. Ricou, for example, praises "the effective counterpoint of her opinions and the objective judgment the reader is encouraged to make which enhances the sense of psychological complexity."[25] Fine, but it must also be recognized that Ricou gives the reader the hardest job in this collaboration. Ross need only provide her opinions, which, in the strictest sense, is all he does provide; it is up to the reader to rise to the bait of encouragement, to struggle for a judgment more objective than hers, and it is finally *this* judgment which not only enhances the sense of psychological complexity, but creates it in the first place. One is left wondering whether the reader's appreciation of complexity is elicited less by the novel than by what the critic has asked him to do. Stephens' antic persona imposes the reader's new tasks even more firmly.

> Before a reader can understand the other characters in the novel, he must examine Mrs. Bentley. She is the narrator, and if the reader takes her at her literal worth, then all the characters become exceptionally clear. But she is a paradox, and there becomes the necessity to probe beyond what she says superficially, and to make conjectures as to her real meaning.[26]

The reader is first promised understanding and exceptional clarity, a promise abruptly betrayed when Mrs. Bentley is revealed as "a paradox," and then, signaled by the cunningly ambiguous placement of "superficially," slyly warned that any problem or conjecturing he does, lest *it* be superficial, had better take account of the difference between what she says superficially and what she says profoundly. With his happy flair for excess, Stephens' persona goes on to claim that the reader's efforts in this direction can even repair flaws in Ross's artistry that must be otherwise conceded: "The only way the reader can realize the portent of all the characters is to let his imagination have full rein. Despite the shallowness of the characters, they are interesting, and at an intense, rather than a cursory, examination."[27] Any interest that can be found in characters called shallow derives here only from the intense quality in the reader's examination, itself possible only if he finally slips any reins Ross might still hold, however loosely, in his hands.

By multiplying both the number and the difficulty of the jobs requisite to the reader's full apprehension of complexity, the recent critics have not only humbled any role for Ross's directing intelligence in the novel; they have also insinuated that Ross has committed certain hostile acts against his reader. A revealing case in point is W. H. New's essay, significantly titled "Sinclair Ross's Ambivalent World" (1969). New begins by confessing that the last line of the novel "haunts" him. "The ambivalence of it puzzles, irritates, confuses."[28] One might think this a reason for rejecting the novel, or at least its last line, especially since New believes that such irritating ambivalence is Ross's "desired aim." But New generously justifies this aim by explaining its effect, and the defence is by now the familiar one. Ambivalence emerges

> out of a carefully constructed web of viewpoints, Mrs. Bentley's and ours, pitted ironically against each other so that we come to appreciate not only the depth and complexity of the narrator and her situation, but also the control in which Ross artistically holds her words.[29]

New's claims about Ross's control and his "careful" construction of *our* viewpoint is compromised a bit by the image of ourselves as gamecocks thrust by Ross, that is, "pitted," against Mrs. Bentley; I'm less sure that "web" makes her a spider to our fly. Our suspicions, however, now aroused, New implies that Ross bloodies us so that he may tease us: "we suspect all of her affirmations, finding in them partial truths that ring ironically against the complex realities Ross ultimately allows us to glimpse."[30] Teasing glimpses make for complexities that can only be suspected, and it is bootless, New assures us, to hope for any more clarity; Ross has deliberately forestalled it: "what Ross does to communicate these ironies and ambiguities is to blur the edges of his images. Absolutes do not exist."[31] Ross's aim, New concludes, has been to deny us not only clarity of perception or understanding, but finally any certainty at all. "The ambivalence is founded in his imagery, founded in the lives of the characters and the nature of their world, germane to the whole novel, magnificently distilling what it has tried to say. When we become conscious of this, we become not only involved in the book, but like the people of Horizon, no matter how apparently sure of themselves, still sensitive to doubt and so to reality as well."[32] If the last phrase means anything, it means that the novel is intended to leave us skeptical and unsure. After being puzzled, irritated, confused, pitted against Mrs. Bentley (gamecock or spider), teased with glimpses of complex reality, bedimmed by images deliberately blurred, made skeptical and unsure, the reader is asked by New to find this distillation magnificent and sensitizing. Ricou, for one, seems willing to do this: "*As For Me and My House*, as W. H. New notes, derives much of its effectiveness as a novel from its ambiguous resolution."[33] But New's demands mean less a canonization of the novel than of its gladly suffering reader.

It is, I suspect, natural for literary critics to recommend books on the same grounds that castor oil is prescribed; the experience is not pleasant, but it may be good for you. If Margaret Atwood is right about quintessential Canadian victimage, it may be even more natural for Canadian critics. In any event, New's position is only the most severe of those from which *As For Me and My House* has been recommended. The early critics inclined to value the novel as successfully realistic and regional fiction, as a graphic evocation of life on the Canadian prairies during the Depression. Edward McCourt, for example, praised the novel's "power to suggest the atmosphere of a prairie region which the reader, whether or not he is familiar with the Western scene, finds wholly convincing."[34] For a reader native to the region, the first pleasure here, however grimly qualified, is one of recognition; Margaret Laurence has testified that "it had an enormous impact on me, for it seemed the only completely genuine one I had ever read about my own people, my own place, my own time. It pulled no punches about life in the stultifying atmosphere of small and ingrown towns, and yet it was illuminated with compassion."[35] McCourt would extend this value to those born elsewhere or too late to know the Depression prairies: "even the most unimaginative of readers must feel the grit between the teeth. . . ."[36] This is by far the most straightforward way to defend the novel's place within a Canadian canon. If the novel succeeds in conveying what it was to live in a significant section of the country at a significant time in the nation's history, however gritty the sensation, then it will contribute to that common, although vicarious experience which creates a group, in this case a Canadian, identity.

But the early critics were also alert to dimensions of the novel which made it more than a valuable regional document. E. K. Brown believed that Ross had "contrived with amazing success to be both local and universal"; the novel is "a realistic representation of a community and a way of living, and no less an insight into powerful and permanent emotions."[37] Brown anticipates the efforts of subsequent critics to expand our sense of a more universal study of human psychology conducted within the novel, but such work has also been marked by a decreasing, and at times a debunking, interest in the book's specifically regional value. The language of transformation is again familiar. New, for example, speaks of "the ironic tension which raises the book from a piece of 'regional realism' to a complex study of human responses."[38] Laurence Ricou, whose chapter on Ross is titled "The Prairie Internalized," contends that "Ross introduces the landscape as a metaphor for man's mind, his emotions, his soul perhaps, in a more thorough and subtle way than any previous writer"; finally, "Mrs. Bentley's landscape is completely subjective."[39] The result is that "Ross represents both an escape from self-conscious local colour and a much more profound, if unconscious, feeling for place."[40] Here, as in New's remark, the terms associated with regionalism grow slightly pejorative; and we edge again toward darker complexities as we are asked to share a feeling for place, a feeling here defined as an unconscious one. McCourt had promised us vicarious participation in the gritty life of the Depression prairies; Ricou offers, by stressing the psychic complications, an even grimmer experience: "An empty, unproductive, and oppressive existence in an empty, unproductive and oppressive landscape makes an intense fictional impact."[41] No doubt, especially when we remember that Ricou sees landscape as a metaphor for man's mind, but if this concussion is urged, not *pro patria*, but for possible insight into the general human condition defined as twice empty, unproductive, and oppressive, there would seem to be less urgency for suffering it.

But the greatest pressure for deregionalization comes not from the interest in the novel's relevance to universally human matters, but, rather more narrowly, from a concentration on the psychology or sociology of the artist figure. In 1960 Warren Tallman raised the point at some length.

> The novel is a study of a frustrated artist—actually, a non-artist—one unable to discover a subject which will release him from his oppressive incapacity to create. The excellence of the study traces to the remarkable resourcefulness with which Ross brings into place the day-to-day nuances of Mrs. Bentley's struggling consciousness as he builds up her account of an artist who cannot create because he cannot possess himself and who cannot possess himself because there is no self to possess.[42]

Tallman is obviously struggling to do justice to Ross's handling of a very difficult problem, the task of credibly portraying a failed artist—such an artist should have enough artistry to convince us that he merits the term, but not enough to be successful. Tallman complicates the matter by introducing the term "non-artist," and further compounds it by his final reductive series which sends Philip Bentley to the vanishing point. As Stephens' irrepressible persona says, "Philip never really emerges as a character, but then maybe that is his condition."[43] As late as 1971, Sandra Djwa listed, among the "disturbing critical issues" still raised by the novel, "the validity of Philip's claim to be an artist."[44] But Tallman goes on to a conclusion that is more convincing because it redefines the issue in terms that are directly relevant to the novel's status within a national canon.

> Certainly there are more deep-reaching portraits of the artist, for in this novel all is muffled within Philip's inarticulation, but none that I know represents with so steady a pressure of felt truth the pervasive undermining of all vital energies which occurs when the would-be artist's creativity is thwarted.[45]

The clear implication of Tallman's judgment was soon announced by Hugo McPherson in the *Literary History of Canada*: "Ross's central theme is the imagination and its failure in Canada."[46] And in *Survival* (1972), Margaret Atwood accepts and explains the novel as a work specifically shaped by and reflective of the nation's peculiar cultural conditions.

> The paradox that confronts us is that Ross, Buckler and Gibson have created memorable works of art out of the proposition that such a creation, in their environment, is impossible. They are Position Three writers naming the conditions of Position Two, making art out of their characters' inability to do so.[47]

The most recent critics have taken some tentative steps beyond Miss Atwood's position, thus initiating a trend that might be called the denationalization of *As For Me and My House*. The quotation from John Moss that begins this essay clearly announced it. The principal method here, of which there are as yet only hints, seems an attempt to probe Margaret Atwood's paradox of an artistically successful portrait of a failed artist in order to uncover its more metaphysical or cosmic implications. Ricou, for instance, has observed that "it is appropriate that a novel which devotes so much attention to life's meaninglessness should have an aspiring artist as a central character,"[48] thus opening the possibility of Philip as a thoroughly postmodern or existential artist enacting cosmic meaninglessness. But the most substantial illustration of this new tendency is offered by David Stouck. Stouck begins by arguing that the novel has not yet been accorded its proper place in the canon precisely because the previous consensus about its regional values was a mistaken one.

> Although in discussing Canadian literature it has become common practice to mention Sinclair Ross as a fiction writer of the prairies, *As For Me and My House* has not been recognized for the remarkable novel that it is,—a book which ultimately transcends all regional considerations.

Stouck's technical quarrel with the original consensus is the familiar one.

> Perhaps the major reason for the limited critical appreciation of the book is for the mistaken belief that because Mrs. Bentley is the narrator, she is the novel's chief character. This assumption relegates Philip Bentley to a secondary role and overlooks the artist's story theme which gives the novel its universal interest.[49]

This is, then, what happens when a reader properly compensates for Mrs. Bentley's limitations: Philip is restored to the centre of the novel and its universal theme of the artist stands revealed. Stouck's version of the kind of compensating required is also used to settle the question of Philip's credibility as an artist: "Mrs. Bentley's viewpoint is a sympathetic one, but at the same time its limitations preserve the mystery that surrounds creative genius; for though Philip is a failure, he is still an artist."[50] I submit that here the debunking of Mrs. Bentley has taken us about as far into the obscure as we should go; released from her viewpoint, the reader must generate and supply the mystery; once surrounded by this fog of unknowing, we are free to imagine anything, even that Philip is an artist of genius. Stouck virtually replaces Ross the artist with the reader as artist. It is no wonder that he claims the novel as "a *Künstlerroman*—which at its core worries the ever-anxious relationship between art and life."[51] Stouck's insistence that *As For Me and My House* is self-reflexive—that is, a novel about itself, a work of art about the work of art—is consistent with a recent trend in international criticism. A typical example is J. Hillis Miller's introduction (1971) to Dickens' *Bleak House* which begins: "*Bleak House* is a document about the interpretation of documents. Like many great works of literature it raises questions about its own status as a text. The novel doubles back on itself or turns itself inside out."[52] But notice also that Stouck's phrasing promises even more trouble for the already burdened reader—worry and ceaseless anxiety about the very enterprise of reading itself. What began with McCourt's prescription for regional grit has become, in Stouck's formulation, a cosmic purgative.

I have tried to show how the new consensus made possible by the debunking of Mrs. Bentley has accelerated the process of canonization for

As For Me and My House. I have also described some of the implications, with emphasis on their disturbing qualities, of this acceleration: a propensity to convert flaws into enhancing virtues; an often tortured complication of critical language, particularly by a penchant for the vagaries of "tension," "irony," "paradox," and "ambiguity"; the deregionalization of the novel, finally by concentration on the artist figure as the centre of universal themes; the progressive enlargement of the reader's responsibility for contributing meaning, with its concomitant humbling of the role allowed Ross's directing intelligence. If *As For Me and My House* is to be accepted into any canon of enduring value by these means, the result will be a singular disservice to Sinclair Ross, the novel, its readers, and, not least, the enterprise of criticism in Canada.

1. Toronto, 1974, pp. 165, 150.
2. In a CBC interview with Earle Toppings now available on cassette tape from Ontario Institute for Studies in Education, 1971, Van Nostrand Reinhold Ltd.
3. Toronto, 1949, p. 99.
4. Toronto, 1970, p. 105.
5. *Canadian Forum*, 21 (July, 1941), 124.
6. McCourt, p. 102.
7. Toronto, 1957, p. viii.
8. Toronto, 1964, p. 133.
9. Toronto, 1965, p. 706.
10. See Winters, *In Defense of Reason*, Denver, 1947, p. 64.
11. Vancouver, 1973, p. 88.
12. Daniells, pp. vi–vii.
13. "Beyond Mrs. Bentley: A Study of *As For Me and My House*," *Journal of Canadian Studies*, 8:1 (February, 1973), 4.
14. "The Mirror and the Lamp in Sinclair Ross's *As For Me and My House*," *Mosaic*, 7:2 (Winter, 1974), 145.
15. Moss, p. 155.
16. The essays by Wilfred Cude, Lawrence Ricou, John Moss, and David Stouck.
17. Cude, p. 3.
18. Cude, p. 18.
19. Moss, p. 157.
20. Moss, p. 158.
21. "Wind, Sun and Dust," in *Writers of the Prairies*, ed. Donald G. Stephens (Vancouver, 1973), pp. 176, 177–178; the essay was originally published in *Canadian Literature*, No. 23 (Winter, 1965).
22. Stephens, p. 180.
23. Cude, p. 4.
24. Daniells, p. viii.
25. Ricou, p. 82.
26. Stephens, p. 178.
27. Stephens, p. 181.
28. In *Writers of the Prairies*, p. 183; the essay was originally published in *Canadian Literature*, No. 40 (Spring, 1969).
29. New, pp. 183–184.
30. New, p. 185.
31. New, p. 187.
32. New, p. 188.
33. Ricou, p. 89.
34. McCourt (revised edition, 1970), p. 102.
35. "Introduction," Sinclair Ross, *The Lamp at Noon and Other Stories* (Toronto, 1968), p. 7.
36. McCourt (revised edition), p. 102.
37. Brown, p. 124.
38. New, p. 188.
39. Ricou, pp. 82, 81.
40. Ricou, p. 90.
41. Ricou, p. 94.
42. "Wolf in the Snow," in *A Choice of Critics*, ed. George Woodcock (Toronto, 1966), p. 62; the essay was originally published in *Canadian Literature*, No. 5 (Summer, 1960) and No. 6 (Autumn, 1960).
43. Stephens, p. 180.
44. "No Other Way: Sinclair Ross's Stories and Novels," in *Writers of the Prairies*, p. 201; the essay was originally published in *Canadian Literature*, No. 47 (Winter, 1971).
45. Tallman, p. 62.
46. McPherson, p. 705.
47. Toronto, 1972, pp. 191–192.
48. Ricou, p. 88.
49. Stouck, pp. 142–143.
50. Stouck, p. 150.
51. Stouck, p. 143.
52. Penguin edition, 1971, p. 11.

Robert Kroetsch's Early Novels

Hazard refused to explain what happened next. I begged him in the interest of logic, of continuity, in the need to instruct and direct future generations, to give me a clue.

The narrator of *The Studhorse Man* (1969) makes a plea that echoes through the reviews of Robert Kroetsch's first three novels. F. W. Watt found his first novel, *But We Are Exiles* (1965), both "powerful" and "incoherent" and lamented that "the motives and needs of the river-pilot protagonist, Peter Guy, remain mysterious to the end." J. M. Stedmond felt that two of the key incidents in Kroetsch's second novel, *The Words of My Roaring* (1966), were "gratuitous" and a third of "little apparent narrative meaning," speculating, however, that these incidents "may be intended to add appropriately modern dark elements to the robust comic scenes." Gordon Roper, discussing *The Studhorse Man*, was moved to apologize for this attempt to explain what was going on in the book: "My transcendental abstracting may make the book seem woolly; it is not. . . , and then explained that Kroetsch was working in a way "which sends out reverberations like a struck bell." I take these remarks (from the *University of Toronto Quarterly* annual reviews of Canadian letters for 1966, 1967, and 1970) as testimony to the fact that Kroetsch's novels contain, and sometimes only barely contain, a verbal energy which is at once remarkable and elusive—an energy often in defiance of logic and continuity which has provoked the reviewers without immediately satisfying them. What generates much of this energy, and much that is elusive about it, is Kroetsch's increasingly keen sense of the difficulties in recreating experience in language. He has insisted, in an interview with Margaret Laurence (in *Creation*, ed. Robert Kroetsch, new press, 1970), that their function as Western Canadian authors is "in making a new literature out of a new experience." And he goes on to say: "In the process I have become somewhat impatient with certain traditional kinds of realism. . . ." Kroetsch's first three novels are interesting in part because they record attempts to capture vivid local experience in styles which probe deliberately and step-by-step beyond the conventional realism and regionalism of the short stories with which he began his career. But they are even more interesting because together they dramatize an intriguing interplay of answers to the question of just how experience itself is to be defined. The question is of interest for any novelist, and his answers to it do much to illuminate his work, but in Kroetsch's treatment, matters of craft are deliberately extended to engage analogous human and moral issues, and his novels become graphic parables of the ways in which efforts to gratify needs, even lusts for significant experience generate moral consequences.

The setting of the first novel, *But We Are Exiles*, is the M. V. *Nahanni Jane* with "one more downriver trip to complete; five hundred miles to run to the Arctic coast; eleven hundred miles to crawl back, bucking the Mackenzie's freezing current, then crossing Great Slave Lake. . . ." The Mackenzie is the novel's most powerful antagonist, its chief characteristic a resistance to human understanding and control. "Man intruded only occasionally on this blur of landscape. . . . The chaos had not yet been resolved into form." Claimed as a highway by men, the river challenges them literally at every turn, "a maze and tangle of channels that confound all but the best pilots; in an epidemic of ponds and lakes and marshes." The best pilots master the river, reduce its chaos to comprehensible form, and it is the pilot's function which is the clue to the task Kroetsch has here set himself—to reduce the endless detail of the river, the minutiae of life on a working river boat, to coherent narrative form. Kroetsch's descriptions of what the discipline of piloting means for Peter Guy, the novel's protagonist, who has spent six years learning his craft, apply pointedly to his own efforts to command his narrative raw material. For example, both the pilot's and the novelist's craft require the acquisition of a new perspective, a process necessary yet painful because of a certain loss of awe. As a novice pilot, Peter Guy had found the landscape beautiful and mysterious in its natural chaos. He had "thrilled to this new unknown within an unknown," but he quickly discovers that the river yields only to "a man with experience and judgment, who could read the meaning in a shade of colour, who could grip the wheel and guess his way below the surface—." Similarly, Kroetsch must discover a way to make his material, originally exotic to the reader, somehow familiar and workaday enough to allow full participation in the plot's adventures without losing a sense of novelty and excitement. The need is for a careful balance. "Boat and river and sky and a thin line of earth and around every bend another bend. All held in delicate and fluid balance by the pilot." What is best in *But We Are Exiles* is its achievement of such a balance in the organization of external detail. The major quality of the third person narrative voice, scrupulously limited so that it enters only the mind of Peter Guy and then only rarely, is a cool precision which has the effect of unobtrusively instructing and refocusing the reader's view. Here, for example, is the novel's second paragraph:

> Peter gave a jerk, another, to set the hooks, his stomach going queasy, and now the grappling-hooks and line and whatever it was

they had snagged began to come up, heavy, still too far down to be seen in the sun-filtering green and then dark of the water; the line curled dripping around his high-topped boots as if to entangle him; the wet, cold line stiffened his fingers.

The care with which the details are made discrete, then set in a precise sequence, the notion of minute changes in tactile and visual sensations, and the barest hint of the emotions which accompany this simple action are typical of Kroetsch's procedures. In much the same way that Peter Guy learned his piloting from the Indian, old Jonas Bird, we learn from Kroetsch "to know a wind spot from a rock riffle, a boil spot from a hidden boulder," and gradually the unfamiliar world of bollards, ratchets, and sturgeon-head scows, of "crooked backs and chars and inconnu," of the Hume River, Aklavik, San Sault Rapids, and the Ramparts becomes an experienced, if precarious, order which allows us to share genuinely in life on board the *Nahanni Jane*.

But if controlling the chaos of the river with the craft of the pilot is deeply satisfying for Peter Guy, and by analogy allows a solution to Kroetsch's major narrative problem, both can be said to use discipline as a means of escape from another kind of chaos. On the river "the pilot's eyes and hands were in isolated yet absolute command. Pure. He wanted to shout the word. This is mine. Storm, ice, wind, rock—those can challenge me. But here a man is defined free from the terrors of human relationships." Guy has become "a white river bum with a river in his head to keep everything else out" in desperate flight from the shock of his discovery, six years before, of the girl he loves in bed with "his best if very new friend; . . . the eloquence of flesh and desire caught dispassionately in the glass mirror inside the door." But escape is finally impossible for Guy; the friend, Mike Hornyak, continues to dominate his life. Now owner of the *Nahanni Jane* and married to the girl Kettle, Hornyak is killed shortly before the action of the novel begins. The search for, eventual recovery, and final disposition of his body and the presence of his widow complicate the boat's already difficult last trip before freeze-up and become the physical counterparts of the characters' emotions as they attempt to weigh and assign responsibility for the series of events that result in Hornyak's death. The situation is resonant and compelling, kept from melodrama by the precise restraint of the narrative voice, and it permits Kroetsch to open such issues as exile from home, the demands of the past as they surface in present guilt, and the nature of collective responsibility. But in the novel these issues are finally and only suggestive because, as representative of "the terrors of human relationships," they remain beyond the limits of a craft that has few resources for controlling them. Like the craft of piloting, which for Guy keeps "everything else out," Kroetsch's choice of method leaves the more profound dimensions of his material in the realm of chaos—provocative, but in the last analysis unclear.

The novel's major characters share the reader's uncertainty about their motives and emotions. Uniformly and credibly laconic, they are unwilling or unable to explain themselves. Peter Guy asks Kettle why she had allowed him to discover her with Hornyak: "'Did you know it was unlocked?' 'Yes.' 'Why?' 'I don't know why.' 'Tell me.' 'I've wondered often.'" Kettle asks Guy to explain the crew's reaction to Hornyak's recovered body which the boat is carrying upriver: "'Why are they all afraid, Pete?' 'I'm not sure.' 'Are you afraid, Pete?' 'I keep wondering. I don't know.'" The limits Kroetsch has accepted make it impossible for the narrative voice to add very much to an understanding of a motive. After a key decision by Guy, the narrator can only report that he made it, "knowing all the time that he did not know why he himself must get back to the boat." Restrained from direct explanation, Kroetsch's method seeks to illuminate inner states by a technique akin to Eliot's objective correlative, a reliance on the precise image of external detail to evoke and thus display the equivalent feeling. The first, tense meeting between Guy and Kettle, after six years and Hornyak's death, is typical. Kettle offers Guy a cup of tea:

> Her elbow brushed his bare arm as she turned to give him a mug. She offered him the mug handle first, her beautiful large hands cupping the mug's chipped bottom.
>
> Awkwardly he accepted, her fingers touching his. They were both silent; then into the quiet of the cabin crashed the high-pitched whine of the motorboats that were dragging the river. Peter bent to glance out the back window.

The requirements here are fairly simple, and the arrangement of detail economically and accurately reflects the shy but reawakening sensuality between the two as it is curbed by their turbulent memories of Hornyak, but like most understatement, it leaves the reader to supply the connections which would carry the moment beyond itself to become part of some larger pattern of meaning. Here Kroetsch clearly shares the belief that a novelist's job is to exhibit and not to explicate, and there is even an explicit hint in the novel that meaning can be genuinely located only in the small, overt patterns of human gesture. Kettle and Guy manage to forget Hornyak only after they participate in an Eskimo drum dance in Aklavik. Kettle explains that "dancing says it" and, of a song she has sung,

"It's the gestures, really, not the words." Then, to forestall Guy's returning memories of Hornyak, she offers her flesh: "'Touch is real,' she said. 'Touch is how we can know.' . . . 'I taste you. I smell you. Even in all the darkness.'" But the situation also makes clear that she is expressing only a variation of Guy's repeatedly shattered hope that the immediate, careful gestures demanded by his craft will somehow exclude the chaos of time, love, and guilt. And the analogy holds. Kroetsch's choice of a restrained narrative perspective, devoted largely to the precise display of detail and gesture, is simply too limited to contain and shape the potentially rich consequences it sets in motion; yet what is most interesting about the novel is that it offers another mode of capturing experience which is an alternative to Guy's—and to Kroetsch's—effort to confine experience through careful discipline.

Mike Hornyak, less a character than a force in the novel, opposes discipline with appetite. He is defined almost exclusively by his lust for fulfillment. "I know what I want. You see that, Guy? I know till I ache from my balls to breakfast." Like Guy, he seeks to master chaos, but his impulse is to consume rather than to control: "'Chaos,' Mike said. 'We've got some chaos to contend with. So hand me that bottle under your seat.'" And Kettle can say of him: "He consumed me the way he consumed everything." Present in the novel only in the memories of others, Hornyak comes to represent the disembodied chaos, "the terrors of human relationships," from which Guy seeks to flee. Predatory in life, Hornyak is preyed upon in death as the living invest him with powers mysterious and destructive, yet fascinating and wholly irresistible. In fact, as the novel's epigraph from Ovid's account of Narcissus suggests and as key incidents confirm, Hornyak is Peter Guy's yearned-for and fated self, the image of consuming energy which causes Guy to move so erratically through the novel: "Running and searching. That was it. He was searching too; even as he fled." As if acknowledging the limits of his chosen method, Kroetsch creates Hornyak as a figure well beyond those limits, a figure who risks all, even to his own destruction, in order to command experience by devouring it. To show the full force of Hornyak's image, Kroetsch finally chooses to enlarge his narrative perspective in order to reflect Hornyak's passionate apprehension of experience, and in doing so, he concludes the novel in a manner well beyond its original restraint, a manner which edges toward impressionistic chaos.

The novel ends as Peter Guy, like Narcissus, confronts his water-held image. Adrift on a barge he has cut loose from the *Nahanni Jane* as she struggles through a freezing storm on Great Slave Lake, released then from his obligation and discipline as the boat's pilot, and alone with the body of Mike Hornyak, Guy returns in memory to the journey west, "wheeling bird-free through the dry prairies," he had shared with Hornyak six years earlier. The memory is recorded as an orgiastic inventory of impressions, the landscape from the angle of a speeding Rolls Royce, a Gargantuan movable picnic, and the wash of a hundred beer parlors between Manitoba and Banff.

> And at Gull Lake a big H turns and turns on top of a big hotel. Turning and turning, an H red on one side, green on the other, like running lights; winding people in off the road. They drank beer at noon. And they looked for the lake at Gull Lake. 'Where's the water?' Mike pleaded to a man with a white walking-cane.

Half comic, half frantic in his plea for life-giving water, Mike Hornyak transforms the experience in Guy's memory from spree to quest. The details of experience are still precisely discrete, but their connections have become urgent, random, and paratactic as Guy's hard-won discipline is displaced by his share in Hornyak's desperate and now almost mythic lusts. The mixture of styles chosen to convey this displacement in turn moves Kroetsch toward a dilemma which he himself phrases in the novel as another of Guy's memories. Guy remembers his father's car "so heavy that when it was moving fast the brakes weren't strong enough to stop it; it rolled and the driver had to wait until it quit. His father delighted in the speed, yet was tortured by the immorality of steering a car that was in fact out of control." Similarly, Kroetsch's problem is to curb the new momentum of the final section into a resolution which will be consistent with the whole narrative. Like Guy's father, he has difficulty stopping it. The experience of the journey west vivid now in memory, Guy at last finds the courage to look at Hornyak's dead face, and the result is his final explosive act:

> And the strength born of his heard laughter: the body toppled stiff from the canoe; hit the water; was lost in the snarl and riot of waves. He did not lock the door, and wrapped in the quilt and tarpaulin he lay in the small canoe. Curled in the quilt and tarpaulin he heard the slamming door, hour after hour. . . . and as it closed he was slammed back into darkness again, the silence again, and the soft delirium of his impassioned motion.

The image is dramatically climactic; something has been resolved for Guy so that he can deliberately take Hornyak's place in the canoe which is both coffin and shelter, but here it stops and the reader is suddenly left to infer the meaning of that resolution. The question of whether Guy survives the experience remains open, but more important is the equally open question of how Guy's final action is to be understood. Is it a final reconciliation between two disparate attitudes toward experience, an acknowledgment by Guy of his essential identity with Hornyak? Or is it a violent usurpation, a repudiation or exorcism of Hornyak's memory and all that it represents? It is impossible to be certain. That the ambiguity of the ending may be intended, that Kroetsch himself may have remained uncertain about the proper interrelationships of discipline and desire in the apprehension of experience is suggested by his next novel, *The Words of My Roaring*, in which he again explores those relationships.

In *The Words of My Roaring*, Kroetsch recreates the Hornyak figure in the person of Johnnie J. Backstrom, thirty-three-year-old Alberta undertaker, novice, and underdog Social Credit candidate for MLA from a drought-stricken, depression-locked prairie constituency, a man "six-four in my stocking feet, or nearly so, a man consumed by high ambitions, pretty well hung, and famed as a heller with women." What was shadowy and therefore sinister about the figure in *But We Are Exiles* is dissipated here by letting Backstrom narrate the novel, voicing the plenitude of his experience in a rhetoric which replaces discipline and precision with a roaring excess. The core of Backstrom's character, like Hornyak's, is the compulsive avidity of his desires. "I have a large jaw and mouth, my appetite is healthy. My eyes are twenty-twenty and so eager they hate to sleep. My ears are wax-free and larger than normal. I consume and I consume." Backstrom's frequent announcements of his capacities are little more than boastful articulations of the Hornyak principle, another way to identify Lear's "unaccommodated man," but Kroetsch has also found a style which fleshes the man, which richly and credibly demonstrates how such capacities function to apprehend and organize, and thus to define particular experience. The simplest element of this style is the miscellaneous catalogue, the inventory of what Backstrom consumes.

> Yes sir, I consumed—pineapple squares and strawberry shortcake, Dutch apple pie and hot dogs with raw onions and whisky and ice cream an sour-cream raisin pie and affection and love and saskatoon pie and generosity and deference and admiration and adulation. I consumed and I consumed.

The itemized contents of the church ladies' food booths at a local stampede and of the audience response to his inspired political speech are focused even as they are confused in the capacious alembic of Backstrom's appetite, and the narrative is rich with these catalogues of local life as they pass through his eager eyes and wax-free ears into language.

But it is another, and more subtle kind of inventory which is Kroetsch's brightest achievement in the novel. The style may depend heavily on the well-worn colloquialisms of the region, but we must see the use to which Kroetsch has put them. Consider Backstrom's explanation for driving his hearse into a telephone pole: "'I had a pretty good jag on. I was drunker than a skunk. I was three sheets to the wind. What a bagful. Right to the gills.'" This is in fact an inventory of the very conventional, once original, still tangy phrases for capturing the extravagant quality of this experience. Here Backstrom is using the clichés deliberately and woodenly in order to bait Doc Murdock, who is both his political opponent and father-confessor, but Kroetsch repeatedly shows us that it is Backstrom's habit to multiply and play with such phrases, and this verbal compulsion in turn convinces us of Johnnie's nagging dissatisfaction with any one of them, his near-desperate urge to name the experience by trying a succession of them. The habit further suggests Kroetsch's own growing impatience with the conventional language of his region. In his modified travel book, *Alberta* (published by Macmillan of Canada in 1968), Kroetsch justifies in part his own efforts to catalogue imaginatively the province in which he was born by saying: "The process of naming is hardly begun in Alberta. We who live here so often cannot name the flowers, the stones, the places, the events, the emotions of our landscape; they await the kind of naming that is the poetic act." Backstrom's occasional efforts to be originally poetic are strained, but he is an adept at folk speech, and the flair with which he tastes, combines, occasionally surmounts, and often brightens its figures in a headlong rush of language gives a new wit and vitality to the old saws. Here, for example, is Backstrom's description of his escape from an embarrassing political debate with Doc Murdock:

> Why embrace the boot that kicks and stomps and tramples you? I simply fled. I confess—I turned at that moment and I bolted. Why turn the other cheek when you can turn both? I took to my waiting heels. I nearly wore the door frame as a collar when I crashed into the open air. I burst out of that prison like a startled Hungarian partridge. I flung myself like so much dishwater into the darkening street.

But Backstrom's ways with folk speech have a function even more important than their transformation of the commonplace by an excess we can savour even as we discount it. As a disembodied Hornyak shows, the danger with such figures is that the more intense their incarnation of voracious appetite, the more they are abstractions—gigantic maws ingesting the world instead of living in it. Without the generous rein of the community's conventional tropes, Johnnie Backstrom might have remained a prairie Whitman, compulsively naming and enumerating his environment in order to make good his boast of containing it. With that rein, Backstrom becomes a credible creature of his time and place. And in fact the community's language is only the most pervasive of the forces which oppose, frustrate, and thus contain his otherwise boundless appetites.

The novel's plot is little more than a string of predicaments for Backstrom—a series of conflicts between his desires and the drought-depressed, wife-nagged, prude-laced, hard-headed world they would consume. These range from the petty annoyances of holes in his socks and dents in his fenders, through the minor embarrassments of an erection in church and the purchase of prophylactics over the counter, through the narrow corners of ordering ten cent beers for twenty-eight voters with only two-forty in his pockets and bidding $128 for a Model-A at a cash auction with even less, to the crowning agony of waiting for the soaking rain he has impulsively promised the constituency in a summer so dry "the fish lose their gills." And here Backstrom is less Hornyak or Whitman than he is Charlie Chaplin, the persistent clown who risks humiliation and defeat because "I wanted to be extravagant once in my life and get away with it. Like a stampede clown, I wanted to duck into my barrel, just in the nick of time. . . . But no, instead of that it was the old misery and woe again." Checked again and again by experience he burns to command, Johnnie's cries of despair are as outrageously lavish as those of his desire: "Gross, gross. My appetites. My longings. My dreams. My deceptions. My fantasies. My Bottomless gullet. My grasping huge fists. My insatiable hunger not just for something but for everything. Gross unto death." But this characteristic rush of phrases, lovingly enumerating his capacities even in the act of condemning them, illustrates the quality which makes the character of Johnnie Backstrom a true comic achievement—he is magnificently incorrigible. He simply refuses to digest the repeated doses of humiliation and defeat, and we leave him struggling with the language to retain his momentarily humble conviction that the soaking rain, which arrived before election day as he predicted it would, was not really of his doing.

This quality is further underscored by Kroetsch's subdued, but unmistakable repetition in this novel of the Hornyak-Guy relationship, this time with the consequences of avaricious desire and careful restraint clearly distinguished. Jonah Bledd, the Guy figure, is Backstrom's best friend "who was always steady as a rock; not much given to laughter, but steady, reliable, levelheaded," and, to point the contrast, "I don't believe he ever quite got loaded, and I don't believe I ever quite failed." Bledd's steady restraint in fact proves unreliable; it fails to sustain him through the shock of losing his job, and he drowns himself. Doc Murdock, "a harsh judge," and one voice of wisdom in the novel, pronounces Jonah's epitaph: "'He was afraid to be a fool. So he was a coward instead.'" Kroetsch has clearly abandoned the restraints he associates with Peter Guy and Jonah Bledd, but the risks he runs in rendering experience as it is present to a figure who passionately dares life, even at the continuous risk of being a fool, are correspondingly great. At times Backstrom is out of his author's effective control and the result sounds too much like a voice that Johnnie himself condemns as "a flatulent windbag," but generally Kroetsch contrives, with a flexible command and mixture of the ribald figures and Biblical echoes of prairie language, to make the words of Backstrom's roaring both credible and engaging. In the process the character becomes memorable, celebrating his experience with comic zest even as it overwhelms him, wisely self-mocking even as he embarks on yet another unwise course.

The creation of Johnnie Backstrom completed Kroetsch's movement from restrained precision as a means of containing experience to more extravagant styles for evoking it. In his next novel, *The Studhorse Man*, the two methods are both present, and the result is an experience both difficult and illuminating for the reader. The novel is ostensibly a biography of Hazard Lepage, a studhorse man dedicated to breeding the perfect line by Poseidon, his great blue stallion. Hazard, like Hornyak and Johnnie Backstrom, is offered as "a man of inordinate lust," "a reckless man," whose motto is upper-case: "NOTHING IN MODERATION," and the problem which seems to face Kroetsch once again is how to order this experience energized by chaotic and imperious appetite without sacrificing its vitality. To do this, Kroetsch uses Demeter Proudfoot, the novel's narrator and Hazard's biographer, but also his frustrated rival in love and at least momentary successor to his mission. Demeter retells Hazard's adventures with all the exactitudes of the biographer's craft; he is indefatigable in his researches into the minutiae of Hazard's past, careful with "mere fact," prodigal with his inventories of localizing detail, and scrupulous in noting that which he fails to discover. Yet his attempts to record a particularly vivid life in a specific time and place are compromised, not only by his frequently lamented inability to collect adequate information, but more seriously by the fact that he is "by profession quite out of my mind." Demeter's profession alerts us to Kroetsch's hybrid method in the novel:

the objective order affirmed by techniques of biography is constantly imposed upon and reorganized by expressions of the biographer's own peculiar appetites—appetites which fuse the pedant's finicky tastes with the libidinous forces alternately stimulated and frustrated by his subject's vagaries. As Demeter puts it: "I myself prefer an ordered world, even if I must order it through the posture of madness. It is the only sane answer to prevailing circumstances." Demeter's posture may be further understood as that of a Peter Guy whose defensive sense of craft has been warped by its response to Hornyak's energies, here those of Hazard Lepage, again the sexual rival whose consuming force is both envied and feared, emulated and repulsed by the man of discipline. Demeter's complex response to Hazard, even more than his violent participation in the climactic events of the plot, makes him an intrusive presence in his own narrative; his self-conscious efforts to escape the limits of disciplined biography with the license claimed by the artist as extreme neurotic are engrossing enough so that Demeter's experience constantly threatens to supplant Hazard's as the novel's subject. And this raises the most serious question about the novel, the question of whether the device of a narrator made unreliable by his self-professed madness is designed to realize the chaotic, but integral vitality shared by Hornyak, Backstrom, and Hazard Lepage, or whether Kroetsch's intention is to show it opposing and finally dissipating that vitality. The answer is disturbing, but inescapable, for Kroetsch is clearly exposing Demeter's narrative as a generally successful act of aggression against Hazard, success marked by the fact that Demeter's actions are in large part responsible for Hazard's literal death.

Just as Johnnie Backstrom is most vivid as he engages the dry prairie world of the thirties, so Hazard is most alive in his frantic efforts to find mares for his stallion amid the distractions of Alberta in the late forties: beer parlors, nearly eight hundred horses loose in blizzard-bound Edmonton, a contest in fancy invective, the RCMP, butchering a pig for a horny widow, a three-day wedding feast, coyote hunters, a poltergeist, and sexual resurrection in an icehouse. These adventures are extravagant to a point just this side of absurdity, yet they remain firmly comic rather than fantastic because they seem grounded in actuality, the flavour of which is most available in Demeter's account when he most effaces himself from it. But Demeter can't let Hazard speak and act for himself, can't let Hazard's world emerge from its antic detail. Demeter's logic is that if "prevailing circumstances" are chaotic enough to approach the absurd, then the usual perspectives must be reversed until madness becomes "the only sane answer" to the need for order. As the consequence of such reasoning, Demeter's madness takes the form of a compulsion to transform his subject, to invest Hazard's extraordinary, but still public adventures with his own private and distorting visions of order and significance.

It is this compulsion which becomes an act of aggression by the artist in Demeter against his subject. This action, threatening to dissolve our sense of an actual Hazard, is begun by reference to the limits of biography, the absence of reliable information which prompts and justifies interpretation and speculation, but Demeter is quick to turn these into alleged deficiencies in Hazard which will sanction the substitution of his own experience: "Fortunately my own experience enabled me to flesh out the bones of his nearly dead memory." Demeter's aggression is further betrayed in his habit of providing fastidious alternatives on the few occasions he allows Hazard to speak in his own voice: "the scene of spring was in that yeasty wind, the high raw odour of mares and spring—... and he said in his crude way, 'that raw bitch of a wind was full of crocuses and snatch.'" Such juxtapositions call attention not only to Demeter straining for eloquence, but explicitly to Hazard's vulgarity, thus preventing the sense of spontaneity which could excuse and even cause our delight in comparable crudities from Johnnie Backstrom. In full flight from Hazard's earthiness, Demeter resorts to a steadily inflationary rhetoric which finally comes near the point where words are separated from their referents altogether. Secure in his bathtub retreat (which he has chosen) in the madhouse (in which he has been confined), Demeter forgets Hazard and reports his own pleasure in listening to the hockey games. This pleasure consists "not only in the air of suppressed and yet impending violence, but also in the rain upon our senses of those sudden and glamorous names," names then woven into a euphonious and extended reverie. Demeter's retreat here to the sheer magic of sounds is his final escape from and perversion of the biographer's task: "I close my eyes against the books and notes and cards and papers heaped about and upon me. My dull task is itself buried in my name-horde." And the Hazard buried under Demeter's name-horde suggests the full extent of Demeter's damage to him. The expressions of Demeter's madness not only displace Hazard as the novel's centre, they rob him of his particularity and thus of his vitality as a character. What was specific in the biographer's view of Hazard comes to seem specious during the madman's flights into name magic; what seemed fact comes to seem factitious until the Hazard who might have rivaled Johnnie Backstrom's solid earthiness becomes as disembodied as the dead Hornyak—a wavering image created by Demeter's narcissistic contemplation.

It is not difficult to see *The Studhorse Man* as a parable in which

Kroetsch deliberately explores once again his own developing conception of the problems, both technical and moral, in capturing the essence of prairie experience in language. And if the novel is properly understood as a display of Demeter's procedures, motivations, and difficulties as an artist rather than as a biography of Hazard Lepage, it suggests that Kroetsch had reached a crucial juncture in his exploration of these problems. He has confessed himself to be restive under the restraints of realism and traditional regionalism—restraints which define the artist's responsibility as mimetic fidelity to some more or less obdurate given existing outside his consciousness. And Kroetsch has reflected his own strong sense of how recalcitrant his material can be, first in dramatizing Peter Guy's struggles to come to terms both with the Mackenzie River and with Hornyak's energies, and then in the physical and social forces which curb and contain the appetites and language of Johnnie Backstrom. But in *The Studhorse Man*, Kroetsch claims, and then explores, a new freedom. By choosing to demonstrate how an artist's consciousness may intrude upon, even substitute itself for, his material, Kroetsch signals a shift in his interest from a mimetic to an expressive theory of art in which the experiencing consciousness is of more concern than that which is experienced. But that he may be uneasy with the implications of this emphasis seems equally clear. By revealing Demeter's enterprise as an act of aggression, perhaps even of revenge against the disturbing vitality of his subject, Kroetsch sympathetically, yet firmly exposes the moral dangers in an expressive theory, particularly the danger of a final solipsism which seeks language to escape the chaotic world of shared human experience by completely denying it. This exposure must have cost Kroetsch some pain, for it is at the expense of his narrator, a figure who obviously fascinates him and whose transforming imagination he has expended much ingenuity to portray. But the case against Demeter's aggression is honestly and dramatically made, and this suggests that the tension between the experiencing mind and the obdurate, chaotic, vital experience it works to capture, the tension variously developed through the first two novels to the direct and destructive confrontation rehearsed in *The Studhorse Man*, remain still unresolved for Kroetsch, still then a source of motive energy for his future work

Some Personal Essays, Mainly Western and Canadian

Praise to the Albany

I sing of the Albany Bar, late of Laramie, Wyoming, for it was more wonderful than McSorley's wonderful saloon, more comforting than Hemingway's clean, well-lighted place, and more lamented in its passing than the tables down at Mory's. For generations the bibuli have celebrated favourite bars as the best possible combination of refuge, creative forum, and all-around lamasery. Let us honour their efforts, for I can no more pass a passable tavern than Mencken or W. C. Fields could go to Philadelphia without hip-flasks. And Laramie (hard Gem City of the Plains to its Chamber of Commerce, but sweet water hole to its surrounding legions of section hands, truckers, cowboys, and tie-hacks) is full of surpassing taverns—Alibi, Poor Bill's Birdcage, Fireside, the Buckhorn, and more. But of all these, the Albany Bar was something special, indeed so absolutely superb as to needs transcend its local fame.

Tosspot memory, running to legend rather than history, has misplaced the Albany's origins. It is known, however, that a bar of that name had been somewhere in town since 1891. The most graceful evidence of its age was a house calendar dated 1907 and illustrated by a Gibson girl with yellow picture hat, parasol, and ample bodice. She was at once muse and alma mater. The great years began in the 1920s with the advent of the incomparable Dewey Bell, first barkeep, then partner, then sole boniface until the end. Dewey opened the doors at 6:00 A.M. to ease the early thirst of the railroaders tending the big 484s that moved the freight over the Sherman range between Laramie and Cheyenne, the steepest grade on the U.P. line. The even dustier trade of minding cattle made the bar into a hiring hall for ranch hands at liberty and laving their tonsils in Albany gargle.

Prohibition had little effect on this occupational therapy; the only marks of the Noble Experiment were some scratches on the backbar from its brief period of storage to elude sequestration by federal agents and an outsized sink with double water pipe to flush and dilute the disappearing booze. From 1928, its last and best location on Grand Avenue faced the rear door of the Gem City Grocery, largest in the Basin, and the grocer increased custom by standing drinks for ranchers in to fill their monthly orders. Its location also permitted citizens to enter for a quick beer, then exit from the alley door convenient to the back vestibules of the three upstairs whorehouses facing Front Street, finally to emerge again from the Albany's innocent front door. Thus were passion and propriety conjoined.

The nymphs departed in the early fifties pursued by a wave of civic outrage over *Redbook*'s exposé of Laramie as Sin City. The alley, once sacred to Venus, became a field of Mars. In fact the Albany's codes duello were so intricate that while the most bellicose tie-hack might amiably overlook direct insults to his mother, once a simple pun became the invitation to step outside. President Kennedy had given a speech in Laramie, several times mentioning Wyoming's newest resource, soda ash. It was perhaps inevitable that the bar's glee over his Boston pronunciation escalated suddenly into whose ash could whip whose, not personal, you understand, but as a fair test among political partisans.

On lazy afternoons the Albany became the club parlour of as venerable a troop of pensioners as ever murmured barracks' tales under the arcades of the Invalides or the Royal Chelsea. The stories were often rousing—for some had helped Pershing chase Villa through Chihuahua—but as often they meandered among the reticulations of aging livers, lights, and prostates. It is significant that the noon to four shift, the peak hours of these gentle revels, was for years conducted by a bartender named Magnus Sandman. Indeed two ancients slipped from life in the bar, one while dreaming in the back room's Morris chair. On the first occasion, Dewey summoned an ambulance, reporting his clearly dead patron as prone to seizures, a prudent phrase used thereafter to cover every emergency.

Until 1964 the Albany's diurnal round closed at eight to facilitate Dewey's nightly games of pan-ginney at Hicks's Card Room on Front Street. In that year more custom accumulated when Floyd Shaman, hitherto auxiliary bartender, persuaded Dewey to remain open until 1:00 A.M. to attract a new clientele, principally Floyd's fellow art students at the university. Again a name proved propitious, for Floyd had the magic. He dispensed the sweet medicine with such geniality that the late crowd evolved tribally. The artists were soon joined by the university's Outing Club—its modest title misleading because it included alpine climbers of no small skill—and then by students and professors from the English and history departments, traditional centres not only of the humanities but, some said, of the ripest grog-blossoms in academe.

Such categories, however, obscure the remarkable individuals so gathered. There was, for example, another Dewey, yclept Drollinger, a diminutive painter whose habit of wearing his glasses across the top of his bald head gave the impression of dual vision, one pair of eyes firmly forward, the other cocked aloft for news from the empyrean. There was Pete Sinclair who, as climbing ranger at the Tetons, helped pluck the hapless Appalachian Club off the mountain, an adventure he recorded for *Sports*

Illustrated under the title "The Night of the Blue Devils." There was Paula née Poteau, a pocket-sized Finn with golden hair and a complexion finer than Sèvres, doubly unusual because of Laramie's notoriously desiccating sun. There was Big John Gruenfelder, historian and amazing raconteur—amazing because he had only three real interests: the minutiae of baseball (he had pitched for a Tiger farm club in Durham, N.C.), the annual editions of *Jane's Fighting Ships*, and the English parliaments under the Stuarts. There was Mert Harris, for whom the annual spring kegger in the Vedauwoo rocks was named, largely in honour of his inventive hangover cures, one of which involved inundation with Number Eight cans of orange juice in his morning-after bathtub. Heroes all. In an age of ersatz celebrity, we were content to make our own, encouraging each other's quirks as they helped swell the Albany's celebration. Our tribal instinct was undoubtedly part of the American male's propensity to extend his adolescence, to prolong the boy-gang stage well into middle-age; it was insular and insulating, with more than a touch of macho chauvinism, but it was also a moral alternative to imperialism, ennui, war, ambition, pedantry, ulcers, bureaucracy, and all the other fantods associated with life in the Republic.

The plan and appointments of the Albany made it a natural stage for homemade pageantry. The deviants who design modern bars are in open conspiracy against social drinking. They believe that liquor must be consumed while stationary; why else confinement in captain's chairs, wrap-around vinyl cubbies, or—it is to cry—those *Sitzfleisch* stepstools cramped against bars padded like the dashboard of a new Imperial. This padding is, I believe, open confession that sitting to drink is dangerous. They further assume that indulgence is a guilty and furtive act, and thus contrive windowless sties lit either by candles in red jars or malformed neon.

Once in a dim Fort Collins caravansary I was near hypnotized by a lighted column of what looked to be orange molasses in oil simmering and bubbling on the backbar like the vitals of hell. Further convinced that libido boozalis needs the whip of fantasy, these gentry make each new saloon the cabin of a sailing ship, a Victorian sporting house, or an English country pub. It is all empty theatrics. Woe betide the excited inebriate who actually tries to trim the mainsail, price the girls, or sound the hunting horn suspended above his head.

Let the Albany be a reproach to these decorators gone *mashugga*. It was built for sturdy, workaday humankind. Its spacious precincts were organized and focused by a backbar noble but not overwhelming in dimension. Brought to Laramie over the pass from Loveland, Colorado, it was constructed in the mode of high Western Gothic, yet managed to avoid excess. Its pilasters were Doric, its crenulations chaste, and it framed a triptych of mirrors, the central one a completely unflawed, unadorned four by ten, certainly the largest looking glass in town, but modest by the standards of Versailles. In the early sixties Dewey's own hands had stripped away the layers of varnish to reveal the original grain. The mahogany lusters on the front bar were subsequently kept to a high gloss largely by the motion of working elbows.

And one stood to labour at the Albany's bar, a posture healthful and even comfortable over surprisingly long periods. It is true that in later years a single stool appeared at the bar's nether end, but purists eschewed it and it was occupied only intermittently by a few pregnant women. There were three tables and some chromium chairs along the far wall, but these provided necessary privacy for reading the *Boomerang* or chess, leaving the main floor uncluttered for those leisurely peregrinations which promote fellowship. And the barroom was graced by a marvelously radiant light. In the fifties an itinerant electrical expert had wandered through. On his advice, six units of unshaded fluorescents were installed, each containing four three-foot tubes.

On the first night patrons had to shade their eyes to find the sauce and the Albany's store front windows bathed the street opposite with a brilliance to shame the Eddystone Light. Three units were hastily decommissioned and later Floyd removed two tubes from each unit, his artist's eye having calibrated the exact wattage needed to make mirrors, mahogany, glassware, the brass rail and trio of spittoons into a medley of such gleaming that in its ambience more than one meditating soul found his satori.

The accessories were in perfect keeping. The front windows were periodically dressed by professionals from the breweries—a dying art, perhaps due to increasingly pinched media; the Hamm's bear, once done in plaster, then in plastic, seemed less sprightly in the pasteboard renderings of recent years. Next the front door was a glass-topped candy counter for the package goods, heavy on the favourites, pints of Sunny Brook and Hermitage, but also showing some mildly exotic Tokays and Muscatels. Behind this was a tall tobacco case, serving mostly as pediment for splendid plaster busts of John Paul Jones, Old Crow, and the Black and White Scotties. These had been donated by long departed whisky drummers who had early understood the need, in a university town, to compete with the marble heads of Aristotle, Voltaire, and Newton. The opposite wall was dominated by Dalziel's fine steel engraving of Landseer's *Stage at Bay*. The stuffed heads of a deer, a moose, and an antelope, lent by an Albany widow, hung in the back room, a space separated from the bar proper by a thin three-quarter partition topped by a lattice affair left over from somebody's May ball, and containing a few more tables, the Morris chair, a beer cooler, a Cathedral Wurlitzer whose records had not been changed since 1949, and the Albany's lone toilet, this circumstance making for some antic times between uninitiated sorority girls and the giant U.P. callboy Cody, who was prompt enough in notifying the next-out list but forgetful about the latch.

Sustenance for the spirit, surely, but more staple fare was always available—enormous farm eggs hard-boiled by Floyd's wife, Molly, potato chips, sunflower seeds, Ritz crackers, little pepperoni sticks called hotsies, corn curls, Kraznowski's Polish sausages served still dripping with brine, Fritoes, peanuts, wheat thins, blind robins (tiny fish dried until their species had become confused), pickles, pistachios, Copenhagen snoose, pretzels, oyster crackers, beer-nuts apparently roasted in a coating of Karo syrup before salting, popcorn, pizzas sent in from up the street, fried pork rinds, taco chips, and Slim Jim strips of beef jerky so tough that legend had cowboys carrying them under their saddles for hot meals at the end of the day, but which we softened by using them as swizzle sticks in the beer. These victuals induced thirst and the Hamm's obligingly flowed from the tap at fifteen cents the nine-ounce shell, twenty cents the twelve-ounce schooner, every third or fourth one on the house for regulars, and a shot of Wild Turkey on your birthday. Occasionally the Hamm's *Totsäufer*, the wholesaler or his customers' man, would buy up to four rounds in a row, but even on a normal night, it was possible to maintain a nice buzz for under a dollar and a half, especially since the active ingredient was more active at Laramie's altitude of 7,145 feet above sea level.

Unfortunately, Floyd's custom of Thursday night free lunch, at first helpings of sauerkraut and all-beef bangers, degenerated into orgies of baloney and Wonder Bread when every freeloader in town got wind of its bounty. On Thanksgiving and Christmas the feasts were more intimate; Dewey would peel bills from his back-pocket roll, have a turkey roasted at Dick Eberhart's Home Bakery, and carve it throughout the afternoon with rye bread and German mustard.

To these add periodic nuptial fetes. The first was an evening reception after Sally's marriage to Merle Ihne, an ecologist modeled on Jim Bridger lines who earned his M.A. helping to implant trout with radio transmitters to map their movements. It was on this occasion that the back room was rechristened so the engraved invitations could read "At the Spike Moose Lounge of the Albany Bar." Floyd and his relief, the painter Jerry Glass, wore green satin waistcoats, and a cold buffet was served. A few strays from the day crowd, particularly a Navaho ranch hand named Nelson

Pine, accepted petits fours and Taylor's upstate New York champagne with appropriate gravity and without remarking what clearly smacked of Eastern newfangledness.

There was one formal riot. A kicking specialist who would graduate from the Wyoming Cowboys to NFL fame organized his bachelor party to feature a spot of hippie-bashing, then an emerging form of Western machismo. Some wag misguided them to the Albany. Their full realization of the mistake was interrupted by the arrival of a posse of Laramie's finest. This peacekeeping was effective and so pervasive that everyone, cops, jocks, and regulars, spent the rest of the evening weeping mace tears into the beer. The kicking specialist's second mistake was to allege in court that the Albany was a low bar, unaware that the magistrate had taken his preprandial shots there every weekday for the last half-decade.

Adventure aplenty, but I loved best the ordinary Friday nights. The beat would begin slowly, early arrivals spaced comfortably along the bar in companionable silence. Maybe one idly negotiating with Jerry for a painting, two more mumbling over yesterday's ball scores. About 8:30 Q. Cook, his quiet weekday mien oiled for conversation by preliminary drafts at the Alibi, would begin. His tonal range was impressive; once he sustained a threnody for the Eighty-Second Airborne by reference to both the Sicilian Vespers and the Defenestration of Prague, and nailed the point superbly by leading us in the "Marseillaise" from atop the bar. Q might be joined by Walter Edens' personal Wurlitzer, a rhetoric of suspended periods so extended that wagers could be laid around the possibility of his reaching them, by the poet Jim Cole's laconic reprise of the Cornhusker idioms of his youth, or by Hank Laskowsky's seasonal ragas, key of D improvisations as much "Havanegilah" as Ravi Shankar. "Amazing Grace," overtures for the evening's solo turns. We would hear again of Fred Cannan's tour as naval attaché for NATO, witnessing the sea trials of two new French corvettes; after a series of Gallic arabesques, they rammed and sank each other, engines all ahead full. We would hear again of the stages by which Max Rardin, early proponent of behaviour modification, convinced Art Simpson that bears would be attracted to their hunter's redoubt in the Snowy Range by manhandling a tub of cow guts up there to fester in the sun. They never were. We would hear again of Dave Lawson's schemes for the bluegrass band. (Mercury later issued their single titled "Laramie" featuring Dave singing "Farewell Amelia Earhart, First Lady of the Skies.") Then a pause to ogle discreetly Jerry's latest girl, each more astonishing than the last, especially one stunner with a voice like Senator Dirksen's. Drum rolls and flourishes.

Then, the evening ripening, we moved to the more heavily operatic;

we would relive the details of Frisbie's misstep, an accident finally immortalized in the name, Frisbie's Fall, given the major rock face at Vedauwoo; we would muse over the time that Stu Crothers and a rodeo princess were indelicately surprised afterhours by Brownie, the Albany swamper; we would rerun a footrace between Big John and myself up from Front Street that finished with me prone to seizures at the Albany's front door; and then the whole ensemble, loaded to the scuppers, flawless in our parts, would collaborate in miming once again the Night They Sprayed the Place with Mace. Familiar voices, ritual action, and finally it would merge into that boozy hubbub which can pass for the authentic pulse of community. We dispersed at 1:00 A.M., some to Short's Care for a morning omelet, some to Poor Bill's, an afterhours club more commonly known as Everybody's, some to Q's for bacon and eggs and a little Ella Fitzgerald, and on fine, rare occasions, a few back at the Albany's front door to greet the dawn and Dewey when he opened again at 6:00.

The Albany closed in 1969, the license went to a lounge out on Grand Avenue, the backbar to a discotheque over the Buckhorn, yet it will take its proper place amid the other monuments of its honoured name. Albany is the ancient and literary name for Scotland, for a set of foreign dukes and a scandalous countess who married one of Big John's Stuarts, for a river rising in Western Ontario and a fur trading fort at its mouth, for cities in Oregon, Georgia, California, and New York, for a congress which concluded a treaty with the Iroquois in 1764. It is also and not least the name of a magnificent bar.

For John Quentin Cook, Historian

O, Q, my quiet man, my rare quadrivium,
Inspirit me; the beer-bred calm we shared so long
Is hardly help enough
For I must hymn a Laramie now lost.
My sentiment is baggy, loose, and large,
Yet full of grace from those who loved
The heft of schooners, hoggers, bellied mugs,
The children's mineral garden view of salt in beer,
The comfort of the rail underfoot.
When I remember Plaza Bar, the Alibi,
The Albany, Poor Bill's, and Myrtle's Chicken Shack,
I will speak well.
It's true we wept on Friday nights,
Your back to Hunt's far corner,
Mine to samples of the things for which we wept,
Often you would hum tuneless and look unfixed,
Awash with beer and boredom, but what private tunes
Of Voltaire, Vico, Sicilian Vespers, Burke, or Jenkins' Ear
I never knew.
I like best late night's windy talks;
Sauced enough perhaps I did not hear your words,
But sauced in part by eloquence I had forgot you had,
So silent were you on the sober days,
An eloquence so grand and fit for bars, the
Hippest undergraduate would stare
And hope for scandal.
Edged on each side by Big John G. and me,
Fat bookends for your wit, you would launch out
The realpolitic, excoriating mushy minds of
Liberals, friends and deans alike,
(Clio so stern she had to wait for Friday night).
Solutions to the problems you evolved were quaint:
The Eighty-Second Airborne troops, the qualities of Russian soul,
The cautionary rules of thought, McGee's defense,
Or specifics simple as the sound of Ella's voice.
All one, no doubt, but when the sun came up, as it too
Seldom did for me, it always seemed as if the need
To hear some words beyond the ones I'd heard all week
Was met.

Toward the Margin: Notes in Passing

I am a male of Anglo-Saxon heritage at the beginning of the seventh decade of my life, and at my back I have heard Postmodernist's winged chariot hurrying near. I began as an English instructor in 1955 and, since 1975, I have been a full professor of English. Sometime during that period, I went from Young Turk to Old Toot without, apparently, noticing the transition. It was brought forcefully to my attention in 1983 by Daniel O'Hara's elaborate insult, delivered in the journal called *Critical Inquiry*, and directed against ". . . the long-established and well-heeled, native American, fly-by-the-seat-of-one's-pants critical pragmatists and know-nothings, who have been waiting in the wings ever since the late sixties for such boring annoyances as critical theory, feminism, affirmative action programs, and so forth, to disappear; we then can go back to doing business as usual, waging our polite and sensible battles over the sources and significance of some line in Pound's *Pisan Cantos* or Joyce's manuscript drafts of *Finnegans Wake*." I didn't at first identify with the specifics, but it soon dawned on me, hey, this is my birth and professional cohort he's talking about. I then tried it on to see if it fit. "Long-established"? (yes, if twenty-five years at this University counts); "well-heeled"? (reasonably so); "native American"? (yes, but twenty-five years in Canada); "fly-by-the-seat-of-one's-pants critical pragmatist"? (dead-on, O'Hara, but I choose to call it "principled opportunism"); "know-nothing"? (I emphatically deny membership in this category, a term borrowed from American politics of the 1850s to designate the political exploitation of an instinctive dislike for foreigners—or maybe he means my reaction to Derrida!). Thinking myself a long-established and remarkably tolerant liberal humanist, I was particularly irked by what I was now beginning to think of as "my" attributes—of O'Hara's attribution to me of boredom with critical theory, feminism, and affirmative action programs, but in justice I remembered the occasions when critical theorists bored me silly and when I found myself anxiously hoping that the young votaries in my department of critical theory, feminism, and affirmative action programs would be, you know, well-mannered and civil in their advocacy. I am even willing to admit that my usual sense of "business as usual" is constrained by my early training as a New Critic, a training that emphasized textual minutiae and urged us to keep our own efforts for social justice separate from our professional behaviour, particularly in the classroom. Insofar, then, that my own profile confirms that O'Hara was not beating an entirely straw man, I read on, warily waiting for the Young Turk's best punch. It came soon enough. It was O'Hara's allegation that the power of us Old Toots "is likely to make unavailable, or at least unattractive and ever so much more difficult, a career option that has only just been introduced in the profession and that has been so strenuously fought for—namely, doing critical theory." Power, ha! O'Hara should have spent the last couple of years I've just spent, but again let's be fair. O'Hara may have reason to believe that Jealous Eld makes us enemies of a new career option, an opportunity for young academics to compete and excel in a field unoccupied (because for the most part either unimagined or left to the philosophers) by old-timey students of literature. Under increased pressure to publish and to find a foothold in a profession top-heavy with seniority, the young strenuously pit themselves against the old for the right to do critical theory—there is something heroic in this martial version for both sides, but the heroics have surely faded since the date of O'Hara's insult in 1983—the truth is that, at least in Canada, doing theory has won vocational battles and now commands the high ground. Proof of this observation requires me to segue, not without a certain wariness, into old-fashioned literary history.

My undergraduate history professor, variously and often simultaneously a Quaker, a coal miner, an eccentric, a Methodist minister, a socialist, and a target for Senator Joe McCarthy's spleen had permanently painted on his classroom blackboard this maxim: "History is an evolutionary process with no abrupt breaks or changes." I was thus early persuaded that historians should be wary of identifying the very moment of significant change. Nominalist students of hockey, for instance, might be tempted to mark the arrival of the slap-shot in the NHL at the moment Charlie Boire, a Montreal sports writer, re-christened, in print, Bernie Geoffrion, a notable practitioner of this delivery, with the sobriquet of "Boom-Boom," but this would be to ignore evidence that the slap-shot was introduced as early as the thirties by the late Bun Cook of the New York Rangers (not to be confused with his brother Bill who also played with the Rangers). Nevertheless and aware of the risks, I will now mark the moment (actually the month) when contemporary literary theory, "postmodernism," became fully established in English Canada. (It should be noted here that I claim the privilege that Len Findlay granted to Linda Hutcheon in the December 1988 issue of *English Studies in Canada [ESC]*, namely "... the economy of allusion at work in her use of the term 'postmodernism.' It is referred to in ways that self-consciously represent it incrementally, implicitly, incompletely, because that may well be all that is ever possible anyway. . . .") The establishing moment begins with the March 1986 issue of *ESC*, by definition the most established of our professional journals.

The singularity of the issue was an "Editorial Comment," the first one R. D. McMaster had seen fit to include during his tenure as the journal's editor. The "Comment" explains that this is a "special issue," one "devoted to papers exercising or discussing some of the newer modes of critical theory." The reason given for the special issue is to "scotch" the "complaint that *ESC* is unreceptive to papers informed by recent theory." McMaster continues: "Our intention, on the other hand, is not to 'ghettoize' such papers or reviews. Others are going through the usual process of assessment and those that succeed will appear in due course."

The establishing month was completed from April 25 to April 27, 1986, when a symposium was held at the University of Ottawa, the proceedings of which have been edited with an introduction by John Moss under the title, *Future Indicative: Literary Theory and Canadian Literature*. Those present celebrated the establishment of theory in Canada by abandoning apology for talk about it. During the closing panel Linda Hutcheon said: "At this conference, for the first time in Canada, I have felt that I have not had to stand up and apologize for giving a theory paper." And Robert Kroetsch added: "Another thing that has impressed me here is the high level of assumption possible, with no apology needed on the part of the speaker. This audience obviously knows how to listen, and what it is listening to." Moss's report of the closing panel also revealed some of the ideas that could now, presumably, be assumed, ideas that no longer needed apology. One of these was enunciated by Stephen Scobie, who memorialized "... that godlike Author whose death has been so thoroughly proclaimed that now, when we come across actual small 'a' authors, we are, like the Angels in Rilke's First Duino Elegy, not quite sure whether we move among the living or among the dead." The symposium's celebration of such a consensus seems less smug than, we may imagine, reassuring and even energizing for those present, feelings that would license Scobie's mild joke. But establishment in the spring of 1986 was not yet orthodoxy; dissent was still possible.

One such dissent was registered, also in 1986, by Constance Rooke. In her essay, "Fear of the Open Heart," in Shirley Neuman and Smaro Kamboureli's *A Mazing Space: Writing Canadian Women Writing*, she rejected announcements of the death of the author as both bloody-minded and bloodless: "In both senses it is too stereotypically male—too close to the garrison, too far from the heart ... I am aware that this is just a manner of speaking, but it is not a manner I much like." Rooke may be right; this sort of talk may be "just a manner of speaking." Despite the serious questions about an author's rights and responsibilities raised by the Rushdie affair, surely no one in Canada has violent or lethal designs on our authors' persons, health, lives, or even their literary property. Despite their new small "a" status, Scobie and Kroetsch remain, God keep them, very much alive and will continue to cash royalty (a term that has its roots in "sovereignty") cheques and, together in the Writers' Union, they will continue to resist legislation by any body that would limit their freedom to express themselves—or anything else they wish to write about.

Clearly, then, proclamations of the death of the author are neither descriptions of *une peste parmi les auteurs* nor covert counsels to auctorcide, but if they are still to have force, what is, pragmatically, their point in Canada? (I concede that for some postmodernist theorists, pragmatists are the enemy, as in O'Hara's splendid insult.) Of course motives will be different for each theorist acceding to the death of the author, but each may take at least some colouration from the motivation governing the *locus classicus* of such proclamations, Roland Barthes' "The Death of the Author," first printed in 1968 and translated in the following version in 1977:

> We know now that a text is not a line of words releasing a single "theological" meaning (the "message" of the Author-God) but a multidimensional space in which a variety of writings, none of them original, blend and clash. The text is a tissue of quotations drawn from the innumerable centers of culture... In precisely this way literature (it would be better from now on to say writing), by refusing to assign a "secret"; an ultimate meaning, to the text (and to the world as text), liberates what may be called an anti-theological activity, an activity that is truly revolutionary since to refuse to fix meaning is, in the end, to refuse God and his hypostases—reason, science, law.

Barthes' polemic makes it clear that the author is just one of the concepts swept away by a revolutionary rejection of authority—all authority, any authority—a political ferocity that E. D. Hirsch stigmatized as "cognitive atheism." There is no real evidence in Moss' record of the symposium at Ottawa that the symposiasts took up this revolutionary stance; rather there seemed a willingness to examine what might follow from thinking about literary texts without reference to the conventional role of the author. In this spirit, and before the postmodern consensus becomes orthodoxy, the historian should examine what will be lost by the author's disappearance—and with some urgency, already in Canada working scholars were beginning to talk as if the author's disappearance were a certainty.

R. D. McMaster was as good as his word given in the March 1986 *ESC*, that papers "informed by recent theory" were "going through the usual process of assessment and those that succeed will appear in due course." And so they did, one of which—Barry Cameron's review of a collection of essays edited by Sherril Grace and Lorraine Weir and titled *Margaret Atwood: Language, Text, and System* in the very next, September 1986 *ESC*—assumes the new poetics by mandating the way we must now talk about the author. Cameron begins: "This is a significant collection of essays in the brief history of Canadian criticism because it marks an effort on the part of the editors to shift the ground of critical practice from the New Criticism to a Structuralist poetics or literary semiotics." Cameron clearly approves this effort, but his judgment is that the collection still retains some unnecessary baggage from the past. He frames his judgment in this passage:

> Such an orientation situates the texts under discussion and the discussions themselves in "Atwood". But, except for a declarative eschewing of the biographical function of author, a temptation which everyone in the collection but George Woodcock refuses, it is not clear in what capacity "Atwood" functions. As a residual humanist source of the text, a self-sufficient individual given prior to the text? As implied author? As scriptor? As an effect of the text, an inferred enunciating agent, a metonymic characterization of the text?

I'll come back to this in a moment—it is my sample postmodern text and I must take up its implications for my experience of Margaret Atwood—but let me first end my history of the establishing events by conceding that doing theory is now in—not marginal, but increasing in force as it commands the enthusiasm and loyalty of young academics. To borrow again from O'Hara's impacted martial metaphor, any remaining resistance from Old Toots can only be regarded as a breach of the Geneva Convention, stray shots from a *combat en rètrait*. But the war had casualties other than aging academics. One such casualty may be the shared effort of trying to be unmistakably clear in speech and writing, an effort which I think is still owed to our colleagues, to the general reader, and to our students, especially to our students.

Let me return to my sample text by Barry Cameron. Oddly enough I don't object to the technical disguises he offers for Margaret Atwood—scriptor, implied author, residual humanist source of the text and the rest—God help me, I even seem to understand what he's driving at with each of these terms. What really arrests and puzzles me is his second sentence: "But, except for a declarative eschewing of the biographical function of author, a temptation which everyone in the collection but George Woodcock refuses, it is not clear in what capacity 'Atwood' functions." I've always distrusted the word *eschew*, and it seems to me that the choice of it puts one well on the way to fuzzification already. But the *OED* assures me that the word still means "to avoid, to shun, to keep clear of, to escape." Cameron's sentence appears to assert that everyone else in the collection refuses a temptation that George Woodcock alone accepts. That temptation is defined as declaratively eschewing the biographical function of author. If I'm right so far, this means that George Woodcock alone refuses to recognize Margaret Atwood as a live author, but that all the others accept her as a breathing writer who pens her own books. But that can't be right—Cameron's review makes clear that he is exposing Woodcock as an old-fashioned Old Toot, and celebrating the others as innovative, pioneering theorists. Can it be that Cameron has said the opposite of what he means? That by getting tangled up with *eschew*, he's screwed up his sentence? It is a puzzlement.

Linda Hutcheon has helped me through this puzzle. I have come to trust her as a guide to postmodernism and to theory, in part because of her courage in offering a clear definition of what postmodernism is. She begins her introduction to *The Politics of Postmodernism* (1989) by answering her own question: "What is postmodernism?" After some hefty qualifications, the answer is: "in general terms it takes the form of self-conscious, self-contradictory, self-undermining statement. It is rather like saying something whilst at the same time putting inverted commas around what is being said. The effect is to highlight or 'highlight,' and to subvert, or 'subvert.' and the mode is therefore a 'knowing' and an ironic—or even 'ironic'—one. Postmodern's distinctive character lies in this kind of 'nudging' commitment to doubleness, or duplicity."

Following Len Findlay's lead in conceding to Hutcheon all necessary qualifications, let us exempt this definition from the postmodern mode it defines, trusting that her definition itself is not double, duplicitous, ironic, or subversive; rather the definition seems admirably clear, unmistakable, and straightforward naming a mode or style that is resolutely, deliberately, and philosophically not clear, not unmistakable, and not straightforward. And because postmodernism is here so clearly set out, it uncovers its affinities and antecedents in a manner equally revealing and clear. For example, they reveal postmodernism as kin to the "nudge, nudge, wink, wink" double-entendres of British music hall humour. In another of its dimensions, this mode has affinities with Camp, as articulated first in the United States by Susan Sontag in her 1964 *Partisan Review* essay, "Notes on Camp." There are fifty-eight of these notes; Number Ten reads: "Camp sees everything in quotation marks," and Number Sixteen reads "... the Camp sensibility is one that is alive to a double sense in which some things can be taken." In any of its forms, one can see why this mode might appeal to young academics—not only because it appeals to their ludic *jouissance* and their professional *jouissance*, but because it is, as Sontag notes, "a private code, a badge of identity even," and thus it promotes in-group solidarity by pulling the legs of those oldtimers who don't get it. And that's it, of course—Barry Cameron is pulling my leg, or perhaps our legs.

The duplicitous, ironic, and subversive function of this mode allows for endless postponement or deferral of intent and renders useless any attempt to pin Postmodernist, wriggling or straight. Cathy N. Davidson, for instance, in an essay in the September/October issue of *Academe* called "'PH Stands for Political Hypocrisy," testifies to the efficacy of this function:

> Doublespeak is at the very heart of the PC/PI debates. Consider even the terms, PC and PI [Politically Incorrect], which apparently were coined in the 30's and resuscitated several years ago as ironic, hip and self-mocking terms that intellectuals used against themselves ... As Daniel Defoe discovered when he landed in prison after his satire *The Shortest Way With Dissenters* was taken straight, irony and parody can easily get lost in the polemical shuffle. Just think about those hilariously provocative MLA paper titles (please, Lord let there be something to enliven this year's convention!) that get so solemnly repeated in the media to demonstrate what scholarship has come to and are passed off as proof positive that Western civilization as we know it is going down the tubes. Isn't there a conservative out there with a sense of humour?

Now classified as a "conservative," I devoutly hope so, but I have my doubts. To test it, I looked through the most recent program for the MLA meetings for "hilariously provocative" paper titles but found only one, "The Politics of Literacy in *Moby-Dick* and Other Exotic Members," (nudge, nudge, wink, wink); in truth MLA annual programs used to be funnier, especially after we learned the knack of unpeeling those titles with parentheses cleverly implanted within words, an appealing game combining anagrams with paronomasia.

Let me give the last word on postmodernist self-subversion to our friend and Saskatoon colleague Len Findlay, himself no slouch as a practitioner of postmodernism. In an essay for *ESC* in December 1988, he says this: "I will try to be as clear as possible about complicated questions, and in so doing will deliberately affirm a politics of intelligibility that may at first blush seem hopelessly at odds with postmodernism . . . from my standpoint, 'intense self-consciousness' can and sometimes does obscure matters unnecessarily, indulging possessive (sometimes obsessive) individualism to the detriment of communication, community, and the work that needs to be done." Elusive as the task may be, the work here at hand is still, persistently I might add, the experience of Margaret Atwood, or "Atwood" as we may call her, fingers wiggled in the air to show that "she" is now less than a Derridan "trace."

I am not unacquainted with Margaret Atwood as a human being, but a later remark in Cameron's review prompted me to reassess the nature of that acquaintance. Cameron claims that ". . . we ourselves are signs cognitively available to others and ourselves only as signifiers (visual images, proper names, and pronouns)." This seems a bit strict, perhaps too positivist or behaviourist, but to test the claim I reviewed the relevant signifiers: Ms Atwood and I spent the academic year 1968–69 as members of the same social circle at the University of Alberta. I was well enough acquainted with her to address her as "Peggy" (without, of course, the quotation marks) and I have presumed to recognize and address her in that manner on the rare occasions we have spoken privately since (during the last short meeting, she advised me how to produce a better crumb in my bread-baking). It must be admitted, however, that since 1969 my acquaintance with her has been sustained largely by the signifying images in the media—her photographs; the accolade of a caricature by David Levine in the *New York Review of Books*; the literary journalists' reports; by the inwit of her reviewers and critics—and by the oddments of literary gossip that found their way west. But principally, of course, by her name on the title pages of the succession of books (chosen *because* of her name on them) that I have read with pleasure, some alarm, and increasing respect. During such reading, I have been reasonably careful, I think, to separate my memories of a real-life Peggy from the authorial presence I've felt in these books—in this advised by Ms Atwood herself in a *Malahat Review* interview: "You don't need biographical information unless the work is unintelligible without it. It's most unfortunate that Dorothy Wordsworth kept a diary. I don't care if William Wordsworth ever saw a field of golden daffodils." She has also registered some absurdities that come from speculation about her "biological function" as author: "The public has given me a personality of not having a personality," she is quoted in October 15, 1979, *Maclean's*, "Sometimes they make up things about it like Margaret the Monster, Margaret the Magician and Margaret the Mother—Romantic notions of what's really there keep getting in the way of people's actual view of you." Given this public's propensity for myth-making, Frank Davey may have it right when he chides the public expectation he still feels obliged to meet by including these remarks in the first chapter of his *Margaret Atwood: Toward a Feminist Poetics* (1984) under the title, "An Unneeded Biography." Let us, then, like Davey and, however grudgingly, concede that the reading public will continue to be curious about the flesh and blood Margaret. Even though we may wince when the inevitable Canadian update of the child's game of "Authors" appears with Margaret Atwood's face on one set of cards and even though we will only skim *Maclean's* latest version, chez Atwood, of Elbert Hubbard's "Little Journeys to the Homes of the Great," let us concede that the reading public has the right to celebrate who and what they will. Better her, say, than even "Boom-Boom" Geoffrion.

Excess in the public's celebration of its authors is not, however, the most serious issue that Cameron raises by placing the name Atwood in quotation marks. Cameron approves the effort "to shift the ground of critical practice from the New Criticism to a Structuralist poetics or literary semiotics," and his key maneuver illustrates what that shift means to do to our notion of an author. Despite the New Criticism's effort to rule out inquiries about an author's intentions, the New Critics generally sought to identify, and so to value, the shaping, resolving, unifying mind of the maker in the evidence of what she had made. Cameron, championing a successor poetics, collects from the range of postmodern theory a series of terms that subordinate anything like the old-fashioned notion of "maker" to the text, however made. Is "Atwood" a residual humanist (in postmodernist talk "humanist" is a pejorative) source of the text? Is the quoted entity a self-sufficient individual given prior to the text? Depends, I suppose, on what is meant by "self-sufficient" and "given." Is "Atwood" an implied author? Is "she" (*do* quoted proper names somehow affect the gender pronouns?) A scriptor? Is "she" an effect of the text, an inferred enunciating agent, a metonymic characterization of the text? Such descriptions will seem overelaborate and finicky when applied to Peggy herself; less so when used to situate the signifier "Atwood," and it is thus unfair to quibble with Cameron here, for he clearly means these terms as allusions to the considerable efforts of postmodern theorists to submit commonsense notions of authors and authorship to careful scrutiny with the aim of understanding more precisely how these things work. Notwithstanding all this, although the author may be the first major casualty of the new literary war, others have fallen or been exiled in Postmodernist's struggle to liberate a free, in fact, unlimited interpretation of the text. The text itself vanishes alarmingly in the new mode after providing a mere occasion for semiotic gaming.

Whatever of the high ground of orthodoxy has now been ceded to the postmodern theorists, a fair population of students has also been pushed to the margin, those who are still innocent of the book unmediated by theory and come to us with a joy of reading. A colleague, recently lamenting the dominance of theory in art, told me of his shocking vision of the curated exhibit he soon expects to be hung. The gallery walls are papered from ceiling to chair-rail with the words of theorists, illustrated by postage-stamp-sized reproductions of paintings. When the text becomes just a footnote to theory, I will join the dissenters who love books and seek asylum on the margin.

Introduction to a Memoir

I entered the terrain of Canadian literature a tenderfoot, but with a modest guide. She was Miss Ruth Tabor, the austere librarian of the Oelwein, Iowa, Free Public Library of my boyhood. Miss Tabor pushed a standard unisex kids' list that included *Anne of Green Gables, Jalna,* and Leacock's *Sunshine Sketches*; I read them, but in early memory I vaguely placed Anne in Maine and confused Leacock's folks with Booth Tarkington's. My adolescent grasp of Canadian history and culture was equally shaky. My Auntie Babe and Uncle Chick had taken me to see the Dionne quintuplets when I was seven, but all I remembered was skepticism about claims they couldn't see us because of the one-way glass. I retained more lurid images of Wolfe and Montcalm on the Plains of Abraham, loyally scorned the empire's Loyalists, who had been harried into Canada, and was indignant when I learned that President Polk had, in 1846, given up claims to our manifestly destined northern border with Canada at "Fifty-four Forty or fight." Teenage jingoism notwithstanding, I had a favourable impression of Canadians. My stepfather Max, who had served in both World Wars, often mentioned the "tough little Canucks" he had met, imprinting Canadians on me as both diminutive and pugnacious. And I was lucky in the first live Canadian I met, Bob Kroetsch, my friend and colleague in the Ph.D. program at the University of Iowa, who was tall but tough. We kidded Bob about his Canadian accent (he was thought to pronounce "about" as if it were "aboot"), but he became our leader one summer when he and Jane were housesitting the magnificent Iowa City home of the historian, William Aydelotte. We played croquet on the lawns, endless and fuddled games because we were into our own popskull homebrew. With three weeks aging it had become a beer of considerable authority. We made it with wellwater from the backyard of Eric LaGuardia's house on the edge of Iowa City and aged it in a cave beneath the house. Aydelotte was the son of the most distinguished president of Swarthmore College; Eric was the adopted son of Fiorello, the Little Flower, the famous mayor of New York City; and the cave under the house was reputed to have been used in the twenties by one of Iowa's most prominent bootleggers.

Canada and its culture remained beyond the periphery over the course of my formal training as a reader. In fact my choice to combine an undergraduate degree in history with a growing interest in literature by taking a cross-disciplinary American Studies program for the Ph.D. imposed further blinders by rigidly stopping attention at the borders of the United States A few Canadian details did leak through. For instance, I remember coming across this in a 1923 letter from Hemingway to Sylvia Beach: "I would like to swing a crochet on the mention of Canada. I would like to hit all Canada a coup bas." It stopped me first because I had to look up the French words. I already knew Hemingway was a nasty bastard, but to offer a whole nation a deliberate low blow because he had been outboxed by Morley Callaghan in Paris seemed excessive. But then a pugnacious people could probably look after themselves. It wasn't until 1966 that I was made to acknowledge the depth of my ignorance about Canadian culture. I was interviewed at the Modern Language Association job market by Professor Carl Klinck, who was planning a program in Canadian Studies at the University of Western Ontario and who thought that my degree and my experience teaching at the School of American Studies at Wyoming might be of use. Nothing came of it because I unabashedly confessed that I knew nothing of Canada. It was with these meagre credentials, then, that my family and I had our landed immigrant cards stamped at the border crossing at Carway, Alberta, on August 1, 1968, in order to take up my new job as an American literature specialist, an associate professor in the English Department of the University of Alberta in Edmonton.

The Centennial in 1967 of Canada's founding had renewed interest in the question of Canadian identity, but during that first year I had more trouble with my own. At first I was simply an expatriate in the Great White North, an image now made real for us because during the winter we arrived, Edmonton suffered a record of twenty-eight days straight when the temperature never exceeded six degrees Fahrenheit *below* zero (after 1975 it would have been recorded as *twenty-one degrees* centigrade below zero); having left the United States in part to protest America's adventure in Vietnam, we had reversed the usual defectors' process and come into the cold. But if the weather was freezing, my new colleagues seemed remarkably warm in their welcome. The first hint of hospitality well beyond duty had come when the department chairman, George Baldwin, offered me a "splash"—three fingers of rye—and then a second splash during our interview at the MLA on Boxing Day (the association of pugilism and Canada again oddly confirmed). Once in Edmonton, I began to feel like Monty Woolly in Kaufman and Hart's *The Man Who Came to Dinner*, not quite lionized but certainly taken up, especially by Diane and Frank Bessai, whose noon-hour table at the Faculty Club was a refuge of bibulous, but civilized discourse within the storm. Thus insulated, I was rarely the butt of the new nationalist, anti-American sentiment of the kind documented in Mel Hurtig's *The New Romans*, published that year. The Bessais had introduced me early to their old friend,

Danny Matthews, and I remember innocently and at length explaining to him the generous income tax holiday that the Canadian government was offering American academics who came to Canada, only later discovering that he was the most outspoken public opponent of such policies. Robin Matthews was diminutive and pugnacious, but in our few meetings also unfailingly civil, even charming. There was, to be sure, the odd occasion when I was made to feel like the ravening U.S. invader. At the nether end of a vinous party at Jim Nelson's apartment, I was backed against the refrigerator door by an angry Dorothy Livesay, just introduced to me as the visiting doyenne of Canadian poetry. She castigated my nation in orders less poetic than pungent, and then, I think, she kissed me.

Whatever my public role was to be, I soon felt the advantages of a private one. I was a trained reader with a whole new literature to consume, and I could do it without being professionally beholden to anyone. I didn't have to teach it, I didn't have to write about it, I didn't even have to judge it. In this matter, I was a dilettante again (some say still), free to read serendipitously, at random, and at leisure. It was, at midlife, a unique boon for one passive by nature, and if I am grateful to Canada for many things, this is a principal one.

I was wrong of course. Having set out only to taste Canadian letters, I have over the twenty-five years since discovered that tasting only whets the appetite. And it's my own fault. There is an occupational hazard peculiar to academics. We can't help but have perceptions. In our vanity we are quick to rank them as significant insights, and in our greed quick to hope them publishable, thus adding to the yearly Life-and-Miracle Sheet which generates our increments and promotions. My first such perception was early and fortuitous. While my family napped at the motel in Banff, I sat alone in a tavern, savouring the advent of my first beer in Canada. Remembering Kroetsch's story about ordering a table-top full of beers after a day of harvesting in the Heisler, Alberta, tavern of his youth and noting that this table-top was remarkably small, I so ordered. The barkeep pointed to a sign ("Two to a Customer"). Drinking two, I noticed that the place was decorated in signs explaining what you couldn't do there . . . a whole section, for instance, labelled "for ladies and escorts only." Puzzled but game, I opened my first Canadian purchase, *MacLean's* for August 1968, and read there an account of the death of Blair Fraser in a whitewater canoeing accident on the Petawawa River that last May. Fraser, I learned, had been a distinguished Canadian journalist, and this reminded me that, however much Hemingway wanted to give a low upper-cut to all Canada, he had respected the training he had received from the old-time reporters on *The Toronto Star*. Further reflection produced a dim memory of a Canadian tradition in documentary films—John Grierson and Robert Flaherty's *Nanook of the North* came to mind. Four names in a string often make an academic perception, however simple. Aha, said the perception, Canadians may have a tradition of good documentary journalism. I filed it, but recalled it when Kroetsch sent us a copy of *Alberta*, his entry in Macmillan's "The Traveler's Canada" series, its inscription dated November 18, 1968. I was particularly struck with this passage: "The process of naming is hardly begun in Alberta. We who live here so often cannot name the flowers, the stones, the places, the events, the emotions of our landscape; they await the kind of naming that is the poetic act." Aha, so the need to document was continuing.

This datum was soon conjoined with two more. The Bessais had put me onto *Alphabet*, the wild journal edited mostly by James Reaney (he was reported to require his graduate students to do brass rubbings of local manhole covers). I noticed that some sections were labeled "Juxtaposition: Documentary and Myth." Aha, that word again, now reinforced by Frank's delight in calling attention in the fourth issue to a found poem, James McIntyre's "Ode on the Mammoth Cheese" (over seven thousand lbs.), which began: "We have seen thee, queen of Cheese,/ Lying quietly at your ease,/ Gently fanned by evening breeze./ Thy fair form no flies dare seize." Aha and Aha. A final Aha was the publication of Dorothy Livesay's book of poems called *The Documentaries* shortly after I first met her. The perceptions were coagulating toward an insight, and almost got nudged together when Kroetsch, on a visit, interrupted a beer run to measure and record in his notebook the details of the old rare book room in Cameron Library. He was getting the Alberta facts straight because, as his remark in *Alberta* hinted, he was pioneering in using the family, as yet unsung local detail in fiction. He later reported that one of his Heisler aunts had been flabbergasted when Edmonton's High Level Bridge—why, she'd crossed it a thousand times without much noticing—had actually turned up in *The Studhorse Man*. I now had enough fortuitous evidence to conclude that part of the new nationalist energies of postcentennial Canada were being devoted to a process of documenting the country preliminary to its full use in belles-lettres, a process I knew had happened in the United States in the early nineteenth century. James Fenimore Cooper's *The Pioneers*, for instance, used footnotes to document details of the manners and customs in a new country, and Melville in *Moby-Dick* had to document the whaling industry before he could exploit it dramatically. I also remembered Emerson's remark about Walt Whitman: "I expect him to make the songs of the Nation but he seems to be contented to make the inventories." I had enough to begin serious inquiry, but soon concern for my amateur standing in Canada and a fear that, should I pursue this line, I might become, God forfend, a comparativist, conspired with sloth to lay the matter aside. But it's been in the back of my mind for twenty-five years. It recently occurred to me that my quarter-century of complicated interaction with Canadian literature and its practitioners may constitute a kind of documentary footnote to the national story. Twenty-five years of dutiful sitting at the Faculty Club's "Big Table," the Stammtisch we inherited from Frank Bessai, has permitted me to drink with an enormous number of Canadian writers—many of whom I now count as genial acquaintances, some as bosom friends. In more formal, but very small ways I have contributed to Canadian letters, sometimes reluctantly, sometimes in earnest, but I have been more shaped (and occasionally scored) by them than I had first suspected was possible. The man-who-came-to-dinner has become a perennial guest, absorbed in the conversation if for no other reason than its long duration, and occasionally contributing a remark. I am bold to think that a brief documentary record of some of this colloquy might be of interest and even some use to my hosts.

A Passion of Poets

My full introduction to living Canadian letters came with participation in a conference encryptically titled "POET and CRITIC '69 POÉTE et CRITIQUE" and held at the University of Alberta from November 20 to 22, 1969. Originally conceived as a small public occasion to celebrate Dorothy Livesay's forty years as a poet (since the publication in 1928 of her first chapbook, Green Pitcher), it quickly spread, became bilingual, and nationwide. Some twenty-five poets/critics were finally invited to speak or read, and about one hundred seventy-five conferees paid the registration fee (a memo from the organizers read: "If the ten dollar fee sounds steep, remember it includes the reception Thursday, the banquet Friday, the lunch Saturday noon, and the play that evening"—and it was seven dollars for students). Three levels of government funded the event to a total of ninety-seven hundred dollars, not quite renaissance munificence, but still impressive. Alberta then was on a roll. Fueled by oil royalties and the new nationalism, we were hellbent on becoming what in the eighties our administrators took to calling "a world-class university." Congressistes/delegates were greeted with a U of A folder welcoming them in five languages, including Russian and Chinese, several oversize postcards of campus landscapes, and a mini-tabloid featuring views of the recently built Tory Building (named for U's first president, not the political party). There was a letter included from Pierre Elliot Trudeau, the most poetic of Canada's prime ministers, beginning with this unattributed quotation: "There is a pleasure in poetic pains/ Which only poets know."

Maybe, but on this occasion the poetic pains were largely suffered by the organizing committee, especially by the three co-chairmen, Dick Harrison and Rudy Wiebe of the English Department, and Brian Dobbs from French. Their files are a fascinating record of the planning, begun in April of 1968, for such a conference. Start with the assumption that this was to be the largest gathering of Canada's creative crop ever, and then imagine the pains taken, crises suffered, frustrations endured, the gritted-teeth tact necessary to deal with outsized poetic egos, and, before the invention of E-mail and the fax, the sheer weight of paper necessary for these delicate negotiations. The plans to induce Marshall McLuhan and Anne Hébert to attend with promises of honourary U of A degrees collapsed; the Canada Council grant was twenty-four hundred dollars short of the plea (as Earle Birney put it: "the cancow didn't come through with the full milk order"); Leonard Cohen, on a roll of his own, was unavailable, and finally they had to find local billets for those who couldn't afford the rates charged by the convention hotel, the CN's grand Hotel Macdonald, of thirteen dollars for a single and seventeen for a double. The organizers' files also and inadvertently reveal the strains that may have prompted the title of the conference and certainly set its covert theme. After all the dealing, the actuality was still one of the biggest Canadian literary fests yet, but the necessary compromises multiplied the number of potentially explosive pairings: French/English, poet/critic, established poets/young mavericks, academics/the rest of humanity—to these add the tense pairings that were emerging in the late sixties: women/men, hawks/doves, marijuana/alcohol, royalists/nationalists, oppressed/oppressors, East/West, Canada/U.S.—perhaps all this to placate the sponsoring governments' official policies of multiculturalism, certainly true of a set of ethnically diverse poets/critics included to take the edge off the English/French focus. What emerged was more a hope than a theme: put these pairs in one place and something interesting was bound to happen. And it did. I had volunteered, was made Equipment Manager, impartial aide to either side of any pair, and found this offered an incomparable back-stage view (principally of the three cochairmen reasoning together at the top of their lungs). These organizers upped the ante one more time by encouraging an "anticonference" to occur during the true conference, an idea suggested to its organizer, sessional lecturer Ed Turner, by Wilfred Watson, the oldest maverick professor in the U of A English Department. Let's begin with the anti-conference.

On Friday, November 14, six days before the conference was to open, *The Edmonton Journal's* Leisure section carried a full-page preview; there were three stories: one about Dorothy Livesay with a good-sized portrait photo; another about the conference titled "A poetic potpourri to alert academics and the public" with three smaller photos of Irving Layton, Eli Mandel, and Earle Birney; and a third about the anti-conference, illustrated with what most commanded attention on the page—a picture occupying the whole of the upper-right-hand quarter. It was of a shapely brunette, nude (save for a bikini bottom), her hands crossed modestly in front, and her back to the camera. Visible in the lower-right-hand corner is a bearded figure with a gloved hand painting words on the nude's back:

BODYSSEY
BODY
 ODE
BODES
BED
 ODYSSEY

Neither figure was identified, but now it can be told. The nude figure belonged to Lynn Weinlos, then one of our graduate students, later part-owner of the most comfortable bookstore in town, and now a very respectable high-school teacher. The poet/painter was my old friend and former colleague, Stephen Scobie, one of the cleverest men I know, and practitioner then of concrete poetry, although in this instance the gloved hand suggested that he was working in an unfamiliar medium.

The story went on to indicate that the anti-conference "is open to any unknown poet. So far twenty-five have signed up to present their works. They'll speak anonymously from behind a screen to 'protect' them from the established poets expected to attend." There was also to be a variety of multimedia performances and talks: "Pot and Poetry," "Who's Whore in Canada," and "Vancouver Robots San Francisco Style." "Three students concealed by refrigerator cartons will be walking about and talking with the audience. And there will be dancing to lights. 'It's a modern McLuhan thing,' Turner said." I wasn't sure about the refrigerator cartons, but the rest of it convinced me that this was going to be a gilt-edged, tree-calf, hand-tooled, rebelliously orgiastic youthquake of the kind I had left behind in the States. The reality was disappointing except for Lynn, now in a one-piece black bathing suit with cut-out circles in the back and sides, and being painted by several hands; The student newspaper, *The Gateway*, story ran a picture of one of them belonging to Bruce Bentz, my American buddy from U of A Art and Design Department. But lest my advanced age even then be suspect, here is an eye-witness report from Barry McKinnon, then a twenty-five-year-old maverick poet from Prince George, B.C.; it appeared as part of his coverage of the conference for *The Gateway*, on December 5, 1969. McKinnon's anticipation had been greater than mine: "Great. Let's hear the revolutionary screams and take our ties off, take our clothes off, throw our polite schedules and portfolios away, drink some honest wine, touch girls, etc., etc." And his disappointment was even greater: "But everybody's dressed except for a girl in a bathing suit getting her body painted. Everybody's come to see it happen. In another room there is a rock band and folk singers, and in another people dance interpretively in front of an egotistic video tape, and in the last room all the 'failed poets' are trying TO READ above the groovy confusion. No one hears or sees. A bomb wouldn't help. It's already exploded."

The conference proper began more auspiciously with a keynote address by D. G. Jones titled "In Search of America: Canadian Poetry, French and English." It was eloquently balanced, giving equal weight to poems in both languages while finding time to mention Wallace Stevens, Frost, Allan Ginsberg's *Howl*, and offering special praise to Whitman's vision of his America. Jones argued that, despite their many differences, both French and English poets in Canada were in search of the land, *la terre*, in a way that confirmed my perceptions about the Canadian documentary impulse. He cited, for instance, a line from a poem by A. M. Klein naming the poet as "the nth Adam taking a green inventory." Jones was followed by a Table Ronde with Pierre de Grandpré, Gatien Lapointe, and Guy Robert. I followed their French at some distance, but mostly admired their elegance. The last event of this crowded afternoon was a round table in which the casting dynamics quickly became clear. Henry Kreisel, our sage raisonneur, was the calming moderator; Eli Mandel uneasily found himself the protagonist, with the young maverick from B.C., Bill Bissett, gleefully playing his gadfly and nemesis, and Margaret Atwood was, as she said, "the token woman on this panel," but managed to seem one of the Fates, maybe Atropos. Mandel started with a provocative description of the present poetic scene, "one where we have a choice being presented to us between hallucination and gentility." According to a transcript from the audio tape (one obviously done by an inexperienced transcriber), he then added: "On the one hand, we have hallucinated poets; on the other hand we have our gentile poets." Then Bissett, according to Stanley Cooperman's report of the conference for the *Vancouver Sun*, "in ways too mysterious to mention, turned himself into a truck," but by this time I was hallucinating and had wandered off to gird up for the evening's reception and readings at the Faculty Club.

The reception began at eight p.m., the readings at nine-thirty. Hoping that my four years of college French would fit me for bilingualism, I bought a drink for Jean-Guy Pilon and engaged him in a twenty-minute conversation that exhausted us both, him from receiving my French, me for producing it. At its end I was mumbling "d'accords" to his eloquence. The report of the conference by John Richmond in *The Montreal Star* spoke of the "gentle Brownian movement of poets and critics," a term that explains the nice buzz most of us had on board as we gravitated to the Saskatchewan Room (for the river, not the province) to hear the readings. Rina Lasnier, Irving Layton, and Pilon were also to read, but the star of the evening was Dorothy Livesay. *The Montreal Star* promoted her to the "Marchioness of Canadian Poetry" for the occasion, and she looked the part: a red satin gown, a sort of golden Marie Antoinette wig, and an elegant cane because of a fall on the ice the week before. She began by referring to the Eli Mandel/Bill Bissett dust-up: "I was rather distressed this afternoon to see a schism developing. . . ." She raised her arms in a bow over her head and said that really "they're all on the same arc," which even at the time I thought a good pun. Then, reaching across the generation gap, she recalled being offered a joint by a Vancouver poet, and responding that it wouldn't do any good because she didn't inhale, thus making explicit in 1968 a rationalization for his behaviour about that time made in 1993 by President Bill Clinton.

Miss Livesay then read several poems, and when she had finished one called "The Dream" and containing a unicorn, an angry voice from the back shouted "That's bull-shit, Dorothy, and you know it!" Unsure if my role as Equipment Manager included duties as Sergeant-at-Arms, I started toward the offender in a sort of truculent Brownian movement; others were on their way. We were momentarily stayed by what was probably the only possible riposte; our giant comparativist and poet, Ted Blodgett, shot back: "Well, Yates, bull-shit to your bull-shit." Someone whispered to me, presumably in explanation, that both were Yanks. My impulse was to pitch Yates in a snow bank, but by the time I got there Gerry McCaughey, who, with size thirteen feet, had flown Spitfires in the war, was quietly talking him down—it was, I saw, the Canadian way.

I later learned that the provocateur was J. Michael Yates, head of the creative writing program at the University of Victoria, and later still, read, in a part of Barry McKinnon's report that didn't make it into *The Gateway*, something that led me to surmise that, while the rest of us came to the readings with a nice buzz on, Yates was nursing a nasty bun. McKinnon testifies: "There are a lot of important people here tonight, including the head of a creative writing department who Charlie politely asks, 'What are you doing at a Canadian Writing conference?' since he impolitely noticed that this guy is an American (like many academics hired in the amusing Canadian wilderness, with its funny vocabulary of prairie and mountains, etc.). Then this guy says, 'I don't know if this is the proper place to punch you out or not,' and he really means it, so Charlie and I back off into a corner where they store the chairs."

Abandoning Yates to cooler heads, I wandered back to hear the final reading from Irving Layton, who had been represented to me as a writer specializing in shocking his audience; he certainly seemed diminutive and pugnacious. But the only thing that he said that was even mildly shocking was this simile: "A good poem is like syphilis; it takes days before it reveals itself." I was more impressed by his voice, and it moved me to make a distinction of my own. Maybe Canadian poetry could be divided between the older generation, e.g., Layton, D. G. Jones, Birney, and Livesay, whose articulation hinted of early training in elocution, and who pronounced the word "poem" as having two syllables—or at least a marked diphthong—and the youngsters who insisted on pronouncing it as "pome," the way Bill Bissett spelled it (as in *Pomes for Yoshi* [1972]). A small perception, granted, but probably the only kind possible at the end of a long, gala evening that ended with most of us deep in the sauce.

The first serious demands on the Equipment Manager occurred on the second afternoon when Earle Birney, who was, I soon gathered, deferred to as the Dean of Canadian Letters, took centre stage in a session called "Poetry and Media Mixing." He needed a slide carousel and we hustled one complete with a remote control. Birney said "next," I clicked, and we went on to a new slide. It was going smoothly, but all of a sudden an image on the screen began to blur at the edges. With horror I realized that I'd forgotten to turn the fan on and the damn thing was giving off smoke, gradually incinerating the D. of C.L.'s collection of exotic slides. It occurred to me that this might be grounds for my deportation, but Birney was unruffled, incorporating the mishap into his performance; we even became buddies for the conference. Amid the plethora of poets, he seemed the one to watch.

That evening the Social Credit provincial government, reportedly nervous but respectful of the university eggheads, gave the conference a banquet at the optimistically named "Eldorado Room" of the Macdonald Hotel. It was genuinely grand, my first experience of a dinner with a toast to the Queen (Bill Bissett left at this point, but I had been carefully briefed by Raymond Grant, my Scottish colleague, to make sure I held my wineglass over my waterglass; that he had, however, omitted the reason was made clear to me by a nearby Hanoverian). Birney turned up in a blue satin Cossack shirt and I stuck to him like a Rock and Roll groupie. When our table of eight had finished the three bottles of wine allotted to it, Birney asked for more. The waiter begged his pardon but said he would have to pay for it. Birney rose to his considerable height, raised his fist at the head table, his radiant shirt and eyes flashing, and shouted "Death to Social Credit," then stalked out. The remark was variously reported by the newspapers, one recording it as "To hell with Alberta's government." But I was a witness and ask skeptics to remember that poets are better at curses than reporters. In that instant Birney went for me from D. of C.L. to the revolution's leader.

I didn't, however, follow him because the after-dinner reading was my first opportunity to hear Margaret Atwood. My wife and I had become friends with Peggy and her husband, Jim Polk, also in their first year at the U of A English Department. Jim was from Miles City on the plains of eastern Montana, played the harpsichord, and had the driest of wits, which issued later in his novel, *The Passion of Loreen Bright Weasel* (1981), a book unjustly neglected by Canadians. I had gathered that Peggy was a promising poet, and she sort of fitted my boyhood notion of the part because she was then in her Victorian period, featuring scarves and/or high collars set off by black chokers and antique brooches (some said she later took up the biker look). She was warm and friendly, except on antic occasions when I foolishly introduced her as Mrs. Polk, perversely pleased at having caused a glint in her remarkable eyes. I was also a touch chilled when she opened her banquet reading with this remark: "I'm a separatist. I want to separate from the United States. Which is a bit difficult since my husband is an American." My irritation with what seemed gratuitous Yank-bashing gave way to my fascination with her reading voice, a flat and measured monotone that I had first heard from T. S. Eliot reading his poetry on Caedmon records. Someone had convinced me that Eliot's choice was deliberate, a way of letting the rhythms, sound values, and line endings emerge from the page. In Atwood's reading, the choice seemed even more appropriate because the affectless voice somehow conveyed the menace latent in the simple situations her poems often recounted. She was, I decided, a category apart, somewhere between the "po-ems" and the "pomes." The combination of Birney and Atwood heartened me: Canada was becoming both a more lively and a more complicated place than I had first imagined.

The session on "Canadian Poetry in Other Languages" the next day was anticlimactic, pretty dull except for the presentation of Eskimo poetry (we had not yet learned to use "Inuit"). Rudy Wiebe began by playing some songs and chants of Arctic peoples originally recorded on wax cylinders by Diamond Jenness. Rudy was followed by Mary Carpenter, from Sachs Harbour on Banks Island in the Beaufort Sea, and she began this way: "Would you all like to stand up with your hands up?" We did and she pointed an imaginary machine-gun at us and went "rat-a-tat-tat-tat. Okay, you can sit down and be resurrected." She identified herself as an Eskimo poet writing in English, read several of her poems and left us with this: "I am pleased to be sharing these moments with you. You people seem very comfortable. You cry about being dominated by Americans. We Eskimos in Canada cry because we are dominated unjustly by our fellow white Canadians." Clearly the oppressed/oppressor pairing was getting more complex as the conference went on.

That afternoon we gathered downtown at the Edmonton Art Gallery to hear the final set of readings. Those poets who had early functioned as critics or panelists and a few others were now to read in the main auditorium, and then the audience was to break up into three parts to please the rest of the attending poets eager to be heard. We started late, the featured poets each read longer than scheduled, and the long afternoon got longer—Livesay again, Birney, Doug Jones, Peter Stevens, Lionel Kearns,

Elizabeth Brewster, Michael Ondaatje, Bill Bissett. I remember the performances of only Bissett and Ondaatje. Bissett did some chant poems that transformed him into something like a Kwakiutl shaman. I liked them. As my friend the Norwegian philosopher Herman Tennessen said of Heidegger's prose, Bissett's "stylistic rhythm has the peculiarly mesmerizing effect of kettledrums finding a short-cut, as it were, from the receiver's tympanum directly to his volitional layers." I also liked the performances in later years when "The Four Horsemen" came to town. Rafael Barreto-Rivera, Paul Dutton, Steven McCaffery, and bp Nichol worked as a sound poetry ensemble that seemed a primal link to my kindergarten joy in rhythm bands, where, as teacher's pet, I happily whanged away with my castanets, bird whistles, and tambourines, while my less fortunate colleagues were relegated to the triangle and wood block. I had been waiting to hear Ondaatje because, attracted by his titles *The Dainty Monsters* and *The Man with Seven Toes*, I already knew and thought well of his work. He concluded by reading from his as yet unpublished "The Collected Works of Billy the Kid," and I was hooked. Ondaatje's work, growing in reputation over twenty-five years, indicates that Canadian readers were also hooked, ready to embrace this exotic cosmopolitan.

Before the favoured poets had finished, I was out in the hall hustling the music stands borrowed to provide lecterns for the three groups. Suddenly out of the auditorium door burst Stanley Cooperman, sore as a boil. As he stormed from the gallery, he shouted back at me: "The next time I come to this son-of-a-bitchin' town, they'll have to pay me to read!" I took this as a summary of what all the unestablished poets must be feeling. Poor Stanley. I had known him casually in the States, occasionally having a drink with him during the Modern Language Association meetings. He was a good guy, but I thought he had taken Normal Mailer's *Advertisements for Myself* too seriously as a model for his behaviour. He had earlier made it clear to the organizers that his reputation as both an American and a Canadian poet made their failure to invite him as a featured player an insult, yet at the conference we amiably exchanged expatriate chat (he had come to Canada in 1965).

As his final outburst hinted, I surmised that he was feeling more in exile, more alienated than I was or Ondaatje from Sri Lanka seemed. Stanley's prophecy did come true: he did return to Edmonton to read in the early seventies, and he did get paid from a League of Canadian Poets grant for touring poets, but he read to an audience of four. The depth of his sense of wandering, of being an alien in Canada, was fully expressed in his book called *Canadian Gothic*, which came out in 1976. Like John Berryman, Stanley had invented an alter ego as the speaker of his poems, one Cappelbaum. Here is the conclusion of "Cappelbaum Takes Out Papers":

> Margaret Atwood,
> permit me to introduce myself:
> "rootless" poet, age
> 5,735 years:
> show me the way to go home.

I was saddened but not surprised when I heard of Stanley's suicide in the late spring of 1976.

As the afternoon staggered on, the three groups become one as exhausted delegates slipped away to the Faculty Club to refuel for the conference's final event, the performance that evening of Wilfred Watson's play, *let's murder Clytemnestra according to the principles of Marshall McLuhan*. My own tanks refilled, I had great difficulty in following the play, but Wilfred's notes to the published text, in the collection of his plays called *Plays at the Iron Bridge or the Autobiography of Tom Horror* (1989) may give the gist of it: "It is to the School of Fine Arts at Banff that Electra comes, with her nineteen heads.... Electra wants to confess, and perhaps expiate, her guilt, the Greek sin of rationalism. Backwards and forwards grammatologized by the postmodernists with whom she has taken refuge, it has driven her mad ...." The play space was the old Studio Theatre in Corbett Hall, the director was Bernard Engel, the set was flanked by two banks of television screens, and the actors were mostly students. I assumed at the time that the director's inspiration might have included "The Performance Group," which had received international press the previous summer in New York doing "Dionysus in 69," a play featuring nudity and interaction with the audience. I was aware of it because it had been directed by a maverick acquaintance from Iowa City, Richard Schechner. *Loss Moidur Clytemetcetc* (as the French title was printed in the conference program) tried as much partial nudity and interaction as was possible in what was still Bible Bill Aberhart's Alberta. A character called Samuela, for instance, was accurately described by another as "wearing very little make-up and very little of anything else." As might be expected from a weary, but momentarily topped-up audience of critics and poets, the reactions were audible, rude, and frequently obscene. Near the play's climax, the actors worked up a hullabaloo of chanting and dancing and they obviously were under direction to mingle with and engage the audience. It was, for this particular evening, a mistake. I remember the near-terror in Samuela's eyes as she struggled to remain in character and yet elude the questing hands of poets and critics alike. The conference, all who remained seemed to agree, had been a howling success.

I may have learned many things from the conference but they must have been ephemeral; at least I can't find them in my memory, but two perceptions stayed with me because later events confirmed them. Despite equal billing in the conference title, there was abundant evidence during its three days that Canadians were uneasy about the office of the literary critic, especially the evaluative critic. Nobody, of course, loves a critic, but the organizers' efforts to generate some critical confrontation came a cropper even in the early planning stages. Invited as a critic, Miriam Waddington, for one, was disturbed, insisting that she considered herself "primarily a poet": she did not attend. A tentative plan for conference events had included a section called "Confrontations" to feature Irving Layton and Milton Wilson on the poetry of Earle Birney, and then Birney and George Woodcock on the poetry of Layton. Layton seemed game, predicting that "sparks, poetic and otherwise, ought to fly," but both Birney and Woodcock were indignant: Woodcock flatly refused the role assigned "since I do not feel that gladiatorial contests are the proper activities of poets and critics." And Birney likewise felt he and Layton were being "forced into the role of literary critics publicly judging each other," and concluding he had no interest in that kind of "academic circus." In the course of his rejection he collapsed the category of critic altogether; for him the plan implied, falsely, that "there is a special species called a critic." Fair enough because it became clear to me that the invited participants wore as many hats as Wilfred's Electra had heads; many seemed quite willing to act as a critic, but not to be taken for one. I was a bit surprised, then, when I came across this in Birney's "Creativity Through Fiction," the text of a CBC talk he had given in 1965: "There are exceptions, but it's largely true that the notable poets of our western heritage have been also 'men-of-letters,' an out-dated but honourable term which few Canadians have ever earned." Birney may have been right about the pre-1965 scene, but as the careers of those I'd met at the conference developed, it was clear that most were becoming multi-media writers, persons-of-letters. Peggy Atwood, for instance, went from poet to descriptive and/or thematic "critic" with *Survival* (1972) and then became internationally famous as a novelist. Perhaps the survival of humane letters in an enormous country required a relatively small literary cadre to share the duties, but the defect of this virtue may be that busy as they are, the role of critic takes low priority. Or perhaps the literary needs of what I once heard described as the "senior emerging nation" required critics who were primarily historians, ordering and arranging the new riches. Certainly the "critics" speaking at the conference generally contented themselves with cultural inventory, literary history touched up with a bit of thematic definition. But I had yet to worry this further.

The second perception was more visceral. During his evening reading Layton announced that he had found a choice bit of graffiti in the men's room. We waited delightedly to be shocked: "May no man speak ill of his brother." Layton then explained that, after all, this was Alberta, the Bible land. I didn't share the laughter because his sarcasm suddenly crystallized for me what I had been feeling as mild but unmistakable condescension from our Eastern visitors. Not yet a Canadian, I discovered I was linked with Alberta as a westerner. One result of my conference resentment was that when, in later years, I encountered buttons that read "Alberta Libre," or heard, during the oil crisis, "Let the eastern bastards freeze in the dark," I was less charitable than the measure wisely advised by Layton's graffiti.

Despite the full spectrum of literary light present for the three days of the conference, my own experience of it had been darkened by the death of Frank Bessai four days before. I had known Frank for only fifteen months. In late September of 1968 he had begun to complain of a tingling sensation in his wrist; medical inquiry led to the discovery of a cancerous brain tumor. Frank had been quick to help me with Canadian matters, but his stoic and wry humor in dealing with his deteriorating condition taught me more about life. He was fond of quoting his father, a laconic German farming near Southey, Saskatchewan: "Every man carries his own hide to market." During the winter of 1968/69 I had volunteered to drive him to the Cross Cancer Clinic for chemotherapy treatments. One morning, a morning brilliant with ice crystals in the sun, I was struggling to get him into the cramped front seat of my Rambler, and after my clumsy manhandling, he smiled and said, "The world still looks good to me, Mort." Dorothy Livesay, on each of the two occasions she read, dedicated a poem to Frank. I remember only the refrain of the first of these: "We are not at home here." I took it as having a special reference to my situation because I may have been luckier in a new country than Stanley Cooperman: I had Frank Bessai to help me feel at home in Canada, but more important, to teach me much about being at home anywhere in a world that still looks good to me.

Where I Was Coming From

Academics get paid for teaching, but they get promoted for activities loosely embraced by the term "research." In order to measure my collisions with Canadian letters, let me go back a bit. My research record began in the most conventional way with a note published in a 1965 issue of *American Literature*, the major specialist journal in my field. In a single paragraph of nineteen lines, I argued (persuasively, I think; at least no refutation has ever surfaced) that because they share a mania for introducing people to each other, Captain Truck, a minor character in James Fenimore Cooper's *Homeward Bound* (1838), was likely a model for Captain Boomer, a minor character in Melville's *Moby-Dick* (1851). It was a minuscule perception, but wholly my own, and remember that this is exactly what I was trained and licensed by my community to do. And I was, in those more spacious days, amply reinforced and rewarded, first with fifty free offprints, each with an extra title page, some of which I proudly sent off to my former teachers. One, Professor John Gerber, responded by quoting a line from Emerson's letter to Whitman sent in thanks for a free copy of the first edition of *Leaves of Grass*: "I greet you at the beginning of a great career...." If Gerber was being ironic, he was also urging me on, but the edge of his tone seems to have cut short my sending the offprints around because I find, with some embarrassment, that I still have about thirty of them left.

I continued to labour in such scholarship, but in the spring of 1964 an odd chain of events began that nudged my academic practice in a new direction. In the spring of that year I was surprised to receive an invitation from one Dr. Forrest J. Berghorn, a name unknown to me, to lecture to a group of sixty Peace Corps volunteers at a training session to be held in Gainesville, Florida, that coming July. Berghorn suggested that I might lecture on "The Performance and Folklore of Capitalism." Nonplussed by such a title, but game because we American-studies generalists could swat up any topic, I accepted. After all, one of my role models, the distinguished Harvard professor, Henry Nash Smith, had defined American Studies as "principled opportunism." Only later did I learn that Berghorn's suggested title might have been a clue that he had mistaken me for another Ross, a law professor at Wyoming who has apparently known Thurman Arnold, the author of *The Folklore of Capitalism* (1937; reissued in 1968). Arnold had begun his career in the Wyoming Law faculty and had gone on to become the assistant attorney general in charge of the Anti-Trust Division in Franklin Delano Roosevelt's administration.

Berghorn had also promised first class, round-trip fare (it came to $281.60), expenses (they came to $28.40), and a fifty dollar honorarium, and so in July I jetted to Florida, my first time in the American South and my first commercial air-flight. I was savouring the luxury of first class until somewhere over Texas a voice over the intercom said that "there's a li'l ole mud-puddle jest ahead, and we're agona sashay round it." I ordered a double, suddenly alarmed that I was in midair among good ole boys, especially the cracker driving the airplane.

Safely on the ground, I was to lecture to the trainees on two successive evenings, and Berghorn warned me that they would be near exhaustion because of their strenuous day training; for example: Portuguese lessons, calisthenics, "community development" (that day learning to build animal pens from scrap material), and all this conducted in Gainesville's heat and humidity that both hovered around one hundred. They had already been doing this sort of thing for six of a twelve-weeks training course. I spent the two days up to my neck in Berghorn's screened-in pool marveling at the variety and size of the insects battling against the mesh, wondering if it would also keep out gators, and trying to think of ways to lighten up the evening meetings. The lectures went well enough, largely because of the good-natured vigour of the trainees, some of whom with enough left to outdrink me at an after-hours beerstube. The Peace Corps had received its share of brickbats. One pundit had dubbed it Kennedy's Kiddie Korps and ex-President Eisenhower called it a "juvenile experiment," but the trainees, most with new B.A. degrees in a surprising range of subjects, seemed so eagerly ebullient that some rubbed off on me. The trip had been my share, however small, in the optimistic visions of Kennedy's postwar Camelot.

Back in Laramie I was further energized because I saw that I could mine the lectures for a new, at least for me, kind of essay. At least one of my insights in preparing them still seemed genuine. I had argued that Hugh Hefner, founder-editor-publisher of *Playboy* magazine, was really Benjamin Franklin turned inside-out and brought up to date by a reversal in the needs of American capitalism. Presiding at the birth of an infant institution, Franklin had helped to create new-world capital by preaching the prudential or squirrel virtues, industry and frugality. Hefner, working in a mature capitalism which required endless consumption of its products for continued growth, was still the economic moralist, but now preaching an ethics of prodigality and leisure. The naked girl on *Playboy's* gatefold was what the old hucksters called the shill to lure the marks into the tent where they could be schooled, not in getting, but in spending. Cheered by apparent success in reaching my Brazil-bound audience, or at least keeping most of them awake and occasionally laughing, I resolved to try for both a light touch and for the common reader, that genial generalist my own liberal arts education had claimed to be creating. I was also convinced that the Ph.D. dissertation had impacted, pinched, and crabbed my written style and, emboldened by Peace Corps and Camelot, I would get my stylistic guns loose with this essay. I had enormous fun writing it and still like reading it, although a taste for one's own prose is a bad sign.

I completed the essay under the title "Poor Richard and *Playboy*: Brothers Under the Flesh," and decided to seek publication for it in a "review" journal. In the early sixties there was still a surprising number of these periodicals catering to something like the common reader. I made a list of twenty-four of them and started soliciting from the top down. The rejection slips from *The Atlantic Monthly* and *Harper's Magazine* were printed, but those from *The Reporter, Saturday Review*, and *The Nation* were more personal and encouraging. In the essay, I had made some fun of the megabillionaire, J. Paul Getty, who was then Playboy's Financial Editor, and Nora Magid of *The Reporter* wrote that it might amuse me to learn that Mr. Getty was their landlord. Finally, after three months of bouncing around, the essay was accepted by *The Colorado Quarterly*. Its editor, Paul Carter, soon became a friend and one of my favorite Rocky Mountain characters, largely because he was a genuine curmudgeon with an amazing flair for invective. I once heard him refer to a colleague as "that lily-sucking defalcator." The essay was published in the Spring 1967 issue, and Paul paid me ten dollars (but billed me for reprints).

In May of 1967 I got a memorandum from Paul telling me I was responsible for The Quarterly's largest—and only—single order, enclosing as further explanation a copy of a letter from Anson Mount, *Playboy's* "Manager of Public Affairs." Mount explained that the dean of the School of Journalism of the University of Illinois had sent him a copy of my essay. He wondered if perhaps I had found a key to Hefner's motivations and personality. He asked for fifty copies of the issue because he wanted to pass out the copies to all the members of his staff. The topper came when soon thereafter I received an invitation from Mr. Mount to lunch, on my next visit to Chicago, at the Playboy Club, to tour the new Playboy Building (the old Palmolive Building on North Michigan Avenue that I had known as a boy because my Auntie Babe and Uncle Chick often called my attention to the Lindbergh Beacon that circled from its spire), and to tour Mr. Hefner's offices, the four-story brick and greystone Playboy Mansion at 1340 North State Parkway that had been featured in so many of the magazine's photo spreads). How could I, a student of Mr. Hefner as cultural phenomenon, refuse?

I was next in Chicago for the Modern Language Association meetings in December. Dressed in a tasteful summer sportscoat (with olive and tan vertical stripes) purchased with the Peace Corps honorarium, I prepared to go backstage at Hefner's empire. I met Anson Mount, a fireplug-shaped good ole boy with outsized spectacles, at the Playboy Building; he immediately asked me to call him Smokey. I asked him what the "manager of Public Affairs" did. He said that he wrote the magazine's NFL football prognostications ("Pigskin Previews") in the fall and handled Playboy's relationships with the "Church." I didn't press him even though I was uncertain about where I fitted in, but his tour of the establishment was so friendly that by lunch-time we were buddies. I later learned that Smokey had taken on his present eminence in the organization because of his skills in handling the clergy who had become vocal in their criticism of Hefner's secular hedonism as he formally developed it in his "Playboy Philosophy," a 250,000-word series that began in December 1962, and ran on for twenty-six installments in successive issues of the magazine. Smokey had even enrolled in a summer course at the Episcopal Theological Seminary in Sewanee, Tennessee, ostensibly to study, but actually to entertain the clergy for miles around with a well-stocked bar in a southern version of the Playboy Mansion. The editorial offices we toured were sleek, decorated in Danish curvilinear furniture and what were surely beyond life-size photos of gatefold Playmates of the Month, although it also displayed a fairly impressive collection of contemporary art, largely by Chicago artists. It was easy to distinguish the junior staff from the senior editors; the former were uniformly what we now call hard-body handsome; the editors by contrast were a scruffy-looking crew, grizzled veterans who had long become immune to the flesh around them. I complimented Robie Macauley, the fiction editor, on the quality of the stories published in the magazine (recent issues had included work by P. G. Wodehouse, Nabokov, and Isaac Bashevis Singer). He may have sensed that I found this a bit incongruous because he was defensive in explaining that *Playboy* paid the highest rates "in the world" to writers.

Smokey sensed something else—that I was near sensuous overload—and he walked me to lunch at the Playboy Club on East Walton Street. After the sleek efficiency of the Playboy offices, the premises seemed a bit tacky, but might have looked better at night. Smokey had written in an early letter that he considered the club a drag; he had also observed that women enjoy the Playboy Club more than do men, a sentiment which made me wonder if Smokey was in full control of his feelings. Once seated, we were approached by a statuesque brunette in a Bunny outfit. In a throaty voice, she said to me: "Hello there. I'm your Bunny, Roberta," and when she brought our drinks she did the famous Bunny Dip, a modified back-bend made necessary by the structural stresses of her costume. She was, despite her intimate claim, our waitress.

Heady stuff for a kid from Iowa, but Smokey had even more planned. We cabbed to the Playboy Mansion, were scrutinized by the television camera over the stoop, admitted and lifted to Hefner's executive office. His personal secretary greeted me with: "Oh yes. You're the fella that wrote that funny little piece about our Hef." (Not quite the right note, I thought.) And then the personal secretary's secretary took me on a tour of the house, Smokey lingering behind in case Hefner should wake up; the master of the house, reportedly up all night working, was sleeping at 2:30 in the afternoon. I never did meet Hefner, but his mansion was something indeed. A. C. Spectorsky, Hefner's copublisher of *Playboy*, had said that the mansion was decorated "in early garish," but to my academic eyes, it was true state-of-the-art swank: theatre-quality film projects, a hi-fi panel that looked like the controls of a 747, a game room crammed with the latest pinball games, a pool abutted by a secluded nook called "The Woo Grotto" and reached by a firehouse pole to slide down from the floor above. It was a big house, but only two other living creatures were stirring. The first we encountered was a sleepy-eyed girl in a pink chenille bathrobe with hair curlers to match having her breakfast in the baronial dining room. My guide shouted to her: "On tour, Honey" and she replied something which I caught as "aw-raght." The guide then explained to me that several of the waitress-bunnies from the Club were housed in a dormitory under the eaves in the former servants' quarters now known as the Bunny Hutch. The other living creature we found on the last stop of the tour, a beat-up, unfinished two-car garage (the kind we all knew as kids) at the back of the house and containing an equally beat-up ping-pong table and a friendly, but smelly St. Bernard named Humphrey. The guide explained that what Hefner really liked to do for recreation was play a few games of ping-pong and romp a bit with Humphrey. Over the years since, this image has remained as poignant for me as Gatsby standing alone on his dock in West Egg, in part because it was confirmation of a point I had made in my essay. Franklin anticipated Hefner in ways other than economic; he was the first American master manipulator of his public image. Even Franklin's lapses from public industry were done with an eye to public response. In keeping with the pattern of reversal, I had claimed that Hefner concealed his undeniable industry behind his public image.

I was disappointed, but it's probably a good thing I didn't meet Hefner in the flesh because he remains, like Gatsby, a fabulous character for me, in small part of my own making—and there is some evidence that I may have had an equally small part in making his own image of himself and his empire. In August of 1969 Wayne Warga reported remarks by Hefner made at a Hollywood press conference. Warga began: "to put the whole magazine into perspective for his listeners, Hefner casually equates *Playboy* with *Poor Richard's Almanac*," and then quoted Hefner: "When Ben Franklin created *Poor Richard's Almanac*, he was creating an ethic for a have-not society. *Playboy*, on the other hand, is creating an ethnic [*sic*] for a prosperous leisure society." I was a little stung at not being credited, but I chose to take his remark as evidence that I had convinced him that he was a true avatar of Franklin. I had to wait for final evidence until "The Playboy Interview" with Hefner in the twentieth-anniversary issue of January 1974. Near the beginning of his remarks, Hefner said: "An article in a university quarterly a few years ago offered an interesting comparison between *Playboy* and *Poor Richard's Almanac*." Again personal pique at his failure to credit me gave way to a subtler, certainly a more self-flattering perception. If Hefner had me floating unnamed and disembodied over an article in an unnamed university quarterly, didn't this somehow make me the disembodied voice of what he now regarded as community wisdom?

My adventures with *Playboy* were making me ambitious: maybe I'd found my métier. I could now see myself becoming a well-regarded, perhaps even a celebrated commentator and critic. I would remain the careful researcher, but develop this new style in order both to instruct and to delight the general reader, gradually building an audience in the big quarterlies. Such confident hope was exhilarating, but it was also dogged by long-ingrained doubts, to understand which requires a short digression into my boyhood.

Up until my seventh year my childhood was midwestern normal— what I remember of it is idyllic, but then my parents suddenly divorced, my father acquired a new wife with a built-in family, and then died when I was twelve. Thus was I raised, as a single child in a single-parent family, by my gentle mother, Isabel, who never weighed more than one humdred pounds and who wore herself even thinner first selling Avon products door-to-door and then as a seamstress sewing buttons on bachelors' shirts, a service of the local laundry. Denied a pension by the divorce, her single income never exceeded two thousand dollars until she was rescued when I was sixteen by her marriage to Max Crane (I now believe she had several offers to remarry but delayed accepting one until she found a stepfather I might like). The remarkable thing about my life with her was that I didn't really suffer from our poverty, largely because we were sustained by our community. The eight thousand souls of Oelwein, Iowa, were mainly railroaders and those dependent on the railroad, The Chicago

Great Western Railway, the two main lines of which intersected there and thus required what I was told were "the largest locomotive shops west of the Mississippi." My grandfather was an engineer; my father, known in his circle as Easy-Going Ross, a switchman, both convivial and well-liked. It was the town's habit "to look out after" such men's survivors. Every year when school opened, for instance, the principal clothier would select a suit for me and charge my mother's account its wholesale price (she tried to pay at least two dollars a month until the next fall); periodically the owner of both the town's movie houses, the Grand and the Ritz, would give me free passes, good, however, only on weekdays. I had my pick of after-school jobs—assistant baker, chief carrier for the *Oelwein Daily Register*, and odds-body janitor in some places where I scrambled to find things to do in order to justify the job that had been invented especially for me. In retrospect I am grateful for all this, but it is also clear to me that I was, with some stoicism, learning a station in life. Despite my mother's protective impulses, I had become a step-child of the whole community, and the experience made me, if not timid, then cautious and wary in my dealings with the world. This posture, I think, also reinforced a midwestern boy's democratic skepticism of anybody or anything that smelled of excessive ambition. In this spirit, I knew that I had no prospects for college when I graduated from high school and was quite content when two buddies and I were offered G-45 jobs by an FBI recruiter as file clerks in the Washington headquarters (the lure was a rumoured one-to-fifteen ratio of men to women in the nation's capital). The summer after graduation and before reporting to the FBI, I worked construction. One noon-hour, as I was negotiating a wheelbarrow down a two-by-eight plank, a dapper and diminutive man awaited me at its foot. He offered me a full scholarship including board and room jobs at Cornell College in Mt. Vernon, Iowa. I took it: goodbye FBI, hello American opportunity. Only later did I learn that my high-school principal, the minister of our Methodist church, and the president of my father's union, the Brotherhood of Locomotive Trainmen, had conspired to get me into Cornell. Certainly generous of them, but a bit deflating to what I seemed to have then seen as my own naked merits. Further deflation was to come before I left for Cornell. My great-aunt, Betsy Ross (yes, she was named after the famous flag seamstress), who had also been my eighth-grade English teacher, invited me for tea. After sniffingly observing that Cornell was a pretty fancy school and that I was lucky to be sent there, she added some advice: "Your Grandfather's [her brother] downfall was liquor; your Father's was women; I don't know what's left for you but you'll do well to remember that the Ross men WERE ALWAYS WEAK-WILLED." When I became emboldened by my success with the *Playboy* essay, I was also dogged by the long-standing suspicion that great-aunt Betsy had been warning me against going beyond my station, against ambition. But I was off to a new country; I would make my reputation there as a respected and widely read critic (being in Canada would allow me to say "internationally respected"). And I remember secretly, in my heart of hearts, whispering defiantly to my long string of benefactors, "I'll show these Canadians a thing or two."

A Memorial Note for Marian Engel

My first impression of Marian did little to dispel my midwestern prejudice that creative writers are difficult people—as Huck says about *Pilgrim's Progress,* "interesting, but tough." Odd bits of her reputation had preceded her arrival at the university. She had recently received the Governor General's award for *Bear,* which someone had told me was about a love affair between the title character and a librarian. I had seen, in *Books in Canada,* a blurry picture of her dressed in a cheerleader's outfit—it didn't say why. After her arrival, I first met her where I meet most Canadian writers—at the big round table in the lower lounge—and I knew she was going to be difficult. It was clear, even on that first occasion, that she could outdrink me. She had apparently learned to smoke cigarettes from Humphrey Bogart, and this seemed to accentuate her disconcerting habit of squinting into the middle distance during conversation. At first I felt she was looking over my shoulder for more interesting company, and then I concluded that she was ignoring our punch lines while waiting, more or less patiently, for her turn at bat. All this seemed further complicated by her recent divorce, to which I attributed her apparent ambivalence toward men—or at least me; she was alternately flirtatious and hostile and sometimes, oddly enough, both at the same time.

These first impressions coalesced for me during the evening of a party she gave for the English Department. She greeted us at the door like Texas Guinan and Mae West rolled into one. She was clearly about eleven ahead, and in fact retired even before the party got moving. Aha, my prejudice said, but then I noticed and ate my way through an amazing range of pastries that she had spent the day baking. It dawned on me that she had overprepared because she was as leery of and nervous about us Western academics as I had been about her. What seemed to me the genteel company of the lower lounge may have figured for her as the Longbranch Saloon—a posse of critics for hire, or worse, a clutch of literary theorists. Had she toughened herself in order to meet us on this Western ground?

So I looked again. And in the months that followed I discovered that the glassy stare increasingly gave way to a truly dazzling grin. I came to see this grin as the signal of a number of qualities that I still value. I discovered Marian's rare animation of mind and spirit. I discovered her disinterested compassion that did much to help me over a troublesome time in my own life, and I discovered her penetrating and ranging wit, a wit and intelligence that makes a tough world bearable for others, no matter how tough we think ourselves.

Eulogy for Mort Ross

Dear Family and Friends of Mort Ross,

I think of Mort Ross as seated at a table.

When I first met Mort, sometime in the 1950s, in Iowa City, he was seated at a table in a famous place called simply, Irene's. Needless to say, he was not there alone. He was, even then, uniquely able to create community. Among the graduate students in English and American Civilization, there at the University of Iowa, he was, by virtue of his generosity and his refusal of any need to compete, the centre towards which we gravitated. Mort was the first native-born Iowan I met, there in Iowa, and he came to represent a kind of caring that I credited to the whole Midwest. Most of us were from exotic places—like New York or Alberta. He was from a place I recall as being named Oelwein. I couldn't find it on my atlas, thinking the place was created by Mort's ability to tell stories—and Mort told stories.

Sitting in Joe's Restaurant and Bar on a Friday evening, having the luxury of a small steak called half-a-Joe's—since none of us could afford the huge full meal—we, his fellow students, had the pleasure of sharing his talk for hours on end. One time some of us drove all the way to the neighbouring state where he was vacationing with his wife, Kettle, in her hometown, Gary, Indiana. We drove for half a day to picnic on the shores of Lake Michigan, and to talk and listen. We were lonesome.

Mort's father was a union leader employed by the Chicago Great Western Railroad. Mort's sense of fairness bespoke his connection with and admiration for his father. In a world where we were studying literature, Mort insisted that literature is connected, directly and wonderfully, with life.

He would make his career by reminding us of that connection, insisting that we take seriously the stories we read—and tell. There in that university town just a few miles from the Mississippi River, near Hannibal, Missouri, near the locales of Mark Twain's stories, Mort was a kind of Mark Twain, reminding us with his soft chuckle that in our various obscurities we live important lives.

Mort left Iowa to become a professor. When I met him again, this time at the University of Alberta, he was, again, at a table. At Mort's Table. Home was something that Mort could carry with him. He was its embodiment, and to sit down at his table was to feel at home.

One summer my wife and I were going away from our house in Victoria and we asked Mort and Janis if they'd like to loaf for a few weeks on the West Coast. They agreed. I returned to find that Mort had coaxed and shaped my rocky garden into the elegance of a poem. I was surprised to think of Mort as a gardener. And yet I should have known—he was a gardener, always, showing the same care for the physical world that he did for people. He had listened to Whitman, and in his own version of the Whitmanesque he cared for the grass, for the varieties of moss on a stone, for the shapes of rosemary.

Mort was a member of the editorial board of NeWest Press. A board is, in one of it definitions, a table. Mort was strangely quiet at that table. He enjoyed being the board's secretary, as if by that act he might collect a new provision of stories. And yet he wasn't quiet at all. Because his presence—his listening presence—reminded us that the books we publish and the immediate world around us must connect.

As a member of that editorial board, Mort was the model of what an editor might be. He had a rare ability to persuade an author to make changes. He could, by the quiet magic of his elegant prose style, persuade writers that the beautiful revisions were their own.

That was one of Mort's precious accomplishments. As a teacher, as a writer, as an editor, as a drinking companion, as a friend—he persuaded us that we had things to say and lives to share—and he persuaded us there must be a deliberate grace in what we do. And by the way—when you saw Mort dancing you realized the absolute grace of his seemingly awkward figure.

During the past few years, Mort was under contract to NeWest Press—to write his literary memoirs—his recollections of a life spent reading and making literature in the United States and Canada—and particularly at the University of Alberta.

How might he ever have accomplished such a project? It seemed impossible. We, his friends, confounded him, always, by sitting down, by filling our glasses, by beginning to talk.

And yet, now, we complete his project by continuing on.

We sit down together, again, and over and over. We remember his gentle grimace that seemed to signal a reluctance to speak. We remember his soft voice, inviting us into the circle of conversation.

Love, in one of its varieties, is a kind of communal discourse that takes place at a table. Mort Ross showed us that. Janis Watkin showed us that. Together, they showed us how to make love grow.

Robert Kroetsch
31 December 1995

Writings of Morton L. Ross

1965:
"Captain Truck and Captain Boomer." *American Literature.* 38 (November, 1965): 1-4.

1966:
"Alan Swallow and Modern, Western American Poetry." *Western American Literature.* 1 Summer, 1966: 97-104. Reprinted in *The Literature of the American West.* ed. J.G. Taylor. Boston: Houghton Mifflin, 1971: 66-72.

"James's 'The Birthplace': A Double Turn of the Narrative Screw. *Studies in Short Fiction.* 3 (Spring, 1966): 321-328.

1967:
"Poor Richard and *Playboy:* Brothers under the Flesh" *Colorado Quarterly.* 15 (Spring, l967): 355-360. Reprinted in *Puritanism and the American Experience.* ed. M. McGiffert. Reading, Mass.: Addison-Wesley Co., 1969: 211-217.

"Hawthorne's Bosom Serpent and Mather's Magnalia." *Emerson Society Quarterly.* (2 Quarter, 1967): 13-14.

1968:
"'Manners:' An Addition to the Vocabulary for American Studies." *Bulletin of the Rocky Mountain Modern Language Association.* 22 (March, 1968): 15-22.

"Walt Whitman and the Limits of Embarrassment." *Forum* 6 (Fall-Winter, 1968): 27-34.

"For John Quentin Cook."

1971:
"What Happens in 'Rappaccini's Daughter'." *American Literature.* 43 (November, 1971): 336-345.

"Thoreau and Mailer: The Mission of the Rooster." *The Western Humanities Review.* 25 (Winter, 1971): 47-56.

1972:
"Bill Gorton, the Preacher in *The Sun Also Rises.*" *Modern Fiction Studies.* 18 (Winter, 1972-73:) 517-527.

1973:
"The Common Pursuit of True Judgment." Keynote Address, Third Annual Conference on Composition and Literature, University of Wyoming, Summer.

"Robert Kroetsch and his Novels." *Writers of the Prairies.* ed. Donald Stephen. Vancouver: University of British Columbia Press, pp. 101-114.

1974:
"*Moby-Dick* As an Education." *Studies in the Novel.* 6 (Spring, 1974): 62-75.

1975:
"Praise to the Albany." *Colorado Quarterly* 24 (Autumn, 1975): 145-152. Reprinted in *Intersections: Essays in the Sciences and Humanities.* eds. Stephen D. Scott, Don Perkins, and Erika Rothwell. Scarborough: Prentice Hall Allyn and Bacon, 1998: 243-48.

"Cooper's *The Pioneers* and the Ethnographic Impulse." *American Studies.* 16 (Fall, 1975): 29-39.

1976:
"Form and Moral Balance in Franklin's Autobiography." *Ariel.* 7 (July, 1976): 38-52.

1977:
"The Arrogating Self." *The Compass.* #2 (December, 1977): 75-80.

1978:
"The Canonization of *As for Me and My House*: A Case Study." *Figures in a Ground, Canadian Essays on Modern Literature Collected in Honor of Shelia Watson.* eds. Diane Bessai and David Jackel. Saskatoon: Western Producer Prairie Books, 1978. pp. 189-205. Reprinted in *The Bumper Book.* ed. John Metcalf. Toronto: ECW Press, 1986. pp. 170-185.

1979:
"What Do You Know About Canadian Literature? Shame On You!" Ninth Annual Conference on Composition and Literature, University of Wyoming, Summer.

"Yvor Winters and the Fallacy of Imitative Form." Rocky Mountain Modern Language Association Conference, University of Utah, Fall.

1980:
"Covering Canadian Writing." *Essays on Canadian Writing.* #20 (Winter, 1980-1981): 80-85.

1981:
Frederick Garber's "Thoreau's Redemptive Imagination," *Canadian Review of Comparative Literature,* 8 (December 1981): 544-547.

1982:
"American Public Styles: Community and the Private Heart," The Edmund Kemper Broadus Lectures, University of Alberta, February 3-4, 8-9.

"On Evaluation." *Canadian Literature.* #92 (Spring, 1982): 78-83.

1985:
> "A Memorial Note for Marian Engel."

1987:
> "The Northern Boundary." *A Literary History of the American West*, eds. J. G. Taylor et al. Fort Worth: Texas Christian University Press, pp. 1000-1013.

1988:
> "Emerson's Unenlightened Child: Some Corrective Notes." *American Transcendentalist Quarterly*. (September, 1988): 89-96.

1991:
> *Sinclair Ross and His Works*. Toronto: ECW Press, 1991. 42 pp; co-published in *Canadian Writers and Their Works*, eds. Robert Lecker, Jack David, and Ellen Quigley.
> "Toward the Margin: Notes in Passing."

1992:
> "Introduction to a Memoir."

1993:
> "A Passion of Poets."

1994:
> "Where I Was Coming From."
> "A Memorial Note for Ralph Ellison."

Acknowledgements

Quotations from *But We Are Exiles*, *The Words of My Roaring*, and *The Studhorse Man* by Robert Kroetsch in the essay "Robert Kroetsch's Early Novels" are reprinted by kind permission of Robert Kroetsch.

"*Robert Kroetsch's Early Novels*" reprinted with permission of the publisher from *Writers of the Prairies* edited by Donal Stephen © University of British Columbia Press 1973. All rights reserved by the publisher.

"Bill Gorton, the Preacher in *The Sun Also Rises*" *Modern Fiction Studies*, 18 (Winter 1972) reprinted by permission of *Modern Fiction Studies* and Purdue University.

"*Moby-Dick* As an Education" *Studies in the Novel*, v. 6, Spring 1974. Copyright 1974 by North Texas State University. Reprinted by permission of the publisher.

PRINTED AND BOUND
IN BOUCHERVILLE, QUEBEC, CANADA
BY MARC VEILLEUX IMPRIMEUR INC.
IN MAY, 1999